'No One Likes Us, We Don't Care'

'No One Likes Us, We Don't Care'

The Myth and Reality of Millwall Fandom

Garry Robson

Oxford • New York

First published in 2000 by
Berg
Editorial offices:
150 Cowley Road, Oxford, OX4 1JJ, UK
838 Broadway, Third Floor, New York, NY 10003-4812, USA

Berg is an imprint of Oxford International Publishers Ltd.

Library of Congress Cataloging-in-Publication Data
A catalogue record for this book is available from the Library of Congress.

British Library Cataloguing-in-Publication Data
A catalogue record for this book is available from the British Library.

ISBN 1 85973 367 0 (Cloth)
1 85973 372 7 (Paper)

Typeset by JS Typesetting, Wellingborough, Northants
Printed in the United Kingdom by Biddles Ltd, Guildford and King's Lynn

Contents

This book is dedicated, with many thanks, to Paul Gilroy, Les Back, John Hargreaves, Terry and Sheila Robson, Marta and Isabelle, and the memory of Harry Cripps.

Preface

'Millwall fandom' has been the focus of surprisingly little serious examination. There can be few groups about whom so much is assumed and so little known, and this fact alone constitutes the Millwall fan as a being of intrinsic sociological interest. Given this, it might be predicted that a study of Millwall would yield fruitful results in the sphere of representations and stereotype-construction on the one hand, or the subculture of 'deviant' masculinity on the other. Yet I have chosen to prioritize neither of these perspectives, having acknowledged, early in the research on which this study is based, that Millwall was microcosmically brimming over with conceptual issues of the utmost sociological significance. These relate to some unresolved, core dilemmas that the discipline of sociology has faced since its inception. In particular there is the question of how, exactly, do we classify, render and interpret varieties of working-class experience? and then unravel the ontological status of the forms of identity and consciousness that are bound up with those experiences?

I have sought to deal with these challenges by developing a theoretical–interpretative framework sensitive to the particular patterns of orientation and communication characteristic of my subjects. First, and drawing heavily on the work of Pierre Bourdieu, I have used the concept of embodiment, of the corporeal self as the primary site of social memory and cultural reproduction, as an interpretative tool with which to locate and explicate that characteristic working-class sense of the past incorporated into and living on in the present. On this basis I argue that 'Millwallism' functions not as an 'invented' or otherwise arbitrary subculture but as a locally grounded and demotically framed structure of feeling with broad social–historical sources.

The temporal, spatial and social mobilities to which working-class life has been subjected in recent decades have not been sufficient to dissolve these distinctive structures of feeling and orientations towards the world – or what may be objectified and reified from without as 'traditions' – because they are adaptive, inter-generationally reproduced and practical. I have therefore framed my interpretation of Millwallism's characteristic modes of reflection and expression with the use of the indispensable concepts of *practical consciousness* (Bourdieu 1977, 1992) and *restricted linguistic code* (Bernstein 1971, 1975). The work of these two sociologists in particular has shaped the present project, and attended its evolution from nascent possibility to completion. Few, if any, of their peers have so clearly, commitedly and persuasively examined and laid bare the psycho-social sources of working-class (or 'first world', but non liberal–individualist) consciousness and communication. Indeed, the contempt in which Bernstein was for so long held by his ostensibly 'progressive' opponents merely emphasizes the ideologically mistaken and/or epistemologically unsound approaches to working-class life that have dogged sociology for so long. Practical consciousness and restricted code, considered as interpretative tools, have enabled the development of a heuristically appropriate framework for the examination of a communicative universe that does not surrender its perspectives and experiences to abstract, objectivist analysis.

An important consequence of this approach has been to understand working-class social identity as most fully constituted, and therefore apprehendable, when it is set in inter-subjective motion. Millwallism is organized, first and foremost, around the congregational liberation of embodied cultural personality and the communicative practices that best express it. The extended focus placed on the historical and cultural backdrop to the development of Millwallism is not arbitrary, but integral to the presentation of an unusually full account of the broader social uses to which football fandom might be put. Detailed examination of these social sources supports my contention that 'belonging' – more usually regarded as the *raison d'être* of participation in studies of football fandom – represents only the starting-point of activity at Millwall. I have decided to take that activity seriously as genuinely, rather than notionally, ritualistic, and I have demonstrated the extent to which Millwallism draws upon anthropologically widespread and recognizable techniques and practices. An analysis of the relationship between embodied cultural dispositions, social memory and the mnemonics and mimetics of match-day participation exemplifies the distinctive theoretical–interpretative approach to largely implicit and experientially dense phenomena that I have tried to synthesise from disparate elements.

I have positioned football in a consciously delimited way as the practical medium *par excellence* of the continuing expression and celebration of the core practices and concerns of embodied masculinity in a specific working-class variant. It is almost impossible to overstate the significance of the game in its more extended sense in the maintenance and reproduction of these practices and in the informal cultural practices of working-class life generally. My interest in the game has therefore been primarily in the area of continuity of practice among these groups in their implicit resistance to and negotiation of modernity and its consequences, but without any particular focus on the hooligan phenomenon; the existing literature can be regarded as having by now exhausted the sociological potential of this particular sphere of activity. It is rather in the area of the deep connectedness to social background (Taylor 1993) and the relationship of football to broader and deeper sources of consciousness and experience that any originality in this work resides. I have tried to provide an account of the game that demonstrates the extent and depth of this embedding, so that it can be seen less as a discrete leisure pursuit than a core and pervasive ingredient in particular kinds of personality formation and sociality.

It is for this reason that I have presented two variants of social identity, the 'Millwall fan' and the 'south-east Londoner', as genuinely interconnected. The former, in a sense, synecdochically exemplifies the latter. This link is perhaps most interesting, beyond the obvious fact that Millwall is a concretely situated cultural institution, for the parallel processes of mythicization to which each have been subjected. The Millwall myth has been variously rejected, embraced or more ambiguously accommodated across the spectrum of Millwall fandom, and chimes closely with the broader mythology and sense of dramatized and notorious social identity long familiar to working-class men in south-east London. The development and negotiation of the Millwall myth, from within the fan-community, should therefore be understood as a particularly intense, rather than novel, experience of dialectically inflected and experienced social identity.

Introduction: Practical Consciousness, Beautiful Game: Working-Class Men, Football and Modernity

> The site of identity formation in cultural studies remains implicitly in and through cultural commodities and texts rather than in and through the cultural practices of everyday life. This, then, is where I want to end, with a plea for identity ethnography in cultural studies, with a plea for carrying out interactive research on groups and individuals who are more than just audiences for texts.
>
> Angela McRobbie, *Postmodernism and Popular Culture*

> That competitive edge got me into fights at school, even at primary school. There's always that myth when you're kids that the best footballer is always supposed to be the best fighter. It's stupid, but I know it's the same all over the country because I've talked to other players who found themselves in the same situation.
>
> Ian Wright, *Mr. Wright*

The field of what might be called 'football studies' has, despite its exponential growth throughout the 1990s, yet to convincingly come of age. Though there is much talk of taking football seriously as a terrain of cultural activity – frequently accompanied by the old adage about it being a matter of 'life and death' – there is still a dearth of sufficiently detailed British work connecting the meanings of the game to its customary social sources. While it is recognized that, for many fans, football must somehow have a part to play in their experiences of social 'identity', it is still the case that the generic and ontologically lightweight conceptual figure of the 'fan' dominates analysis. However, fans are people, the majority of them grounded at the deepest experiential levels in highly specific and regionalized cultural formations. The depth of identity-experience characteristic of some of these contexts cannot be conveyed by approaching their links with particular clubs as though the latter are simply external symbols or sites of emotionally saturated consumption. A significant factor in this failure to connect football to the very deepest sources of social personality lies in the more generalized inadequacy of sociological conceptualizations of working-class consciousness and experience. Only an increased anthropologization of sociology will enable the latter to fulfil its largely neglected promise to reveal the experiential densities of working-class life. The present study argues for the reinstatement of just that enterprise, on the understanding that 'working-class' (like its concomitant, 'bourgeois') is, first and foremost, a metaphor for continuing streams of variegated but anthropologically distinct experience which have been neither adequately defined nor interpretively handled by the customary, tortuous excursions into the minutiae of socio-economic categorization.

The key concepts through which the requisite sensitizing of sociology has been made possible derive from the work of Pierre Bourdieu. An operationalization of the fundamental heuristic categories of practical consciousness, *habitus* and embodiment is, therefore, central to everything that follows. These interpretive tools are particularly useful and important given the contemporary over-investment in the idea of the discursive in sociology and cultural studies. I spell out in the following the ways in which these ideas inform the methodological and interpretative framework to be applied to the analysis of Millwall Football Club, an informal cultural institution within which the themes of class, masculinity and the dialectics of social identity could scarcely be more central. The experiential–semantic field around the club through which these themes find articulation – what I call after Christan Bromberger (1993) the Millwall *Collective Imaginary* – has therefore been the key empirical site of the research. The primary focus of the examination of this locally inflected cultural institution is on the specific modes of masculine experience, social practice and identity for which it provides a dramatic and vital expressive context. Though I will be taking pains to identify some of the general sources of working-class male experience where I take them to be relevant, I do not intend to make Millwall fans stand in for all working-class men. It is in its particulars that the Millwall phenomenon is most interesting and deserving of attention

Masculinity, Cultural Continuity and Football

It is difficult to overestimate the significance of the role played by association football in the lives of millions of working-class men and boys over the last hundred years. This intensity of emotional investment in the game since its professionalization in the late nineteenth century is explicable, primarily, as an expression of the need to sustain modern contexts in which the core elements of pre-modern male subjectivities and cultures could survive and flourish. It is this which gives football its decisively masculine aspect, and the patterns of practice and expression that have historically surrounded the game their particular characteristics. The growing interest and participation in football culture among women should be understood in this context, and awaits careful sociological elaboration. However, the focus of the current work is firmly on the emergence of football as a demonstrably masculine domain. The gradual tightening of bourgeois cultural hegemony throughout the latter half of the nineteenth century ensured – in its tendency to constrict the range of arenas in which such subjectivities could find public expression – that for many men football would become an extraordinarily highly charged focus for powerful undercurrents in the passage to modernity. Its unique role in these processes has made football perhaps the most highly charged sphere in public culture, and one which has no parallel as a vehicle for what is usually an implicit celebration and maintenance of specific and enduring class-based moral forms.

Arguing for football as an historical vehicle of embodied cultural reproduction necessitates a marginalizing of contemporary debates around the nature and causes of hooliganism, the focus of so much of the formative football literature (e.g. Clarke 1976, Dunning *et al.* 1988, Marsh *et al.* 1978, Taylor 1971, 1982). I proceed from the view that 'football hooliganism' and match-day disorder in general have at their core no inner truths or obscure causes awaiting revelation. The nature of the game, and the social sources from which it draws, adds itself quite naturally to 'periodic excess and the carnivalesque'[1] (Armstrong and Giulianotti 1997: 8), and has done for centuries. Robert Malcolmson's (1973) account of popular recreational forms demonstrates that the close identification of football with drunken rowdiness and violent local conflict was well established by 1700, and that attempts to suppress and control the game in the interests of the growing requirements of labour discipline and the consolidation of puritan ideology were also well under way by this time (Malcolmson: 90, and see also Elias and Dunning 1986).

The struggle over permissible forms of bodily practice, emotionality and morality for which football has provided a focus has been therefore a long and bitter one. Most striking in it is the apparent irrevocable passion demonstrated for the game by plebeian/working-class men, which even public school codification (Hargreaves 1993) and the attempt to incorporate into the game the cult of the aristocratic gentleman did not diminish. The deep hunger amongst working-class men for the playing of the game (Cunningham 1980) around the time of its professionalization in 1863 appears to have been too extraordinary to explain away in terms of mere leisure. Few activities offered such men the opportunity to express a deeply embodied need for physicality, competition, visceral collectivity and ludic expression. The culture of the modern professional game soon came to reflect these things in heightened public form. Football, having been re-appropriated from the gentleman-amateurs of the public schools, entered the twentieth century, first and foremost, as a celebration of intensely male working-class values, 'where skill and cunning were valued, but hardness, stamina, courage, and loyalty were even more important. Fairness and good manners were not held in high regard' (Holt 1989: 173).

The tensions inherent in the growth of the professional game in the most intensive historical period of bourgeois missionizing and class 'conciliation' should not, however, be overlooked. They reflect the wider tensions around working-class 'respectability' so characteristic of modern class relations, and militate against any simple view of football as a repository of immemorial values and practices. The possibility of the carrying over and adaptation of pre-modern popular traditions is important here, for it indicates the (structured–improvisatory) role played by varieties of working-class *habitus* in the dialectics of cultural orientation. The possibility that durable – and transposable – embodied cultural dispositions may be reproduced over time and in changing contexts means that we must search for a third way of apprehending the realities of modern football culture – as neither pre-modern merry English nor convincingly modern/respectable, but as existing somewhere between the two, containing elements of both.

The relative autonomy from adult supervision enjoyed, historically, by young working-class men frames the critical space of social practice here (e.g. Suttles 1971, and Willis 1988). This space frequently exists as a temporally anomalous lacuna, resistant in frequently heightened and exaggerated ways, to the onward developmental march of the 'Civilising Process' (Elias 1982). The possibility of deep and intransigent cultural dispositions being subject to embodied reproduction – often beneath the level of improving material culture *and* explicit consciousness – is passed over by the 'latent evolutionism' (Horne *et al.* 1987) of this theory, especially as it is employed in the 'Leicester' model of the social development of football. In this (Dunning *et al.* 1988), it is claimed that the incorporation into working-class experience of increasing standards of material comfort and security entails the inevitable concomitant of the 'adoption' of respectable values (Dunning *et al. 1988*: 130). However, the realities of working-class respectability, especially where men are concerned, are far more complex and ambiguous than this suggests.[2] The ontological depth of the relatively recent historical 'adoption' of some of the symbols of gentility must be weighed against the (ever-present) cultural imperatives which tend to press hard on the social experiences of young working-class men.

I would therefore suggest that the practical nature of many masculinist class formations and social processes has led to the development of forms of consciousness in which the genteel and its opposites may be loosely unified. This is not the 'double consciousness' (Gilroy 1993) experienced by groups even less smoothly integrated into the structures of modernity, but a consciousness in which the oppositional, counter-bourgeois sensibility is overwhelmingly conveyed in implicit and mimetic ways in the use of the body itself. Eschewing anti-capitalist and utopian rhetoric, this masculine obsession with playing and watching football highlights the unarguable historical fact that the social definition of sport has itself been a central terrain of class struggle, 'part of the larger field of struggles over the definition of the *legitimate* body and the *legitimate* use of the body' (Bourdieu 1991: 360): definitions, that is, of legitimate and illegitimate culture and subjectivity.

The overwhelmingly apolitical nature of the (sub)culture surrounding football attests to its status as a primary – and primarily – practical–cultural sphere.

The fact that football culture had to wait until the fanzine explosion of the late eighties (Jary *et al.* 1991) for any meaningful, internally generated textual elucidation exemplifies this status. 'Football' is a set of practices within which implicitly counter-hegemonic and sovereign masculine identities may be lived and articulated in embodied demonstrations of social competence, grace and excellence. Absolutely central to what are the frequently obscure but nevertheless internally coherent social cosmologies of young working-class men, football – as Ian Wright observes – is thus impacted with meanings and experiences. And embedded as they are in more dense and extended social 'backgrounds' (Taylor 1995), these elude discursive articulation: for the existential grounds of such experiences are not straightforwardly accessible. In this sense, the game can be understood metaphorically as an experientially and symbolically condensed set of practices that contain and express a more general mode of consciousness and sense of reality – the feel for the game of football connects to the feel for the game of practical–collective life:

> The habitus as the feel for the game is the social game embodied and turned into a second nature. Nothing is simultaneously freer and more constrained than the action of the good player. He quite naturally materialises at just the place the ball is about to fall, as if the ball were in command of him – but, by that very fact, he is in command of the ball. The habitus, as society written into the body, into the biological individual, enables the infinite number of acts of the game – written into the game as possibilities and objective demands – to be produced; the constraints and demands of the game, although they are not restricted to a code of rules, *impose themselves* on those people – and those people alone – who, because they have a feel for the game, a feel, that is, for the immanent necessity of the game, are prepared to perceive them and carry them out. (Bourdieu 1990: 63)

The meanings which inhere in participation in the game may therefore be seen as transposable to the other spheres of activity in which practical mastery – predicated in general in working-class contexts on what tend to be the cardinal virtues of physical readiness, personal capability and the conquest of contingency – defines the bases of social participation. Thus the *best footballer*, with his innate charisma and aura of improvisatory excellence,[3] should also be the *best fighter*. In this interpretative universe a single movement may mimetically summon up, beneath the level of explicit awareness, an entire aesthetics of masculine presence and social cosmology, instantiating identity and belonging for those with access to the appropriate frames of experiential reference. For these crucial and characteristic elements in working-class male culture, played out daily in parks, football stadia and elsewhere, circulate in a space significantly beyond the word; beneath its contemporary veneer of rule-bound and high-performance modernity, the game remains a practical medium *par excellence*, encouraging all participants to 'reflect on the limits of "rationality", provoking the heart that aches and memories that linger' (Archetti 1992 : 233).

These themes continue to characterize football even in the current age of hyper-modernization, increasing commercialization and cultural complexity. The growth of new markets and the extension of involvement in the game to previously disinterested sections of the population (Goldberg and Wagg 1991, Williams 1994) should not obscure the persistence of its practical nature at ground level. Though the terrain of supporter culture *appears* to be changing with unprecedented speed, it is too early to take, for example, Richard Giulianotti's (1993, 1996) notion of 'post' fandom as an evenly distributed or widely characteristic phenomenon. Here, the power of the written word is once again adjudged to carry all before it in its culturally transformative power, and to recast the nature of football supporting itself. The notion that the emergence of the fanzine phenomenon constitutes a definitive 'epistemic break' (Armstrong and Giulianotti 1997: 212) with prior traditions of support is a dubious one: for anarchic humour, self-deprecating irony in support, criticism of club and league authorities and supporter-protests did not begin in 1989 – at least not at Millwall. And though growing numbers of individuals characterizable as (ironic, distanced) *post-fans* do clearly exist, it is far from clear that the bases of participation for the majority have radically changed. This is likely to be most true, as is the case with Millwall, of small and medium-sized clubs with little or no appeal beyond their own historical and social-ecological limits.

It is perhaps easy to forget, now, the hard times prior to the renaissance and new-found respectability of football in the nineties. Since the war, the durability of the dispositions and orientations accommodated by the game have enabled it to survive as a vital and exemplary sphere of embodied masculine culture. The game has held onto its deepest meanings in the face of genuine tragedy, intermittent moral panics, bourgeois indifference (at least until Italia '90), leftist–intellectualist opprobrium,[4] Margaret Thatcher's war against it (Armstrong and Young 1997) *and* the liberal–progressivist attempt to undermine competition and incorporate sport into a generalized culture of therapy.[5] It may be that, having survived these things, it will be the increasingly grandiose and accelerating processes of commercialization now sweeping through the game which definitively weakens the link between football and the practical masculinity that has always sustained it. And though there are indications that something of the kind is beginning to happen at Millwall, football in general still appears able to accommodate, if no longer unambiguously express, these core elements.

This accommodation consists, most significantly, in the continuing capacity of individual clubs – as historically vital cultural institutions in working-class life –

to offer contexts for the generation of highly specific, ritualizing communities of interpretation and expression. The nature, scope and detail of such communities, and the manner of their accomplishment on the basis of embodied cultural expertise, await the kind of sustained sociological–anthropological treatment and interpretation required by their subtlety and depth. The recent anthropological turn in British football studies has begun to address this shortcoming, with Richard Giulianotti (1993. 1996) and, in particular, Gary Armstrong (1998) producing sophisticated analyses of relationships between fan communities and their local social sources. Indeed, the latter's combination of interpretive sophistication and insight borne of fine-grained local knowledge make it a benchmark study of both 'football hooliganism' in general and its workings at the level of a specific club. This study attempts something different; eschewing a focus on the detail and mechanics of match-day disorder – about which there is little new to be said – I examine and connect the social sources of a locally inflected masculinity to the minutiae of the ritual activity characteristic of Millwall's *Collective Imaginary.*

Interpreting the Collective Imaginary

The experiential bases of participation in what I will call 'Millwallism' are of a depth too great to be contained by notions of *invented traditions* (Hobsbawm and Ranger 1993), *imagined communities* (Anderson 1983) and their narratives of more or less arbitrary belonging. Rather, I want to suggest that the declarative act of belonging is the beginning rather than the end point of participation in football-based rituals at intensely localist clubs like Millwall. The fact of belonging exists not as a climactic end in itself but as a basis for something far more extraordinary and compelling: the heightened experiential activation of the varieties of social consciousness and embodied identity that make such belonging itself possible and structure its expression. For it is not in the waving of banners, the painting of faces or the other increasingly common paraphernalia of football 'carnival' that the affective centre of ritualization at Millwall is to be discerned.[6] It is, in this sense, less an invented tradition of more or less arbitrary symbols than the collective context for a drama of lived identity derived from deeply personal experience. Understanding this requires an examination, in detail, of the ways in which this heightening of experience is collectively achieved via subtly and strategically applied versions of anthropologically widespread techniques of ritual practice.

Like many clubs of its size and kind, Millwall is the site of a particularized expressive subcultural community. Defining such an interpretive community as exists at these clubs as 'imaginary' is not, as I will demonstrate, to construct it as fictional or even primarily 'discursive'. Though the individuals who make up its membership cannot be viewed as a geographically homogenous grouping, the club's cultural community is bound together by specific understandings of class, masculinity and local history. Put differently, the fact that the majority of Millwall fans no longer live in the immediate locality of the ground does little to reduce the importance of the club as a primary symbol of the area and the patterns of culture forged within it. Christian Bromberger's idea of the 'Collective Imaginary' is a useful starting point in defining such a community, involving as it does the

> Identification of the team or club with an ideal image of collective life . . . this team is perceived, through its playing style, as a symbol of a specific mode of collective existence, and not as a simple sign (arbitrary) of a common belonging (Bromberger 1993: 118).

The expressive community that constitutes itself at a football club on this basis does indeed exceed in significance the mere explicit, discursive assertion of a common belonging. For if it is characterized by the expression and affirmation of particular and symbolically charged local identities and orientations it also has the potential to do something more. Via a powerful and transformative process of ritualization, the Collective Imaginary may summon up and experientially actualize that identity. The ways in which what I will define as *commemorative ritualization* operates at Millwall is best approached through a brief look at the relevant thinking of Bourdieu (1977), Paul Connerton (1989) and Maurice Bloch (1989).

Connerton notes – and this is crucial to a critique of the hermeneutic approach to enacted cultural forms – an overwhelming tendency to focus attention on 'the content rather than the *form* of ritual' (1989: 52). He regards this as a basic misinterpretation, and argues for the primacy of form. The basis for this prioritization of form over content is to be found in Connerton's belief in the efficacy of particular forms of communicative practice in ritual contexts:

> Once we begin to consider the form of ritual, as distinct from the form of myth, we come to see that ritual is not only an alternative way of expressing certain beliefs, but certain things can only be expressed in ritual. (1989: 54)

The two key spheres integral to the distinctive communicative form of ritual are what Connerton calls *habit-memory* and *incorporated practices.* These closely parallel Bourdieu's *habitus* and *bodily hexis*, and are worth examining closely both to illuminate these parallels and to inform that framework for the interpretation of quasi-formal ritual,[7] which Bourdieu elides in favour of the concept of *ritualization.* Connerton underpins his approach to forms of communicative ritual consciousness via an examination of three distinct forms of memory. The first two, personal and cognitive memory, are closely identified with fully articulate and explicit self awareness and as such define an area that '. . . the hermeneuticists have standardly been trying to recover and interpret' (1989: 29). This focus on full articulation, explication and reflexive access to, in Basil Bernstein's terms, the grounds of individual experience,[8] is defined by Connerton as 'conventionalism'.[9] It is the third category, habit-memory, that such approaches in contemporary social theory have tended to ignore.[10]

But what, given that personal memory has been studied in connection with (verbally articulate) individual life histories and cognitive memory with investigations into universal mental categories, are the dimensions and characteristics of habit-memory? To begin with, and in contradistinction to personal memory, it is structured collectively and is implicitly performative. It is collective, Connerton argues on the basis of an examination of Maurice Halbwach's (1980) work on social memory, because the idea of individual memory itself – as a discrete and separable phenomenon – is an abstraction almost devoid of meaning. This (and here again there are echoes of Bourdieu) is due to the fact that

> Groups provide individuals with frameworks within which their memories are localised and memories are localised by a kind of mapping . . . no collective memory can exist without reference to a socially specific spatial framework . . . our memories are located within the mental and material spaces of the group. (Connerton 1989: 37)

It is this fact of collective orientation – so much a feature of many non-bourgeois, locality-focused groups – which makes ritualized communicative forms of sociality so powerful and, in fact, possible. Ritual emerges in Connerton's conception as, like class itself, not a thing but a process. Its essentially commemorative nature means that ritual is not a discrete or isolable socio-cultural 'event', but rather an extension of the everyday, a collective practice premised upon the summoning up of an operational and activated holistic (bodily, affective) experience of group identity and 'tradition': 'Images of the past and recollected knowledge of the past are conveyed and sustained by (more or less) ritual performances' (Connerton 1989, 37). I want to stress that in this conception 'tradition' is neither simply 'invented' nor part of a 'discursive' group representation. Ritually expressed identifications such as those in evidence at Millwall are far from being fictive, in the sense of being creatively brought into being out of novel or disparate materials. Rather, they are rooted in habitual group experience and, in this sense, significantly *commemorative* in both Connerton's and Bourdieu's terms – as public expressions of embodied cultural orientations and imperatives. It follows that freezing and isolating out specific ritual 'moments' (songs, chants, crowd activity etc.) as if such expressive 'content' were primary, makes little sense. To think of Millwall fans' ritual practice as a 'text' awaiting retrieval and hermeneutic 'interpretation' is to miss the point. It is not merely what songs, chants or bodily performances *say* that is significant: it is also what they *do*.

The Research

The overwhelmingly practical and largely implicit nature of the forms of cultural practice exhibited at and around Millwall present a serious challenge to the ethnographer. In order to arrive as closely as possible to the experiences and meanings that underpin these practices I have employed an interpretive framework derived from a synthesis of historical, textual, interview and participant–observational methods. The analysis is diachronic, concerned with identifying not only salient themes in the history of the club, but with a broader historical conception of the cultural formations out of which its supporter-culture emerges. Examining the distinctive varieties of class *habitus* characteristic of these processual histories has been important here, but is by no means definitive, being well beyond the range of this study.

There is no doubt that these class-cultural formations have been, and continue to be, subject to broad and perhaps accelerating processes of change. It is the continuing valency of customary (though adaptive) experiences of identity and practice, however, which demonstrates the usefulness of the concept of *habitus* as the link in the dialectic between the subjective and objective components of class and between past and present, structure and practice. Millwall fan culture should therefore be thought of as expressing important themes in both specific and general processes open, to some degree, to the future. *Being Millwall* is thus one way in which some individuals may choose to collectively negotiate – as meaning generating agents-in-the-world – the uncertainties of rapid demographic and social change from a standpoint of practically cultivated 'ontological security' (Giddens 1979: 219).

At the core of this practice are experiences of embodied culture inaccessible to language. Recent developments in linguistics and cognitive psychology (Johnson 1987, Lakoff 1990, Lave 1988), which have been extensively mulled over by anthropologists yet remain curiously marginal to literary sociology and cultural studies, have added weight to the practical/embodied conception of culture and practice, and to the view that 'words of themselves do not reveal the semantic densities of experiential space' (Hastrup 1995: 32).

In light of this, Bloch considers the methodological implications of seeking to render non-sentential knowledge in the medium of writing. To do so is, inevitably, not to reproduce the knowledge of the people being studied but to transmute it into an entirely different logical form. Such a transmutation might, of course, be meaningfully achieved to some degree – it is after all possible to describe things that are not linguistic – but the onus is on the ethnographer to explicitly acknowledge the act of cognitive translation involved. 'Perhaps', Bloch suggests,

> we should make much more use of description of the way things look, sound, feel, smell, taste and so on – drawing on the realm of bodily experience – simply for heuristic purposes to remind readers that most of our material is taken from the world of non-explicit expert practice and does not only come from linear, linguistic thought. (Bloch 1991: 193)

This I have attempted to do in those chapters containing empirical description. I have sought to convey the multi-sensory, experiential density of particular events via a poetic–suggestive mode, in recognition of the limitations of naturalist descriptivism (Clifford 1994). This, in its way, is a further example of the near-redundancy of the word in both experiencing and rendering heightened modes of collective-ritual activity still characterized by mytho-poetic imaginative sensibilities and primitive-classificatory interpretive systems. The language-based analyses of interview and fanzine material are nevertheless critical in marking out the dimensions of the contexts in which embodied practices are played out – with the proviso that the unbridgeable epistemological gulf between experience and explicit knowledge is recognized. Drawing on Bourdieu, Hastrup makes the critical point that cultural identities can be elicited neither from the spoken nor the written word. It is in social memory, and not in texts, that the 'rules' and strategies that underpin action are situated. If recollection is embodied rather than written, the implication follows that the place to look for 'identity' is in collective social experience:

> Giving privilege to words as clues to identity, history, society or culture is to commit an epistemological error. Identities are stored in practice; it is the '*habitus*' of a particular people that is the basis for that intentionless convention of regulated improvisation, that lends some degree of coherence to their world. Taken by themselves words are only a limited means of entry into this world. We have to observe and analyse how they are put to use, and how their implicit symbolic capital is put into social play. (Hastrup 1995: 41)

My interpretation of these social sources and interactive practices is on the basis of a biographical steepening in the relevant social spheres. A native of south-east London myself, I have been a fan of Millwall for over thirty years, I have attended innumerable games both home and away and engaged in more discussions and conversations about the club than I care to remember. I therefore enjoy some degree of access to the broad sphere of embodied cultural practice submitted to analysis here. Indeed, it was the dissonance generated by the collision of dispositions inculcated in me by a working-class background and a relatively late exposure to academic culture and language which has led to a preoccupation with practical–cultural consciousness. While I do not claim to be the true and only exegete of this medium, I have a foot in both camps, and have developed a perspective on relations between what appear to be incommensurable modalities of consciousness and experience. Perhaps, then, I have straddled the ontological gap between words and social processes, and thus made the experiential density of this sphere of social practice available to the reader. The extent to which I have made accessible something of the experiential density of this sphere of social practice, situated firmly as it is on the other side of that gap, is for the reader to judge.

The full-time ethnographic research was conducted over two years, focused on the 1995/6 and 1996/7 seasons, while Millwall were playing in what was then the Endsleigh first division. Throughout this period I attended a total of sixty-five games. I travelled to and from games with small and large groups, by train, car, coach, and participated (for the most part soberly) in drinking sessions before and after games. This immersion in match-day activity afforded many opportunities for observation and discussion, and this was supplemented by a social contacts with Millwall fans away from match-days. I conducted, in addition, twenty-five representatively selected recorded interviews with white male fans in domestic and public (pubs, cafes, workplaces) contexts. Two thirds of these interviewees were previously unknown to me. I defined myself here as a Millwall fan writing a sociology book about Millwall fans, interested in locating, as precisely as possible, the nature of the club's appeal and the characteristics of relationships between club and fans.

In the main, the majority of the Millwall-focused textual sources drawn on derive from the same span of time. A small number of the fanzines – both *No One Likes Us* and those of other teams – predate the research period by a year or two, giving an overall span of four years. As noted, I have approached these less as indispensable discursive forms in their own right than as important *indicators* of those socially embedded and practical locations that host the real action. Though they are both a way in to the detail of the culture and increasingly significant in their own right, they are secondary phenomena, and I treat them as such.

The complexities inherent in the attempt to get at the central meanings of Millwallism are reflected in the overall shape of the study. In Chapter One the focus is on that peculiar dialectical relationship between actual experience and apocryphal public myth that characterizes the historical development of the Millwall archetype. This revolves around a consideration of the emergence and circulation of specific understandings and constructions of the club in the general media, the more particular football-based 'fanzine' literature and sociological interpretations of the development of the 'hooligan' phenomenon. Out of the examination of these phenomena and processes emerges the centrality of two themes: specific and continuous patterns of embodied cultural practice, and the relationship between these and place.

The high degree of inter-subjective experiential density that these patterns express are rooted, I argue in Chapter Two, in varieties of *habitus* characteristic of the historical development of inner south-east London. The examination of the most salient among these proceeds from a view of the club as an exemplifying and heightening informal cultural institution centred on their ritual enactment, maintenance and continuing reproduction. Some of the specificities of metropolitan working-class experience are essayed in their historical dimensions and connected to the contemporary understandings and exhibitions of regional class subjectivities for which Millwall provides a focus. These specifics constitute the first stream of what I have called the social sources of Millwallism.

This line of analysis is carried over into Chapter Three and the second stream of Millwallism's social sources – a more general examination of what I take to be the interconnected foundational themes of working-class masculinity, varieties of sociality and the ontologization of place. The concepts of embodied cultural reproduction and social habit-memory are of central importance here to the proposal of a heuristic framework for the interpretation of the social sources of those patterns of consciousness and embodied practice that have underpinned the development of British football culture in general and Millwallism in particular.

Part Two begins, in Chapter Four, with a consideration of the relatively novel sphere of football-subcultural writing in the most significant and popular of the Millwall fanzines, *The Lion Roars*. The historically recent emergence of a relatively stable textual field allows for a numerically rich appraisal of participants' definitions of the central tenets of Millwallism as they impinge upon their own involvement in the cultural life of the club. The focus is on the non-footballing meanings relating to identity and value that inhere in this internally generated material, and on the ways in which these (secondary) elaborations 'thinly' stake out the parameters of the otherwise thickly semantic, experiential universe (Geertz 1975) inhabited by Millwall fans on, especially but not exclusively, match-days.

The (potentially) experientially pervasive nature of the relationship between a commitment to Millwallism and the sense of self is illustrated by the interview-based material in Chapter Five. *Millwall* is considered as an enormously dense and powerful personal symbol central to processes of 'symbolization': the merging of the cultural symbol and the self. It is suggested, in the context of commonly held structures of feeling and socially embedded personal identities that *Millwall* functions, like 'working-class' itself, as both a metaphor for and heightened instance of a specific modality of social being and consciousness.

This merging of symbol and self, I suggest in Chapter Six, is an experiential phenomenon individually known but inter-subjectively generated and sustained, most demonstrably by the collective maintenance of enacted, expressive ritual forms at and around games. Description and interpretation of these forms, situated as they are at the affective and experiential centre of Millwallism, therefore constitute the basis of this final substantive chapter.

Notes

1. The carnivalesque (Bakhtin 1965) dimension of Millwallism fandom is considered in Chapters Four and Six.
2. Work on the *Blades* of Sheffield United (Armstrong and Harris 1991, Armstrong 1998) demonstrates this. Though the class backgrounds, as defined by the authors, of participants in this particular footballing subculture are far from homogeneous or uniform, the patterns of disposition and behaviour exhibited by them demonstrate the important point that even football hooligans can come from *good* lower-middle-class homes. Social mobility need not, in itself, eradicate these kinds of embodied practices and sensibilities.
3. 'Only a virtuoso with a perfect mastery of his "art of living" can play on all the resources inherent in the ambiguities and indeterminacies of behaviours and situations so as to produce the actions appropriate in each case, to do at the right moment that of which people will say "There was nothing else to be done" and to do it in the right way' (Bourdieu 1992: 107). But elsewhere Bourdieu's early, mistaken view that the sphere of excellence is incompatible with the *consumption* of sporting spectacles (1978: 829), represents an uncharacteristic lapse in his usually firm theoretical–intuitive grasp of 'popular' dispositions. Christopher Lasch (1979: 105), writing at around the same time, offers a far more perceptive account of discriminating and active spectatorship: 'Far from destroying the value of sports, the attendance of spectators makes them complete. Indeed one of the virtues of contemporary sports lies in their resistance to the erosion of standards and their capacity to appeal to a knowledgeable audience. Norman Podhoretz has argued that the sports public remains more discriminating than the public for the arts and that "excellence is relatively uncontroversial as a judgement of performance". More important, everyone agrees on the standards against which excellence must be measured. The public for sports still consists largely of men who took part in sports during boyhood and thus acquired a sense of the game and a capacity to distinguish among many levels of excellence.'
4. The contempt with which Ian Taylor (1982), for example, dismisses the lives of 'underclass' football fans indicates the extent to which, despite their rhetorical and ideological attachments, leftist intellectuals have frequently evinced an aversion to any 'incorrectly' channelled masculine vitality.
5. Lasch (1979: 122) observes that the 'anguished outcry of the true fan, who brings to sports a proper sense of awe only to find them corrupted from within from the spread of the "entertainment ethic", sheds more light on the degradation of sports than the strictures of left-wing critics, who wish to abolish competition, emphasise the value of sports as health-giving exercise, and promote a more "co-operative" conception of athletics – in other words, to make sports an

instrument of personal and social therapy'. See Hargreaves (1993, Chapter 8) for an account of the ways in which such perspectives have been incorporated into pedagogic practice in British schools.

6. Millwallism is, in terms of material aesthetic symbols, spare to the point of asceticism. The ubiquitous replica shirts notwithstanding, a Millwall game is unlikely to be a riot of carnivalesque colour. This disdain for the visible trappings of 'ritual' is derived from two broad and interconnected sources. Firstly, a no-nonsense aesthetic sensibility rooted in the (white working-class) metropolitan dislike of ostentation. Secondly, the tendency to understand the essence of ritualization as held in the embodied agent rather than external symbols. When Nottingham Forest fans arrived at the New Den for a vital promotion game, the unfurling of an enormous flag and contributions of a Euro-style trumpeter were met with spontaneous and savage derision. Similarly, the late 1980s craze for inflatable plastic emblems, bananas in particular, barely registered at the Den: Millwall fans, by and large, don't do that sort of thing.
7. Bourdieu invariably maintains a tight focus on the concept of 'ritualization', arising as it does out of everyday consciousness and practice. Though he is not at all sympathetic to notions of ritual as either discrete entity or process located at the level of the supraindividual collective, I would suggest that his model of practice and practical mastery is uniquely suited to an account of the kinds of implicit, practical and ostensibly spontaneous ritual activities in which Millwall fans engage.
8. Bernstein's views on class and language are central to my understanding of processes of ritualization in English football. It bears repeating that Bernstein (1971: 164) argues that forms of socialization *orient* the child towards speech codes that control access to relatively context-tied or context-independent meanings. The most important influence on this process is social class, with working-class children likely to be most sensitized towards particularistic, rather than universalistic, meanings. Misinterpreted as a deficit-theory of working-class language, this schematic model is premised upon a range of characteristics which rather constitute strengths in the context of collective socialities: collective expression, shared (often implicit) meanings, metaphorization of narratives and communalized speaker roles. The implications of such orientations and skills for participation in ritual processes in working-class cultural institutions are obvious.
9. One of Mary Douglas's central assertions in *Natural Symbols* (1973) is that it is an exemplary characteristic of fully reflexive and articulate modes of consciousness that they develop dismissive orientations to the very idea of ritual itself. Such forms of 'elaborated' (in Bernstein's terms), personally individuated, decontextualizing consciousness are essentially antithetical to collective expression and communication. 'Ritual', Douglas observes, 'is become a bad

word signifying empty conformity' (1973: 19).

10. An exception to this in British thinking is to be found in the work of Michael Oakeshott, who distinguishes between two forms of morality. First, there is the 'reflective application of a moral criterion', a form of life which most values self-consciousness, whether individual or social. Second, there is a form of morality which is a 'habit of affection and behaviour'. Conduct derived from such a form is 'as nearly as possible without reflection' or 'nothing more than the unreflective following of a tradition of conduct in which we have been brought up' (Oakeshott 1962, cited in Connerton 1989: 29) This model, clearly, is Bourdieu's 'practical consciousness' – that central component of, especially, non-bourgeois groupings – in another guise.

Part I

–1–

The Millwall Myth and its Urban Context: South-East London as the Land that Time Forgot

> A winter-chill Tuesday in south-east London. Commuter trains from suburban Kent chug out of New Cross Gate station, soon to unpack their contents at Waterloo East a couple of miles up the line. In the other direction, there is the usual snarl of buses and lorries inching their way through the traffic lights on the Old Kent Road towards Elephant and Castle. Between railway and road, as if marooned on an island where progress has passed it by, stands the Den – home to Millwall Football Club for the last eighty three years. If you cut through to the ground from Surrey Docks – or Surrey Quays, as the property developers renamed that little swathe of Rotherhithe – then head down Trundleys Road and Sanford Street, you finally turn right into Cold Blow Lane. Never was a street more aptly named. Through its graffiti-strewn tunnels, past the scrapyards full of clapped-out cars and down to the Den blew the wind of malevolence that provided the public preconceptions of English football in the late 1970s and early 1980s. No ground has been closed down by the FA because of crowd trouble more often than the Den.
>
> Denis Campbell and Andrew Shields, *Soccer City*

The word *Millwall*, I would suggest, is one of the more evocative in contemporary English. It functions as a condensed symbol, widely and indiscriminately used to express ideas and feelings about an entire sphere of activity and experience well beyond the compass of its original meaning. It has become a byword for, amongst other things, violent mob thuggery, unreconstructed masculinity, dark and impenetrable urban culture and working-class 'fascism'. The metaphoric power of the word derives, of course, from the archetypal status of the 'Millwall supporter' as the defining and emblematic 'Football Hooligan'. The archetypal status of the Millwall fan is a vexed and complex one, in which myth and reality have perhaps become so closely intertwined that even some of those most closely involved are unsure as to where the one might end and the other begin. It is a story of violence and mayhem both real and apocryphal, of particular and localized patterns of masculine culture, and of the ways in which popular representations of that culture meet with subcultural self-definition in dialectics of identity. It is also, critically, about a cultural struggle for the right to *embody* that identity.

In this chapter, then, I want to do three main things. First, to demonstrate that Millwall does in fact function as a powerful archetype in what we might call the popular consciousness. Second, to examine the ways in which Millwall fans played a pivotal role in the development of the media narrative of 'Football Hooliganism'. And third, to demonstrate that representations of the club and its fans are inextricably bound up with ideas about a specific urban locality.

Fear and Loathing on the Old Kent Road

> When it comes to fear, there are few things to match being bushwhacked in a dark subway by several hundred Millwall boys. It makes you wonder why you ever became a football hooligan.
>
> Mickey Francis and Peter Walsh, *Guvnors*

> 'Earthquakes, Wars and Millwall reports as they happen.'
>
> BBC Radio Five advertising poster, 1995

In December 1995 BBC2 screened *Decisive Moments: Images from the News.* The documentary focused on media coverage of the Conservative party-leadership contest of that year, and particularly on challenger John Redwood's media campaign. An expert on the manipulation and presentation of photographic images revealed the clumsy and inopportune nature of Redwood's campaign, and demonstrated ways in which the visual impact of various photo-opportunities could have been improved. Examining a picture of Redwood's 'team' – a group shot featuring a dozen or so people – our guide suggested ways in which the composition of the image could be improved so as to make it appear more professional, ordered and 'less like the terraces at Millwall'.

The Same evening (the 28th) saw an edition of the BBC1 comedy sports quiz *They Think Its All Over*. Presenter Nick Hancock introduced the show with a joke about the increase of accidents under the British Rail privatization programme: 'I don't know what's so original about doing trains, Millwall fans have been doing them for years.' The invocation of Millwall in these two widely divergent contexts is both instructive and typical. It attests to the ways in which the received imagery of the Millwall fan is disseminated across a range of popular media forms. It appears frequently enough, and in a sufficient variety of contexts, to have assumed the status of an archetype. Its shorthand and multi-referential qualities allow for it to be used metaphorically in almost limitless contexts. In the kinds of instances exampled above – of which there are countless others, with more being added all the time – the name is invoked in an abstracted, contentless manner. It exists as a cipher, condensing a range of widely disseminated understandings and images into an abbreviated and highly malleable symbol. Before going on to look at the broader media and sociological processes that led to the development of this symbolic status, I will look at the ways in which the symbol is understood, defined, fleshed out and given content in the burgeoning sphere of popular football writing. This will illustrate the ways in which ideas about Millwall are framed and circulated in the football–cultural dialogue of fanzines, magazines and a growing number of popular books.

One of the most significant developments in late-1980s 'renaissance' in football culture (Redhead 1991, 1993, Williams and Wagg 1991) was the emergence of the 'fanzine' phenomenon. By the turn of the decade every league club had at least one such supporter-generated forum for the dissemination of various forms of football and football-related writing. This was an important movement,

> Enabling a 'users' view – and sometimes a radical re-interpretation (or defence) of popular cultural forms to be expressed by people who would otherwise be excluded from any usual means of written expression about, or control over, mainstream institutions in the production of mass culture . . . a particularly potent example of the existence of a continued 'contestation' over cultural institutions. (Jary *et al.* 1991: 581)

While it is certainly the case that fanzines played a critical role in processes of cultural contestation, they have had an equally significant role as textual forums for the circulation of the kind of dialogical subculture previously maintained orally in English football. As repositories of the kinds of humour, lore and apocrypha with which fans have always framed their participation, fanzines represented something new in the culture of the game: fixed, stable and documentary channels of communication *between,* as well as within, clubs. This enables us to look at some of the understandings and imagery by means of which ideas about and experiences of Millwall are conveyed by other sets of fans.

One of the annual staples of fanzine practice is the pre-season review of a club's prospects for the coming campaign. These usually include a guide to those grounds to be visited, and to the kinds of (primarily alcoholic) entertainments and adventures to be had in their environs. The August 1996 issue of Rotherham's *Moulin Rouge* contains the following:

> Millwall – Why us? I mean why? I'm crappin' miself already about the New Den visit. They'll be rightly upset about being 2nd division fare after they thought they'd be premier poseurs. Rotherham town reduced to a moonscape, life as we know it altered forever?

This humourous, mock-apocalyptic style is absolutely typical of fanzine correspondents as they contemplate their impending doom in south-east London, and fanzine culture is saturated with examples. What is perhaps most interesting in accounts of these games is the invariable focus on Millwall's iconic urban context. *Forest Forever* (Nottingham Forest) wonders:

> How can four clubs, all located within five miles of each other geographically, be so socially distant from each other? Unassuming Charlton, Wombling Wimbledon, Suburban Crystal Palace and then savage, nasty, malicious Millwall. I'd read and seen all about the problems Millwall have with their fans but nah, I thought, hooliganism's on the wane isn't it? Perhaps it is, generally, but it's alive and well and truly kicking in Deptford and Peckham.

Arsenal's *The Gooner* is more strident still. The report relates, like the foregoing, to a highly charged and important fixture. The correspondent has been intimidated, and clearly considered himself to have been in real danger. This is beyond dispute – there was very real 'trouble' after this game. What is interesting for present purposes is the language and imagery used to convey the experience:

> I hope you all made it back in one piece from The Den on 10th January after our FA Cup 3rd round victory over Millwall. Wasn't the atmosphere horrendous? They can build as many new grounds as they like but the supporters will never change. And what about those Dickensian surroundings with water dripping from the dank viaducts? . . . Getting away from the ground after the match was like being on manoeuvres in some enemy infested outpost of Vietnam . . . And by the way Mick (McCarthy), we're not *supposed* to be a Premiership team, we are and have been for 75 years, which is 73 years longer than your shabby underworld outfit. Good riddance and so long.

These kinds of ways of writing about Millwall and its environs, with its fused imageries of urban decay and sense of Dickensian obscurity and danger are not confined to the sphere of fanzines. In the burgeoning field of football-related literature one highly specialized genre is the memoirs of the reformed hooligan. This trend, originating in the late 1980s (Allan 1989, Ward 1989), is characterized by a widespread dissemination of the subcultural staples around which so much of fanzine culture revolves: a carousel of reputation and myth, claim and counterclaim, tall tales and journalistic despatches from the front line. Millwall tends to feature largely in these accounts, the legendary status of its fans of the seventies secure. As Colin Ward reminisces,

> The word ['Millwall'] sent shivers down my spine; the hardest fans in the land. They had once taken the Everton end in an FA Cup tie. Everyone knows dockers are tough . . . when it (the whistle) blew we shot out of the exit towards our car. Every street looked the same: bleak and uncompromising. At every alleyway we passed we were fearful that Millwall fans who knew the area would emerge. (Ward 1989: 29)

Ward later declares that, while it was one thing to defend your 'end' against attack, 'it is quite another mixing it on the streets against Millwall' (1989: 95). The iconic status afforded Millwall fans in these matters is clearly apparent. More recent contributions to the genre continue the trend. The Brimson brothers (Brimson and Brimson 1996) offer an 'insider's' guide to the aetiology and dimensions of football-related violence. In addition to noting that 'Millwall away is one of the most dreaded fixtures of the season', and that 'the very name Millwall has a thuggish ring to it' (1996: 107), the authors provide a broad historical perspective:

> It is common knowledge that there are a number of clubs whose fans have been at the forefront of football violence for many, many years . . . the mere mention of the names of these teams evokes memories of trouble caused throughout the country . . . two of the most infamous sets of fans are from East London, and they are, of course, West Ham and Millwall . . . what still holds true . . . is the reputation of this club's followers as one of the most violent groups of supporters in existence. Moreover, the original Millwall mob, the F-Troop, who used to wear some very strange headgear, remain possibly the most feared firm ever seen at an English football ground. (1996: 105)

An analysis of these accounts reveals a very solid – indeed invariable – core of themes and images: the mythical status of Millwall fans' exploits and adventures, especially in the 1970s; a darkling urban iconography in which danger lurks around every corner; and the association of a legendary toughness and capacity for violence with particular occupational and cultural groupings such as *dockers* and *gangsters.*[1] It becomes transparently clear, given all of this, that the Millwall myth is as much about a sense of place as it is about the history of a discrete cultural institution. Popular conceptions of the urban ecologies of south-east London circulate, as we will see in the next chapter, well beyond the area itself. They are as likely to appear in the *Daily Telegraph* – 'the immediate area was so run down that the building of a football stadium could only improve it . . . if you added a couple of street urchins you would almost be back to the era of Charles Dickens' (quoted in *The Lion Roars,* no. 41) – as in the scurrilous ravings of fanzine correspondents. They have received their most explicit and forceful articulation in one of the additions to the hooligan-memoir genre (King 1996). In this ostensibly fictionalized account of a Millwall–Chelsea game at the New Den, the Chelsea-supporting narrator crystallizes many of the prevailing understandings of Millwall in their rawest form:

> We're building up for Millwall and it's going to be nasty, yet we respect Millwall somehow, deep down, though we'd never say as much, knowing New Cross and Peckham are the arseholes of London . . . As far back as our memories go Millwall have always been mad. Something special, mental, off their heads. They've got their reputation and they deserve it, raised on docker history spanning the century. A hundred years of kicking the fuck out of anyone who strays too far down the Old Kent Road. (1996: 225)

The narrator provides these brief historical speculations in order to contextualize what follows. Chelsea's 'boys' have come to south-east London to test themselves against the might of Millwall's 'firm'. Millwall-Chelsea games, like those against West Ham, have indeed been characterized by high levels of violence over the years, as the respective firms fight for supremacy of the capital. As the Chelsea firm enters the environs of the New Den the narrator describes, from his west-London perspective, a very different city:

> Millwall's in a corner of London where time stands still even if they do have a plush new ground. The streets and people remain the same and Cold Blow Lane was a wicked place full of nutters, and the New Den may look flash but it's full of the same old faces standing in the background waiting patiently . . . we're putting ourselves on the edge and when you're in south-east London it's a fucking long way to the bottom if you get thrown off . . . through streets they know like the back of their hands. This gives them the advantage because you could get lost for days in the blocks, houses, empty yards. There's no colour in the buildings, bricks identical and wasteland overgrown, rows of broken walls and broken wire, smashed glass and rusted metal, dull new houses that remind me of Bethnal Green. It's a fucking joke thinking about Millwall's flash stadium set in amongst this shit . . . It's fucking eerie this place. Full of decaying dockers in flat caps bombed and left to rot under a collapsed London. (King 1996: 225–7)

The tone and imagery could scarcely be more gothic or apocalyptic. Even if we accept that exaggeration is the primary effect of this rather bravura style, the symbols and imagery through which a sense of particular place is rendered are commonplace, and continuous with other accounts. This part of London is clearly drenched in a specific kind of folk-taxonomic mystique. I will argue in all that follows that this mystique is derived from the peculiarities of south-east London's historical development. There is an important sense in which certain generalized ways of thinking about and representing the area precede the development of the Millwall myth, and that the latter was to some extent drafted on to some of these pre-existing frameworks. I will argue that these historical and cultural themes were framing contexts for the central position occupied by Millwall in media and folk accounts of the development of football hooliganism as a distinctive phenomenon from the late 1960s on. A brief social history of the club will illustrate the extent to which it has been inextricably bound up with these broader processes.

'Soccer Marches to War': Millwall and the Birth of the Modern Hooligan

Pre-history of the 'Hooligan'

> 'DON'TS, for Spectators'
>
> DON'T advise players how to play or what to do. The players engaged by directors will doubtless have had some previous experience of the game. They are taking all the

risks; you, personally, are quite safe behind the touchline. DON'T give advice to the referee. He has to give his decision quickly, and, like the rest of us, he makes mistakes. Always respect his decision; the game will be much better for doing so. There is plenty of room for good and reliable referees. Why not try and pass for one yourself? It is by no means an easy job. DON'T imagine the Directors and officials are not aware they can and do make mistakes. Rely upon it when found they will be remedied.

DON'T swear or use bad language of any description in the hearing of others. It is not nice for ladies to hear, and it does not raise you in the estimation of other would-be friends; besides, the Directors don't appreciate it. They are endeavouring to cater for all. Try not to spoil other people's pleasure. DON'T make what may appear to you and your friends to make 'funny' remarks respecting our own or visiting team. Such are not asked for by the Directors or players. Remember there are people quite as funny as yourself present, who wish to follow the game.

From the Millwall Christmas programme, December 1919

'DON'T DO IT, CHUMS'
DON'T ever invade the playing pitch – keep your seats and places on the terraces – keep off the grass.
DON'T throw soil, cinders, clinkers, stones, bricks, bottles, cups, fireworks or other kinds of explosives, apples, oranges, etc. on the playing pitch during or after the match.
DON'T barrack, utter filthy abuse, or cause any physical violence to the referee and his linesman inside or outside the Den.
DON'T barrack, utter filthy abuse, or molest in any manner players of the visiting team.
DON'T barrack, utter filthy abuse, or molest in any manner the players of the Millwall Football Club.
DON'T assemble in small or large numbers in the streets adjacent to the Den
DON'T deface or remove Warning Notices which are posted within the Den.

From a Warning Notice issued by the Millwall, 1949–50

Once again we are seriously perturbed by the irresponsible behaviour of certain groups of unruly teenage supporters . . . This sort of thing must be stamped out for the good of Millwall and the game. We are not exaggerating in any way thc unruliness of these young people. Even our own genuine supporters have been shocked and shamed by their behaviour and unless it is nipped in the bud now decent civilised supporters will stay away, and this is something we can not afford to happen.

From Millwall *v.* Swansea programme notes, April 1966

The foregoing quotes, spanning a period of almost fifty years, were all directly and pedagogically aimed at the entire body of Millwall fandom. The most striking, and significant, thing about them – changes in tone and language notwithstanding – is the apparent continuity of the forms of behaviour to which they are addressed. Foul language, missile throwing, vandalism, large street 'assemblies' and occasional violence. These are, of course, the staple activities of what came, from the mid-1960s on, to be known as Football Hooliganism. Much of the sociological literature devoted to football over the last twenty years or so has revolved around one important question: what factors, if any, distinguish the phenomenon as widely understood as emerging at some point in the 1960s from some earlier patterns of football supporting? The work that has most closely addressed this question (for example Clarke 1991, Dunning *et al.* 1988, 1990, Taylor 1982), from divergent perspectives, has found some degree of consensus. While the existence of crowd disorder and violence is widely acknowledged to have been of a piece with the early development of the game, accounting for the emergence of contemporary Football Hooliganism has been a more fractious problem. In particular, it is worth drawing attention to some of the more useful aspects of the work of Dunning *et al.* at Leicester. The greatest virtue of this body of analysis lies in its detailed historical focus and consequent stress upon the significance of continuities in relationships between class, masculinity and English football. The idea of continuity – though probably overstated in the 'Leicester' model (Williams 1991: 177) – is crucial. For it is clear that the structural and expressive characteristics of the modern hooligan differ significantly from his clinker-throwing, abusive and sometimes violent antecedents. What is less clear is the extent to which both draw upon fundamentally similar orientations towards the body, language, collective ritual experience and an (adaptive) aesthetics of class. In what follows I want to do two things. First, to illustrate the ways in which these four interdependent spheres have characterized the cultural development of the Millwall fan-community from the early part of the century. Second, to look at the ways in which these distinctive – though not unique – modes of cultural expression and practice at Millwall came to be defined as exemplary and emblematic in the construction of the contemporary hooligan-paradigm.

Millwall Athletic Football Club, amongst the first in London, was founded in 1885 by workers at Morton's preserve factory on the Isle of Dogs on the north of the Thames in east London. The majority of the founders were of Scottish origin, and chose blue as their colour and the Lion Rampant as their emblem. Like many of its early northern counterparts, Millwall was closely identified with particular proletarian occupational groups, in this case with the docks (Murray 1988). It was not until 1910, following a succession of ground changes as support expanded, that the club relocated south of the river to New Cross at the Den.

As anticipated, the bulk of support for the club was soon derived from south of the river, from Bermondsey, Rotherhithe and Deptford – a very similar constituency of dockland support to that previously obtaining on the Island. The social origins of the club's support at this time, then, were firmly located in the proletarian masculinism of the period and area, providing a highly specific social context for the formation of the identity and culture of the club; the significance of particularized, regionally inflected supporting traditions in English football is now widely recognized (see, for example, Clarke 1991, Williams 1991). Millwall fans have thus been characterized by extreme and voluble raucousness and toughness throughout the club's history. These characteristic patterns of support and the cultural orientations which they express have been very closely associated with Millwall throughout its time in south London. Sufficiently distinctive to have been consistently noted as such by a long succession of observers since the 1920s, the ways in which these patterns have been reproduced within the club and understood without it must be at the core of the attempt to account for the development of the Millwall archetype.

Though Millwall fans were clearly far from being alone in their capacity for unbridled fervour (Dunning *et al.* 1988: 14), from the 1920s on their reputation for raucousness, passion and occasional violence came to be expressed in terms of the now familiar and historically continuous theme of *intimidation*. In 1920, following a fractious encounter in which the Newport goalkeeper was pelted with missiles before being 'flattened' by a 'useful right hook' (Murray 1988: 83), the Den was closed by the FA for the first time. Events were followed closely in the national press. The report of the special meeting that imposed the two-week closure stated that

> The commission is satisfied that missiles were thrown by a section of spectators and that there was a considerable amount of disorderly conduct, bad language and intimidation of the visiting players. (Murray 1988: 83)

This was the first of what was to become a league record of five ground closures (and three substantial fines), with all but one occurring between 1920 and 1949. The second occurred in the 1934/5 season in response to the 'pelting' of Bradford Park Avenue players, and followed a number of warnings relating to spectator misconduct in previous seasons. The club felt this to be an especially harsh decision and would only refer to an 'alleged incident' (Murray 1988: 115). After the game a number of fans, incensed by Bradford's robust style of play and perceived refereeing inadequacies, gathered outside the ground:

> A crowd of nearly 4,000 strong assembled. There were shouts and catcalls, and the crowd began to chant 'We want the referee.' (*Sunday Pictorial* 25.3.34)

After this early example of referee-intimidation – something with which Millwall fans were to become closely associated – few incidents of similar misconduct appear to have been reported until 1948. However, the reputation of Millwall fans as partisan and volatile was consolidated by events surrounding the FA Cup campaign of 1936/7. The fifth round tie against First Division Derby

County (Millwall were then in Division Three South) – witnessed by an unsurpassed record crowd of over 47,000 – saw periodic 'pitch invasions' stemming, in all likelihood, from extreme overcrowding (Murray 1988: 120). These events were relayed nationwide on Pathe newsreels. Millwall's reward for overcoming Derby 2–1 was a sixth-round meeting with Manchester City. A second victory over more celebrated rivals, the 2–0 win sparked scenes of strenuous celebration:

> The Millwall crowd which had 'swayed and roared incessantly' as City were put to the sword, spilled onto the pitch lifting the players onto their shoulders, ecstatically conveying them to the dressing room and it needed a police cordon for Mangnall to find his way to the tub. (Murray 1988: 123)

Less ecstatic behaviour led to Millwall's ground being closed for the third time in 1948 following a game against Barnsley. As far as Millwall were concerned this was another occasion on which poorly received refereeing decisions appear to have been the catalyst for disorder. Late in a fiercely contested game the referee adjudged Purdie to have fouled a Barnsley forward, a penalty and uproar ensuing:

> After the spot kick had made it 3–3 a number of Millwall supporters cleared the wall and ran onto the pitch to remonstrate with the referee. One was stopped only seconds before he could reach the man who had so infuriated the crowd all afternoon. The official was also the target of missile throwers within the ground and as he departed Cold Blow Lane made another wrong decision by admitting his identity to one pent up fan who tried to hit him. (Murray 1988: 164)

In subsequent programme notes the troublemakers were referred to as 'ultra-keen supporters', rather than the disowned 'hooligans' with whom we are now so familiar. These individuals were thus acknowledged as genuine supporters overcome by zeal, an excess of which appears to have been responsible for more serious events at the Den in the following season. The occasion was an incident-packed game in which three of the visiting Exeter team's goals were hotly disputed:

> After the game a gang of between 150 and 200 spectators ambushed referee Meade and linesmen Day and Turner. Mr. Meade claimed he was struck on the back and teacups were thrown. (Murray 1988: 170)

The Den was again closed for seven days, and the club fined £100. The growth of a folkloric reputation was now being facilitated by the widespread reporting of these events in newspapers and newsreels. The tone of many of these reports, however, was far from apocalyptic, and as far as the Exeter game was concerned 'the national press commented on the *game'* rather than the incidents around it (Channel 4, 1989). This focus on the game itself, rather than what were still seen as secondary events, was part of a general pattern. Though the immediate post-war period is widely regarded as a quiet one in terms of football disorder, the tendency to play down and under-report incidents belies the fact that a total of 130 incidents of disorder were reported to the FA between 1946 and 1959 (Dunning *et al.* 1988: 79). If Millwall were not alone in this period in having some disorderly fans, by the 1950s there were clear associations between the club and the more volatile manifestations of support. These associations were to be integral to the development of new definitions of football disorder throughout the 1960s and beyond.

History of the 'Hooligan'

> Millwall is more than a football club, its a way of life
>
> Anthony Clare speaking on *Panorama* Millwall Special, BBC 1977

The account of the chronology of the phenomenon of modern football hooliganism developed by Dunning *et al.* has, in a general sense, become standard. Its theoretical coherence has been criticized from those hostile to its theoretical presuppositions (Horne *et al.* 1987) and, more recently, from within its own ranks (Williams 1991). The status of its empirical content has, in addition, been seriously questioned (Armstrong 1998, Armstrong and Harris 1991, Hobbs and Robins 1991). Of these criticisms the theoretical issues are the more pressing, and relate to the high level of generality at which the (Eliasian–figurational) theory operates, its apparent 'irrefutability' (Williams 1991: 177), and a simplistic 'functionalism and evolutionism which are one sided in the questions raised' (Horne *et al.* 1987: 162)

However, despite these shortcomings this account of the development and construction of the hooligan phenomenon has its strengths. It offers a concise, chronological and useful account of the process. In addition, it is by now the most generally known and consulted general body of enquiry into these matters, and has in its turn affected perceptions and understandings. To some extent it has become a constituent part of the paradigm it describes. It has certainly contributed to a stable terrain of received knowledge about the development of the hooligan phenomenon. In what follows I will use an event-centred narrative account of the emergence of football hooliganism as we now understand it, and reveal the pivotal role enjoyed by Millwall fans in this process.

By the late fifties newspaper reports of disorder surrounding games had begun to alter significantly in tone, with violence becoming more readily defined as being socially problematic and a cause for concern. This process accelerated throughout the early sixties and by the middle of that decade those engaging in football-related disorder were being characterized as 'hooligans'. This sense of a new, emerging panic intensified in the year or two before the 1966 World Cup, at which time there seems to have been widespread concern about the possibility of serious disorder while the eyes of the footballing world were upon England. A significant strain within this developing media narrative saw British fans as becoming 'infected' with the decidedly un-British qualities of intemperance and aggression (Dunning *et al.* 1988: 120).

In 1965 the actions of Millwall followers seemed to signify, and not for the only time, a worsening of the problem and a heightening of the debate. At a game at Brentford in November of that year a dead hand grenade was thrown onto the pitch from the Millwall end. This symbolic gesture evoked some dramatic newspaper responses, most notably in the *Daily Sketch*, which felt that 'the Football Association have acted to stamp out this increasing mob violence within 48 hours of the blackest day in British soccer – the grenade day that showed British supporters can rival anything the South Americans can do' (Dunning *et al.* 1988: 120)

The sense of an emergent menace is palpable in this and other reports of the time, and the 'Leicester' account is invaluable for its delineation of this process. Arguing that the frequency and seriousness of events were by now being routinely exaggerated by a media busily constructing a 'moral panic', it is claimed this kind of attention directed towards disorder '. . . was contributing directly towards its escalation' (Dunning *et al.* 1988: 120, after Cohen 1971). With these observations the authors arrive at the point of the defining of the practices and patterns of football-related activity which gave rise to the popular pre-Heysel phenomenon of the 'Football Hooligan'. The account of 1960s football disorder and the emergence of the 'ends'[2] is presented as part of a continuum of working-class youth and subcultural activity beginning with the Teddy Boy movement of the 1950s (which emerged in south-east London – see next chapter). By the late 1960s the scene was set for one group who were, in many ways, the inheritors of the Teds' mantle, to combine an ostentatiously working-class subculture with an application in the football context and open up the age, in the popular consciousness, of the modern Football Hooligan. These were the skinheads. For the crucial watershed season of 1966/7 our authors note a number of key developments, with the critical moment being the one in which large numbers of northern fans, already beginning to construct themselves into rudimentary 'mobs', 'arrived' in London. This increasing sense of challenge stimulated a higher level of cohesion among the London 'ends'. This was a new and important development. Factors inhibiting its arrival earlier are given:

> In the early Sixties, the away travel of young fans had still been restricted by parochialism and cost. In addition, such Northern fans as had made the journey to the capital had, up until then, retained a healthy respect for home territories, especially in the East End

> dockland areas where the reputation, especially of Millwall fans, had for a long time induced caution on the part of outsiders. (Dunning *et al.* 1988: 166)

The key event in this process occurred not at Millwall but at West Ham, where a huge travelling contingent of Manchester United fans arrived in East London 'seemingly intent on claiming the North's first terrace success'. The disorder and violence that attended this fixture elicited the headline 'Soccer's day of shame' from the *News of the World*. Many similar headlines characterize press reportage from 1967, with 'War on soccer hooligans', 'Courts go to war on soccer louts', 'Soccer marches to war' and 'Soccer thugs on war path' offered by Dunning *et al.* to support their assertion of the importance of events in 1967. The key events at Millwall in that year surrounded an important game against Plymouth Argyle, when Plymouth won at the Den and ended Millwall's extraordinary 59-game unbeaten home run.[3] Angry scenes followed, with windows smashed on the Plymouth team coach and referee Norman Burtenshaw struck by angry fans. High-profile newspaper reports spoke for the first time of the 'Den of Shame', and in November the first perimeter caging was installed (Murray 1988: 211). These events placed Millwall fans squarely at the centre of an emergent media-defined phenomenon. It was a position they were destined to retain long after this initial phase as the association between club and hooliganism solidified. It is, incidentally, worth recalling that it was Manchester United's 'Red Army' who then enjoyed the highest notoriety in the emergent hooligan pantheon – a notoriety which has since faded from public consciousness as that of Millwall fans has grown.

The late 1960s, then, was a critical period in the development of the Millwall myth. The Den became arguably the most feared ground in the country as the result of a unique conjunction of themes: the long-standing folk-reputation of the fans; the confirmation of that reputation at a critical moment in the emergence of a new moral panic and paradigm; the Den's situation in one of the most mythicized urban locations in England; and a very real capacity for disorderly and sometimes violent supporting going back to the early part of the century and which derived from particular patterns of local working-class culture. The ways in which the actual and the mythical are entwined – or, perhaps more accurately, in which the actual becomes *mythicized* – are central to this process. Consider, for example, the memoirs of Eamon Dunphy, who played for Millwall in the early 1970s. These reveal the ways in which these ideas and this imagery may situate themselves *within* the club as a cultural institution:

> The team that Benny (Fenton) inherited was all but unbeatable at home. When you looked around the Den it wasn't hard to see why. The place was distinctly lacking in ambience. Having wound their way through a maze of narrow streets off the Old Kent Road, visiting teams would draw up outside what looked like a derelict factory. Here,

> grey was the primary colour. What wasn't grey needed a coat of paint. The pitch was tight – and bumpy. The visitor's dressing room was dark and narrow, as welcoming as a British Rail loo. Only good teams and brave players survived their introduction to the Lion's Den. And even some of them changed their minds when the game kicked off. At that stage visiting players discovered that the fans were as hostile as the decor. Even small Millwall crowds made a fearsome noise, which chilled the bones of many a hard man who'd come to London believing southerners were soft. This was the wrong part of London. (Dunphy 1986: 17)

Though the folkloric reputation of Millwall and its fans persisted throughout the early and mid 1970s, two events in 1977 and 1978 led to the Den becoming constituted as the defining and emblematic 'spiritual home of football hooliganism' (*Match of the Seventies*, BBC 1, 3.9.96). When in 1977 the makers of BBC 1s *Panorama* decided to contribute to the flurry of media concern and fascination with hooliganism, the reputation of Millwall fans made them an obvious choice as exemplifying subjects. In choosing to frame and interpret the general phenomenon of football hooliganism through the particular culture of a (numerically modest) aggressive Millwall fandom at a time when public concern and interest was at its peak, the programme makers fixed and mythologized the association between the two in perpetuity. The anxious furore generated by the programme was matched by its reception in the less well publicized, informal sphere of hooligan culture: Millwall fans became both a symbol of everything that was wrong with the country in the late, state-of-the-nation-1970s, *and* the ultimate icons in football subculture. 'Harry the Dog', the fiercest Millwall 'nutter' of them all, made for fantastic television: a combination of high-intensity violence and a cinematically thuggish demeanour meant that he quickly acquired a genuinely symbolic status. The defining populist image of embodied Millwall fandom had arrived, and it stayed. Few who saw Harry's one-man assault on the Bristol Rovers 'end' have forgotten it. Interviews with other fans generated an extraordinarily powerful sense of mythically understood invulnerability:

> We're always in the second or third (division) like, but people are frightened of us all over England.

> They're the best supporters in the land. They'll go anywhere. Anyone comes down 'ere (the Den), they'll get slung out, *I tell ya that now.*

Those involved in the running of the club were outraged and hurt, feeling that they had been misled and that their trust in agreeing to co-operate with the filming had been abused. *Panorama* was charged by no less a figure the Dennis Howell, Minister for Sport, with an excessive focus on a small minority of fans and a sensationalist approach. He thought that '. . . it was the most irresponsible programme seen for a very long time' (Murray 1988: 243). The already poor relationship between club and media organizations was permanently soured, and it is this that is at the root of Millwall fans' zealous contempt for the latter.

The framework of definition and interpretation of all matters relating to Millwall set up by the programme has, as we will see, been employed in automatic, shorthand and symbolic ways ever since. A consequent sense of embittered injustice and a defensive wariness of outside opinion are amongst the primary characteristics of Millwall fan culture. With the reporting of disorder at the following year's FA Cup game against Ipswich[4] (Ball 1986: 188, Murray 1988: 245), the pattern was set. Fighting in the crowd on that occasion led to the first closure of the Den since 1949, and probably definitively strengthened a universal association of Millwall with violent mayhem. The year 1978 saw an extremely high-profile game at West Ham, when Millwall were again at the very centre of an apparent worsening of the general situation at a match which

> produced what, up until that time, was the most comprehensive and sophisticated show of force for dealing with spectators at an English Football League match. All told, more than 500 police officers took part (Dunning *et al.* 1988: 178).

It was 1977/8, then, that were the years in which public perceptions of Millwall had become sufficiently fixed and widely disseminated to constitute the *Millwall Fan* as a more or less stable referential symbol (Turner 1967).

Serious disorder attending a fifth-round cup tie at Luton in March 1985 extended and solidified the reputation of Millwall fans still further, to the extent that 'the name Millwall had become synonymous with everything that was bad in football and society' (Murray 1988: 269). Again, Millwall symbolized an apparently worsening situation in a period that saw the reputation of the game reach its nadir (Dunning *et al.* 1988: 246–9). Crucially captured by television cameras, the event was a focus of national attention, significant enough to stimulate House of Commons debate and lead to the creation of Margaret Thatcher's 'Soccer War Cabinet'. It is widely considered to be the symbolic watershed in the post-war history of the game and the battle against hooliganism (Campbell and Shields 1993: 123, Dunning *et al.* 1988: 246, Murray 1988: 269). In the public consciousness the Millwall fan thus became not merely further associated with, but incontrovertibly *representative of* boorishness, thuggery and violent mayhem.

Millwall fans therefore found themselves in the late 1980s carrying a heavy mythological and symbolic burden which the club itself has found difficult to overcome. The development of groundbreaking community initiatives in the late 1980s (Bale 1993: 174, Campbell and Shields 1993: 122, Williams 1991: 182) and successive attempts to improve the image and status of Millwall had only a limited impact on public perceptions, and evaporated altogether when a powerful media archetype underpinning structures of received understanding become operational. I do not define the status of Millwall as *archetypal* for simple effect. Rather, I want to suggest that archetypes perform an important and particular role in the context of ritualized news production.

Paul Rock (1973) has observed how news-focused media practices tend to operate according to a principle of *eternal recurrence.* News, he argues, derives its character largely from the sources and contexts of its production. News-gathering itself, of course, takes routine forms [5] closely linked to those institutions that generate

> a useful volume of reportable activity at useful intervals: The Courts, sports grounds and parliament mechanically manufacture news which is effortlessly assimilated by the press . . . When these assumptions are applied, news can acquire a cyclical quality. If resort is made to developments which are institutionalised, predicted, short-lived and in continual production, news will itself become a series of cycles. The content may change, but the forms will be enduring. Much news is, in fact, ritual. It conveys an impression of endlessly repeated drama whose themes are familiar and well understood (Rock 1973: 68).

Particular well established themes in this process require the kind of precedent-based mnemonic triggers that allow for the full cognitive and affective force of a given phenomenon to be given immediacy and form. It is in this sense that *Millwall* functions as an archetype, with applications well beyond the limits of a discrete cultural institution.The idea of Millwall has come to exemplify and reference a sphere of counter-bourgeois subjectivity and experience generally defined as invalid and transgressive of the normative, liberal–individualist presuppositions of the central institutions of the public sphere (Cohen 1971: 119). The overall context for this is the role of media institutions in the maintenance and consolidation of a definition of social reality premised upon a paradigm of national 'consensus' (Hall *et al.* 1978: 55) and cognitive maps of meaning organized around the primacy of liberal–individualist, bourgeois conceptions of subjectivity and cultural practice. One low-level but continual characteristic of mainstream media production – leaving aside periodic, high profile 'moral panics' – is the recurring validation of these conceptions in an ongoing confirmation of the primacy of the manners of social being derived from them. The Millwall archetype – though it is always waiting to be operationalized in its literal, folk-devil sense as circumstances arise – has by now transcended and outlived its role in the framing of specific, conjunctural panics. It is used rather as an important symbolic marker in the recurring and ritualized media narratives relating to social order and the illegitimacy of particular cultural and moral forms.

Millwall has been critical in this process, for it allows a number of incipiently transgressive themes situated on the major boundaries of 'consensual calm' (Hall *et al.* 1978: 66) – crime, violence and volatile collective culture in the context of a working-class area within *minutes* of the metropolitan centre – to become conflated and condensed into a unitary, exemplifying symbol. This status as a primary symbol expressive of these themes underpins the archetypal nature of the Millwall fan, and has generated the unique burden associated with that fandom. The negotiation of this burden, of this dialectic of ascribed and experienced identity, is at the heart of Millwallism. Few other social groupings – of any description – have had to come to terms with and absorb into their cultural forms so particular and widespread a body of 'knowledge' and opinion about themselves. The Millwall archetype, arising as it has out of a complex interplay of culture and representation, constitutes the *Millwall fan* as a primarily symbolic being. His reputation *always* precedes him, and an awareness of this special, iconic status saturates the sharply self-aware expressive cultural forms generated by Millwall fans, and clearly underpins the emergence of the anthem *No One Likes Us* during the 1980s.

A public, dialogical engagement with reputation and myth is therefore central to the way in which fans constitute themselves as a collective. Millwallism, in this sense, contains the classical ingredients of passionate, local-patriotic English football supporting *and* something which passes beyond them – those collective responses to the reformulation of 'Millwall' as a highly charged and ubiquitous symbol in the cultural politics of the public sphere. This idea of Millwall as a media symbol is particularly important in the context of contemporary developments in the expansion of football into new markets, in a climate in which football would appear to be shedding its working-class iconography and associations at an unprecedented rate. Though the tensions generated in fan cultures by the progressive commercialization of the game are at least as old as the sociology of football itself (Critcher 1979, Taylor 1971), in the late 1990s the game appears genuinely poised on the brink of a definitive and stable breakthrough into middle-class markets. The role of media sports coverage in confirming and validating conceptions of Civil Privatism (Hargreaves 1993: 149), focused as it is upon the cardinal bourgeois themes of individuation and personal achievement through struggle,[6] rather than team effort and the sublimation of the self to the collective – has not left football untouched. The attempt to transform football into 'family-oriented entertainment on middle-class lines' (Hargreaves 1993: 151) should be located in this general tendency of mass media towards the tacit maintenance of consensual–hegemonic maps of social reality.

This is the context into which Millwall, with all its unruly, counter-bourgeois and market-unfriendly baggage, is routinely inserted in symbolic contrast to the prevailing wind of progressive change held to be blowing through the game – even in periods of calm when Millwall fans are not in the news.[7] This is a crucial point to remember in all that follows. The routine and widely disseminated circulation of this archetype in a variety of contexts has been a feature of both broadcast and printed news-production, documentary and entertainment programming, and sociological analysis itself. These developments have, at one level, transformed Millwall from a modest leisure institution to a highly charged and richly connotative symbol independent of the club and its supporters. This has had profound consequences for the cultural life of the club. Millwall fans have had to come to terms with, absorb and work into their expressive and identificatory forms responses to a widely diffused body of information and opinion about themselves and their ostensible patterns of culture. This is the primary extra-footballing characteristic of Millwallism. The dialectical interplay of experienced and ascribed identity is registered, and expressed, on a number of levels within the club, and the examination of these will be central to later chapters. The unambiguously counter-bourgeois tone of the culture has, in its turn, been central to the development of the myth. The geographical context, too, has been crucial, and Millwall's location in south-east London has not been incidental in the elevation of the club to iconic status. Historically this part of London has been characterized by a broader but parallel dialectics of identity, as well as being host to some very particular patterns of masculine working-class culture. In the next chapter I will explore the key salient themes in the historical development of the area, and consider the ways in which they have been culturally reproduced up to the present time. In this way I intend to position Millwall as an exemplary institution of the area and its culture, and flesh out some of the substantive content of the broader cultural processes that find expression there.

Notes

1. See Chapter Two for a detailed discussion of the *Docker*, the *Gangster* and masculine cultural formations in south-east London. With reference to possible significance of the latter in the development of the hooligan phenomenon, Dunning *et al.* (1988: 169) speculate persuasively upon the influence of gangsterism on the fledgling London football firms of the 1960s: 'Traditional working-class animosities between London and the provinces may also have been indirectly spiced in the mid-1960s by the emergence of the notoriously violent Kray and Richardson "protection gangs". More particularly, the "cool" violence of these London racketeers may have provided role models for working-class teenagers and young adult males who moved around the fringes of the London underworld, in that way helping in the formation of a partly older "street smart" backbone for some of the major London ends.'

2. The term 'End' derives from the tendency, established in the 1960s, of the more volatile sections of a team's support congregating on a particular terrace, usually behind a goal and therefore at the end of the stadium.
3. The Millwall 'unbeaten run' remains a source of great pride to fans, and is a central fact of club lore, and the core cosmological sense of what a combination of *committed* Millwall fans and players means and is able to achieve. The Den in its heyday in the late 1960s and early 1970s was regarded as a fortress in every sense, with visiting players and fans required to fight – often literally – for their survival. The unbeaten run strengthened and sustained the sense of Millwall space as passionately intimidatory and physically inviolable. These themes continue to characterize Millwallism and underpin the orientations and expectations of many fans – a source of some dissonance in the context of the far less inviolable New Den.
4. Murray, Millwall's historian, regards the Ipswich disorders as 'the most savage scenes ever witnessed at the Den' . . . and notes the significance of the 'disquieting yet almost inevitable irony that the BBC cameras should be back again, this time recording for Match of the Day but also, as it turned out, for the main news bulletins' (1986: 245). Ball, referring to the same incident, describes ' the most violent, hostile atmosphere I have ever experienced inside a football ground' (Ibid: 190).
5. The geographical proximity of Millwall to the metropolitan centres of news production is surely not insignificant. The juxtaposition of some of the central institutions of consensual–hegemonic culture to a site of its apparent antithesis a twenty-minute drive from Fleet Street has provided not only a symbolic contrast but a readily accessible and easily exploited potential source of news data. If this spatial congruence was not the primary cause of a long-standing media fascination with Millwall, it certainly did nothing to hamper its recurrence once the archetype was up and running.
6. Expressed, most clearly, in an overwhelming focus on *individuals* and the disclosure of their personalities throughout the various media (Hargreaves 1993: 150).
7. Three examples of references to Millwall, collected in October/November 1996 at random from radio, television and newsprint, illustrate this. On 17 October, Radio Four's *Today* programme focused on the club – in connection with an anti-racist initiative being launched on *Tyneside* – as part of a generalized discussion of race and football. No other club was involved, and Millwall was clearly being defined as exemplary in any such discussion. A short interview with a south-London-accented fan was contemptuously undermined by the show's presenter. On 5 November the Channel Four comedy television show *Drop the Dead Donkey* featured the assertion that it was as difficult for the office Lothario to control his genetic predisposition towards promiscuity as it

was to control 'Millwall fans on holiday in Benidorm'. Here the Millwall fan represents not only football hooliganism, but unreconstructed, atavistic masculinity *itself.* On 10 November, the *Observer*, in a report of the Bristol City *v.* Millwall game of the previous day, could not resist a reference to the 'brutality' of some Millwall fans even though the game itself provided absolutely no context for it. It appears that neither moral panics nor ostensible 'news-worthiness' itself are a precondition of the continual circulation of these ways of framing and representing the club.

–2–

The Social Sources of Millwallism: Some Varieties of South-East London *Habitus*

Chain-smoking commuters cross Pearl River to run the factories Hong Kong has built in China's special economic zones. Some have families on both sides of the river: Chinese women still have lower expectations than the wives these plastic-Lion-King tycoons leave behind. There are a sprinkling of Westerners on the ferry too, in search of bargain-basement manufacturing deals or pedalling hi-tech equipment to entrepreneurs in the making. From the other direction come teenage hustlers lugging suitcases full of pirate Cds pressed in army-owned factories, and mainland gangsters in white socks, clutching briefcases and mobile phones.

The two sides of the river are as inextricably linked, and as uneasy about each other, as are Westminster and Southwark, divided by the Thames.

Deyan Sudjic, *Guardian*, 24.6.95

If there is a modern equivalent to early Southwark it might well be Tijuana, the seedy town just south of the Mexican-American border. Each settlement has made its living by becoming the pleasure-ground for a more closely regulated area to the North, and allowed fugitives from its neighbour to take shelter. The Thames may not be the Rio Grande, but medieval Southwark certainly had a Wild West atmosphere. In the taverns, brothels and gaming-houses of Bankside sudden violence was common, and its causes were the stuff of cowboy films: having driven cattle to town, the unwary would take their pay and go in search of a good time, only to meet a greedy lady of pleasure, a card-sharp or a bully. Stage-coaches would arrive with their passengers robbed or wounded, after an ambush by masked men lurking by the roadside . . . This was the flavour of Southwark life for centuries.

Richard Byrne, *Prisons and Punishments of London*

Is it not also possible that within this city and within its culture are patterns of sensibility or patterns of response which have persisted from the thirteenth and fourteenth centuries and perhaps even beyond? Does the passage of the city through time create its own energies that exert a pressure upon our perceptions and our understandings, which is all the more powerful for being normally overlooked?

Peter Ackroyd, *New York Review of Books*, 21.9.95

Peter Ackroyd's question is a fascinating one, and warrants serious consideration. It is possible, I would suggest probable, that particular structures of feeling and patterns of culture have been generated by London, its history and its people.[1] These have assumed specific forms, dimensions and characteristics out of the historical process of the growth of London and its spectacularly novel and distinctive social dynamics. As an historically unique kind of city it has produced unique and arguably specific forms of working-class metropolitan culture, and in this chapter I want to attempt to delineate and interpret something of these processes. However, I approach this with reference to the kind of comparatively prosaic cultural-reproduction theorizing already discussed, rather than in terms of Ackroyd's opaque and supernatural essences and energies. These may or may not exist. What certainly does exist is the lingering influence of that long, complex and processually peculiar historical development that has given the city, and the south-eastern part of it perhaps most of all, it's particular atmospheres, and it's people their particular characteristics and patterns of culture. It is to the specificities of these patterns that we must turn in order to apprehend what, if anything, is distinctive about the cultural orientations brought to Millwall by its fans.

The current chapter should be read, then, as an attempt to develop a detailed historiographical examination of the (spatial, cultural, experiential) situations out of which Millwallism has emerged. I will be seeking, most importantly, to put the notion of *habitus* to grounded and empirical work, in order to offer an archaeology of the situated moral forms and patterns of culture that have given the particular modes of masculinity characteristic of Millwallism and south-east London their dimensions and flavours. Though this may appear to disrupt the chronological flow of the overall argument I am developing, it is vital if we are to get beneath the surface of the observable expressive characteristics of Millwallism and offer an anthropologically *thick* account (Geertz 1975) of their socio-historical bases.

In the introductory chapter I was critical of the thinness and superficiality of much of the sociology of football fandom: here I back up this critique with a sustained attempt to identify and explore the distinctive spheres of experience and cultural traditions to which the people who support Millwall are heir. In this way we may come closer not only to an appreciation of the kinds of people Millwall fans are said to be (as in the previous chapter), but also to the kinds of people Millwall fans are. I hope, in undertaking this exercise, to offer an unusually rich and suggestive account of the elements that have generated the Millwall myth from within. Though this aspect of the analysis will inevitably involve the speculative consideration of processes far removed from the sphere of football, their significance in contemporary manifestations of Millwall-supporting will become apparent later in the chapter – and should be borne in mind throughout the work as a whole.

On the Far Side of the River: The South-East's Place in the Cultural Map of London

The possibility of a collectively generated social consciousness retaining it's integrity, its 'schemes of perception' over time, is critical for what follows: the attempt to identify the dimensions and content of particular forms of class-based 'practical' consciousness, generated by the metropolitan experience, and the lingering manifestations of these in contemporary London life. This attempt to trace the history of some of the practices, sensibilities and orientations of sections of the London working class[2] proceeds from the possibility that they may contain a highly durable core. I am thinking in particular about what appear to be striking historical continuities in patterns of masculine London working-class practice and identity. The heterogeneous and highly differentiated nature of the historical city makes the attempt to develop a definitive, singular *habitus* untenable. It might, rather, be possible to identify a range of historically coherent themes that have demonstrably characterized the development of particular groups of working-class Londoners. It is not possible to provide an exhaustive or fully rounded account of these continuities here, as this would be a vast undertaking. The partial and selective nature of what follows is intended to be a speculative and suggestive account, organized around a number of exemplifying moments in the history of the city.

The focus is on that inner portion of south London that runs along the Thames from Bermondsey to Deptford, and westwards from the river to incorporate the boroughs of Southwark, Lewisham and the more eastern sections of Lambeth. For practical purposes this inner core is what I mean by south-east London. I will concentrate, in particular, on Southwark, the City of London's first suburb (Johnson 1968), and the site of those historically continuous settlements that are as old as the City itself. The patterns of culture that I take to be characteristic of the area are best approached via the social history of those particular localities that grew up from the Middle Ages on the south bank of London Bridge. This is not to claim that Southwark has an utterly distinct identity and tradition, for in particular there are clearly similarities of history and development with east London. What I do suggest is that specific patterns of practice, sensibility and response have demonstrably characterized the development of the area and its people, and have been reproduced over time, though not of course entirely homogeneously or evenly, in such ways as to have generated particular, nuanced inflections of social identity.

It is a characteristic of accounts of the phenomenon of London to stress its uniqueness: its size, transformations, bewildering profusion of peoples,[3] trades and lifestyles, its historically staggering heterogeneity and scope. Raymond Williams is not alone in seeing eighteenth-century London as a distinctively novel kind of place, generating new patterns of social organization, senses of human possibility and modes of consciousness and experience (Williams 1973: chapter

14). This sense of expanding possibility and decisively novel experience was accompanied by the equally powerful and simultaneous pull of the locality.

The bewildering size and variety of London has generated a social patchwork of intensively localist culture and sentiment, a series of highly differentiated social spaces within the city. By the nineteenth century, Richard Sennett observes, London was a conglomeration of 'class-homogenous, disconnected spaces' (1994: 322). Extreme localist identifications in the context of a vast and ultimately unfathomable metropolitan whole thus became a primary characteristic of the historical development of London's working-class communities, differentiating them from their provincial counterparts. It is little wonder, given this variety and diffusion of communities – and of the obscurely folk-taxonomic ways of interpreting and representing them – that so much of London tends to be missing from its social history. This is most acutely true of south-east London, an area which remains chronically underhistoricized. This is primarily due to the fact that socio- historic accounts of London invariably revolve around the easily juxtapositionary cognitive scheme of East/West. These apparently obvious and reassuring polarizations, between rich and poor, grandeur and squalor, light and dark, and order and chaos become translated into contrastive analyses of relationships between West and East London (Walkowitz 1992). South London is marginalized in this conceptual framework by its location on the *other side*, its separation marked symbolically, as well as spatially, by the Thames. The effect of this separation has led to its demarcation as an obscure and unknown space, a region of darkness nestling, in the case of Southwark, hard by the very heart of the Metropolis itself. And when it does appear in social histories of London at all, it tends to do so as a shadowy realm of crime, disreputability and 'incipient decay' (Ash 1971: 39).

South-east London therefore enjoys a specific position in those folk-taxonomic schema that so characterize life in the city. And its close association with 'crime', itself an absolutely central sphere in historical relations between the metropolitan classes, marks it out as an especially significant site in the ongoing dialectics of class and culture, of social identities embodied and ascribed. This particular tradition and iconography, from medieval criminal quarter and pleasure ground to Fagin and the definitive Dickensian criminal warren at Jacob's Island in Bermondsey, [4] from the original nineteenth-century Hooligan to the first 'Teddy Boys', from classical gangland enclave to home of the archetypal football thug at Millwall, marks south-east London out as a very particular and historically significant place.

In his recent social history of London (1994) Roy Porter, himself a native of the south-east, paints a vivid picture of the kind of impending municipal apocalypse now central to debates on the future of the metropolis. The routine and apparently unavoidable litany of those political, economic and cultural ills that are destroying the social cohesion, urban ecologies and healthy civic sociality of contemporary

London life is laid out in stark and persuasive clarity: the Thatcher years; the diffusion and attenuation of local government and resulting infrastructural collapse; unemployment, crime and social division; the awful triumph of the motor car. All of these and more are detailed in Porter's elegiac account of the apparently irreversible decline of the once-glorious metropolis. The shift from post-war corporate cohesion to contemporary chaos is exemplified in his contrastive accounts of New Cross, with the area characterized, in the period after the war, as being a 'stable if shabby working class community completely undiscovered by sociologists' (1994: xiii). These days, however, 'Dossers and drunks litter the gardens, and some of my students were mugged there last year. South London has gained a mean reputation for drug-dealing, racial violence, gangland crime and contract killing' (1994: 9). As a device with which to convey a sense of recent social collapse this typification of the changing fortunes of south-east London is as good as any. However, it misses the vital point that inner south-east London gained its mean reputation much earlier in history than this account suggests, and Porter's florid emphasis on the more contemporary manifestations of this 'meanness' – 'drug dealing' and 'racial violence' – obscures the extent to which 'gangland crime' may well represent a sphere of *continuity* in the life of the area. Porter rightly identifies the area as one to which there accrues a highly particularized system of representation and symbolic imagery, enjoying a distinct place in what we might call the popular consciousness. I would suggest, however, that the central elements of this repertoire – apparent predispositions among the populace towards criminality, violence and generalized disreputability – are rooted in a much longer and more continuous experiential dialectics of social identity, and cannot merely be used to form part of an account of post-war decline.

The story of these ways of seeing and representing south London is a long and complex one, and a detailed account lies well beyond the scope of this piece. However, I hope to demonstrate that particularized folk-taxonomic conceptions of south-east London centred upon disreputability and criminality have been in circulation since the Middle Ages, and that though the dimensions of these are historically variable, the themes and imagery through which they are expressed are continuous. They express a way of thinking about the area which I suggest informs both external attributive representations of it and the symbolic repertoire of cultural identifications subscribed to and utilized by sections of its population. [5] Of particular importance here are archetypal representations of masculinity. Before examining the constitutive elements of these archetypes in detail let us briefly consider, at the level of representational imagery, the highly specific urban ecologies in which south-east-London man is situated. Porter's invocation of the twin markers of meanness and disreputability is characteristic of many accounts of contemporary life in the area. A representative perusal of references to the area in popular writing will serve to illustrate the point.

A 1995 edition of the London listings magazine *Time Out* (6–13.9.95: 33–40) features a series of articles contrasting life north and south of the river. In a range of pieces that are unusual in that they have south London as their focus at all, the explicitly caricatured and stereotypical representations of the respective regions contrast, as we might expect, the civilized north with the backward and barbarian south. These explicit and humorous stereotypes are interesting in the way that they express widely diffused, folk-taxonomic ways of thinking about the area and the profound psycho-social divisions that characterize London life. In an echo of Deyan Sudjic's awareness of the powerfully symbolic role of the Thames in these matters, it is felt that 'The Seine in Paris and the Tiber in Rome pull their respective capitals together, but the muddy waters of the Thames are an impenetrable psychological barrier.' Further pieces develop and press the point home in forthrightly comedic terms. From the perspective of North London, Andrew Mosby tells us that:

> In the south, if you listen to the conversation long enough you soon realise that everyone is called John, Kev or Vanka, and there is an unwritten rule that if you look at someone else's pint its the equivalent of looking at their dick and merits a 'spanking'. Spanking and all other forms of violence, along with television, are the two most popular activities in south London . . . A typical north London car will have either a golfing umbrella in the back or a Panama hat, suggesting a day enjoyed at the races. In south London the norm is a baseball bat or a sawn-off shotgun, suggesting that the owner is a habitual user of anabolic steroids and hoping to commit violent crime if he or she hasn't already. (*Time Out* 6–13.9.95: 35)

Before moving on to recount how, in south London, homosexuality remains illegal and men 'have women's names tattooed on their arms to prove they're not queer', Mosby rehearses one of the central images of the divide; that *black cabs never go south of the river.*

There is no attempt to play down this kind of imagery from the perspective of the south. Rather, Rick Jones boasts that 'No one does much work here. Crime is more or less the only form of commerce.' The Old Kent Road, he tells us, is included on the Monopoly board only because it is where 'Northerners habitually get mugged on their way to the continent'. With some acuity, he later makes a flitting attempt to do something much more ambitious when he identifies Southwark with particular psycho-social states of mind and patterns of sensibility:

> Shakespeare and his tarts, pimps, boys and cronies spent their days scoffing at the pompous struttings of those who went in and out of the city. Today the germ of their cynicism lurks in the S bend of the Thames at Southwark. It seeps, if not into the South Bank arts complex or into the newly built Globe, then out into the tributary streets of unlovely SE and SW postal districts, where untainted youth picks it up like a sexually transmitted disease. (*Time Out* 6–13.9.95: 37)

While these kinds of representations are clearly not to be taken too seriously as analyses of social relations south of the river, they are important for the ways in which they illustrate some of the dimensions of a London-archetypal, attributive and folk-taxonomic way of thinking.

These humorous accounts address what can be without doubt a harsh social reality. The London Borough of Southwark, which constitutes the core of inner south-east London, is classified by the Department of the Environment, using a wide range of socio-economic indicators, as the second most 'deprived' local-authority area in England and Wales (*Guardian* 5.6.94). This fact informs another type of account of the area, in which an awareness of specifities of this urban ecology are articulated alongside a particularistic iconography of working-class/gangsterish masculinism. A widely diffused stock repertoire of interpretation and imagery derives from this. John Williams, offering his 'expert's' view of the Millwall 'hooligan problem' in the aftermath of the infamous Derby play-off disturbances of June 1994, gives us the following:

> I believe it has something to do with the nature of the area where the club is based. It is strongly working-class and a very tough neighbourhood. It has a strongly masculine culture in which young men were brought up to express themselves by being tougher than in other parts of the capital. (*Guardian* 20.5.94)

This sense of a specific and localized type passes over easily from a discussion of Millwall fans to one centred on more generalized patterns of masculine culture and practice. An *Independent* article (15.4.94) on the Brink's-Mat bullion robbery, Britain's biggest ever armed robbery, is representative of these kinds of account, with its routinized invocation of the 'run down council flat on the Bonamy Estate, just off the Old Kent Road' (15.4.94). This specifically understood urban ecology is the context for that 'south-east London gangland which has produced some of Britain's most notorious criminals'. I would stress here that assessing the accuracy or otherwise of these claims is not of primary importance. What is significant is the way in which so many accounts of the area, and particularly of its darkly conceived masculine subcultures, revolve around the manipulation of a particular and consistent repertoire of symbolic meanings and identifications.

Ducking and Diving: Fugitives, Entrepreneurs and Embodied Resistance

Social histories of London have Southwark firmly entrenched by the twelfth century as the resort of criminals and other assorted unruly elements. A sense of two distinct, mutually hostile settlements emerges clearly in accounts of the time. Johnson (1968: 35) notes that the period is characterized by a continual contest between the 'City' and the 'Borough' for civic control of Southwark, and that the presence of criminal communities in the south reflected the far more stringent municipal organization of the former. Thus Southwark became the first site of escape from the juridical rigours of the centre, and the river – easily traversible by boat in times of flight – already exists already in the twelfth century as a concrete and symbolic boundary between north and south, order and chaos, the rule of law and the fugitive colony.

By 1155, the year of the institution of the first City guild, the 'disorders of Southwark were an affront to the increasingly well regulated city' (Johnson 1968: 40). This highlights another important theme in the development of north–south relations, namely a tendency in the latter towards a less formalized, regulated and guilded occupational culture which was premised, even at this early stage, upon an ambivalence towards institutionalized power in the economic sphere. This pattern of dubiously legal, autonomous work in infringement of trade regulations is therefore a second important theme which should be placed alongside those more overtly criminal practices from which it was seldom unambiguously discrete. Here may lie the origins of particular kinds of south-east London *habitus*, and it is perhaps not too far fetched to speculate on the lives and practices of some of these distant forebears of 'Del Boy' Trotter[6] This condition of criminal disorder and civic and economic irregularity in Southwark remained, according to Johnson, 'substantially unchanged until the nineteenth century' (1968: 61).

It was during the period 1550–1700 that, in McMullan's (1984) assessment, the sphere of crime became a deeply institutionalized characteristic of the city's socio-economic structure. Criminal practice, and the kind of social consciousness that must surely have been its concomitant, are in this view deeply embedded historically in plebeian/non-bourgeois cultural formations and must be seen as central rather than peripheral. For McMullan, the growth of an 'opportunity structure' for crime is indivisible from the history of the growth of the City's economy itself.[7] The density of population enabled criminals to become sufficiently concentrated to form 'discrete social networks of their own through which the skills and techniques of crime could be refined and *generationally transmitted*' (1984: 20, my emphasis) in the context of 'an agglomeration of unmonitored and unsupervised enclaves' characterized by weak communal policing, decentralized administration and outright defiance. Primary among such enclaves was Southwark, 'probably the area of London with the most venerable reputation as a resort of criminality' (1984: 56).

This vividly criminal Southwark appears to have found its fullest expression in Elizabethan London, at the time of the emergence of a more fully developed and recognizable type. Elizabethan and Jacobean comedies, says Johnson, produced a new and particular stock character: 'The witty but unscrupulous Londoner' (1968: 63), relieving the guileless of their money. This sense of urban wit and guile, and a theatricalized self-presentation in social interaction, is echoed in the consolidation of another characteristic theme in the social relations of south-east London: a deeply rooted antipathy towards the policing authorities. Johnson relates an account involving seven Southwark ruffians who, 'on seeing the forces of law advancing on them, . . . turned with a cry of "down with the constables", and set upon them as well' (1968: 68). Thus, in 1546, a full four-hundred years after Southwark first gained its unambiguous reputation for disorder, the problem of how to deal with lawlessness in the absence of a strong local authority remained. From medieval high jinks to Elizabethan thuggery to the lionization of police killers in contemporary football chants[8] and the indestructible hatred of the police frequently displayed by members of the south-London gangland fraternity,[9] these themes have been consistent characteristics of very particular kinds of south-east London *habitus*.

Beyond descriptions of this picaresque environment, it is important to speculate on the kind of historically developing metropolitan consciousness being matured in it. These critical themes of fugitive sanctuary, patterns of criminality, widespread 'disreputability', a blurring of the boundary between legitimate commerce and illicit hustling, poverty and squalor and, lest we are tempted to push these points too far, a profusion of relatively stable occupation-based communities, express a stark and difficult social landscape. It was to become particularly so from the late seventeenth century, with the history of proletarian[10] Londoners and their cultures marked, from this time, by an intensifying and long-term struggle over identity and practice, with 'crime' as a dimension of ideological contest at its centre. In thinking about the course of this struggle we can glimpse in perhaps their starkest relief those specific qualities and elements that come to characterize the cultures of working-class London as it enters the Early Modern period.

By the mid-eighteenth century, as Porter notes, London was less a mere city than a novel and exhilarating social phenomenon. It had arguably generated, out if its rule by commerce and cultural entrepreneurialism rather than by King, Court or Church, something unique and extraordinary in the modern period: a confident, sometimes arrogant, proud and frequently unruly metropolitan populace (Porter 1994: 183). This astounding city, this new kind of crowd, of noise, of energy, was generated, for Porter, by a unique 'alchemy of money and the masses, its popular commercialism run by capitalists great and small'. This is a conception of a new London consciousness forged out of the hustle: wit, mental toughness, the impulse to autonomy and an extreme materialism generating a particular kind of metropolitan working-class response to early capitalism.[11] This new people emerge out of what Raymond Williams calls a new *moral arena*: 'As London grew, dramatically, in the eighteenth century, it was being intensively observed, as a new kind of landscape, a new kind of society' (quoted in Porter 1994: 184). Londoners were a new kind of population, forged out of novel and exhilarating social relations and economic arrangements, of the great Metropolis and displaying an acutely proprietary attitude towards it. They were a harsh and difficult people, as Porter puts it, 'in love with themselves'. In the coming times they were to need all of their self-confidence and resourcefulness.

Linebaugh's work (1993) – focused primarily upon eighteenth-century London – develops a critical point made by E.P. Thompson (1963: 64) in relation to 'sub-political traditions',

> popular attitudes towards crime, amounting at times to an unwritten code, quite distinct from the laws of the land . . . This distinction between the legal code and the unwritten code is a commonplace at any time. But rarely have the two codes been more sharply distinguished from one another than in the second half of the eighteenth century. One may even see these years as ones in which the class war is fought out in terms of Tyburn, the hulks and the Bridewells on the one hand; and crime, riot and mob action on the other.

This positioning of 'Crime', Thompson stresses, within patterns of culture and sub-political oppositional sensibility is characteristically a London phenomenon, of a people who 'astonished foreign visitors by their lack of deference' (1963: 64). This places discussions of 'crime' within a much broader framework of social history. The location of the social sphere of crime is thus a highly specific one and is interpreted by Linebaugh as primarily a matter of both practice and sensibility generated in response to the intensifying effects of the early capitalist recasting of social relations in the early eighteenth century. This latter process had particular implications for the London working class for whom the long term struggle over social practice, culture and identity was especially acute. Resistance to the confining and oppressive effects of this emergent form of economic and social reorganization – premised upon the institution of private-property rights and of the wage – took place in London primarily in the realm of sub-political, 'criminal' action. Criminality can therefore, at least in part, be interpreted as a vehicle for the expression of a particular kind of class consciousness, and not merely a matter of illicit economistic practice pure and simple. For sections of the population the practice, the idea and the *consciousness* of crime has been an important oppositional sphere in which struggles have been fought over not only material realities but embodied social identities themselves. Elements of this sub-political culture of crime – as a means of making a living *and* an important realm of activity in the process of resistance to bourgeois cultural hegemony – continue to linger here and there in London, and nowhere more so than in the south-east.

The early eighteenth century in Europe was, of course, defined by Foucault (1977) as the age of the 'great confinement'. Linebaugh concurs, but identifies important countervailing tendencies at the level of sub-political resistance:

> Doubtless, incarceration, in its many forms and for many purposes, was a major theme that can easily and exactly be particularised for London in the early eighteenth century. Yet the theme of incarceration brought with it the counter theme of excarceration. As the theme of incarceration was played out in workhouse, factory, hospital, school and ship, so the counterpoint of excarceration was played out in escapes, flights, desertions, migrations and refusals. (1993: 23)

The refusal of subordination, Linebaugh thinks, was a characteristic of the London labour force, and we have already encountered those earlier expressions of a particular social consciousness – a proprietary metropolitanism, lack of deference and history of relatively autonomous occupational practice – which would have generated such attitudes. It is this refusal of subordination which militated against any easy institutionalization of Londoners during the age of confinement, and explains, in Linebaugh's view, why 'new experiments in industrial organization, like the factory, were placed outside London' (1993: 24).

The popular culture generated by this difficult and resolutely non-bourgeois urban population was vivid, colourful and often explicitly focused on the widely circulated exploits of emblematic superstar criminals. The greatest of these was Jack Sheppard, a housebreaker and specialist escaper who, Linebaugh notes (1993: 8), was once the single most well-known name from eighteenth-century England. His adventures were circulated and followed in the media of that 'other' history of

> historians, pantomime and song. The oral history of Sheppard has maintained his memory within human contexts where books were scarce and working class resources for an independent historiography were non-existent . . . At a time when economists have been hard put to explain how the labouring people could actually live given the wage rates that prevailed, Sheppard's life can raise the question of the relationship between thievery and survival. (1993: 8)

The long and spectacular career of Sheppard, and his status as an emblematic figure, can tell us a good deal about the experiences and responses of the London labouring classes from which he emerged. When in prison under sentence of death, for example, and harangued by the Newgate prison authorities to concentrate his energies upon spiritual preparation for his impending afterlife rather than further attempts at escape, Sheppard replied that 'one file's worth all the Bibles in the world' (1993: 38), which alerts us to other important characteristics of the London consciousness that will be considered presently: irreligion and a steadfast materialism. After his execution Sheppard became an even greater folk hero, 'to be used for bitter political satire or to be admired for his tenacity and indomitability. His elevation to fame was a rise neither with, nor without, his class. Almost as a figure of sport, he attained an "individual fame" that united the "mob"' (1993: 38). The stories of Sheppard and others found their way into archetypal representations widely circulated in the popular consciousness, and 'The popular theatre of Southwark or Bartholemew Fair kept cockneys laughing at themes of repression and resistance' (1993: 38).

'No City of God': Competitive Working-Class Individualism and Responses to Bourgeois Evangelism

The nineteenth century arguably constituted for working-class Londoners a period of change still more intense, and a consideration of its major developments adds some further strands to an analysis of the relationships between class, consciousness, (often implicit) resistance to increasing bourgeois cultural hegemony, and crime. I want to look briefly at what was happening in south-east London whilst the social landscape of the nineteenth-century city was being utterly transformed, in particular at some of the types of activity – that is, largely *criminal* activity – which if anything provided a kind of continuity of response to changing material realities in the period following the 'great confinement'.

Jones (1971, 1983), Pearson (1983) and Himmelfarb (1973), amongst others, have examined the social, political and economic processes that underpinned the 'Condition of England' debate of the latter part of the nineteenth century. Interest in the conditions of the poor and outcast[12] of London was central to this debate, as were historically continuous attempts to define, redefine and shape thinking about class, culture and identity. The impulse to categorize and interpret London's various plebeian groupings, which finds its fullest and most detailed expression later in the century in the work of Charles Booth, crystallizes in mid-century in the work of Henry Mayhew. There are clear problems, as Himmelfarb (1973: 708) demonstrates, in simply using Mayhews' descriptions of London street life as unproblematic historical or proto-sociological data. His work, however, if treated with caution, palpably demonstrates two main themes: first, an obsessive and essentially prurient bourgeois interest in the lives of the swarming Victorian underclasses and their means of subsistence; and second, the apparent existence of a plethora of vivid and highly differentiated criminal subcultures. One of the most prominent – though not the only – sections of the city in which the latter appear to have thrived was, as we might expect, inner south-east London.

Throughout his work Mayhew demonstrates a particular penchant for the area. Apparent swarms of thieves and swindlers, many of them street children or 'arabs', were operating in the 'New Cut, Lambeth and Borough' (1862: 133). This latter area, just south of London Bridge, is characterized as the site of a subculture of 'Irish-cockney teenage thieves' (1862: 142) and of the practice of 'snatching with violence' (1862: 234) – which Mayhew regards as the Victorian equivalent of the highway robbery of Sheppard's era. A set-to in the New Cut reminds us of the already noted and deep-rooted reservoir of anti-Police sentiment, with a crowd forming against arresting officers and urging 'let 'em go' (1862: 138). The Thames, on both its south and north banks towards the east, is the focus of a teeming riverside underworld almost too widespread and complex to categorize. The impression conveyed by Mayhews' work, in fact, is of a set of highly differentiated criminal subcultures (in south-east, east and central-north London) almost as heterogeneous and arcane as the city's virtually incomprehensible employment structure. One thing is clear, however: if Mayhew is in any sense a credible witness of the street life of nineteenth-century south-east London, the criminal proclivities of large sections of the working-class were both a continuing feature of life in the city and, in the workings of particular kinds of *habitus*, consistently adapting in terms of practices and strategies of survival to rapidly shifting material realities.

The position of south-east London is even more central in accounts of law and disorder in the latter decades of the nineteenth century. Pearson's (1983) account of Victorian 'hooliganism' begins on familiar ground, noting those

> fierce traditions of resistance to the Police in working class neighbourhoods, so that not uncommonly Police attempting to make street arrests would be set upon by large crowds – sometimes numbering two or three hundred people – shouting 'Rescue, Rescue' and 'Boot him!' (1983: 74)

This is from a *South London Chronicle* report of 1898. This period is characterized for Pearson by an early media panic centred on an emergent 'hooligan' phenomenon. His account is generously illustrated with archive material from south-London newspapers, indicating once again the pivotal role that the area played in shaping historical understandings of law and order. In 1899, for example, Clarence Rooks's *The Hooligan Nights* located the origins of the 'hooligan gangs' – in an echo of Mayhews' 'Irish-cockney teenage thieves' – in 'Irish Court' at the Elephant and Castle (Pearson 1983: 255). While the details of this account of the birthplace of Victorian hooliganism are a matter of dispute, the point is made: that in 1899, the 'Elephant and Castle' was understood to be sufficiently coterminous with disorder, violence and criminality to make it a primary site around which bourgeois anxieties and folk-taxonomic attributive schema could be focused. This is the period in which it was said that the gangs of south London wore 'boots toe-plated with iron, and calculated to kill easily' (Pearson 1983: 77), a good sixty-five years before the emergence of the 'Skinhead'. Press reports of London street life at the time of the 1898 Bank Holiday were filled with accounts of assaults and robberies, pick-pocketing, gang fights,[13] stabbings, vandalism and 'free fights'. In one of the latter, 'a Bank Holiday bust-up in the Old Kent Road . . . consumed the energies of 200 people' (Pearson 1983: 81).

The territorial imperative was often a feature of such disturbances. One of the most important characteristics of nineteenth-century London was, as we have seen, the intensifying development of disconnected and class-homogeneous urban spaces. The parochial and localist sensibilities fostered by this pattern of development were informed, in part, by particular occupational sensibilities and cultures. Charles Booth, in his carefully microcosmic accounts of the various parts of London, repeatedly stressed the staggering multiplicity of traders, and the localization of their trades (O'Day and Englander 1993: 104).

At no point in his vast analyses of the labouring people of London does Booth purport to provide generalizable insights into the nature of life in the metropolis as a whole – a recognition of the fact that the specifities of its patchwork of communities rendered such a task untenable. He constantly stresses heterogeneity, diversity, multiplicity and smallness of scale as the main characteristics of the London occupational structure. O'Day and Englander, in their survey of Booth's work, note that 'Neighbourhood and community – patterns of sociability, of language, of dress and politics – often reflected the needs and norms of the trade' (1993: 122).

Given this, the proletarian London of the nineteenth century is probably best viewed as a collection of discrete, parochial, intensively localist, occupation-based communities, reflecting nuanced differences of speech, comportment and, to an extent, sensibility. This was the period in which a folk-taxonomic, cognitive map for the apprehension of the metropolis – an impossible proposition, given its magnitude and heterogeneity – would have become profoundly nuanced, complex and arcane. This patchwork of distinct communities is one of the primary characteristics of nineteenth-century London, and nowhere would the sense of locality have been more keenly experienced than in the south-east, with its highly particularized, characterized and continuing spatial *and* cultural status, operating as an obscure *other* to the metropolitan centre. A peculiar fusion of elements, then, appears to characterize this London: a profusion of deeply entrenched criminal subcultures; the heterogeneity of its non-institutional, small scale enterprises; the lack of a genuinely cohesive, 'corporate', class consciousness; and the primacy of localist, parochial and differently nuanced urban socialities. To these we must also add irreligion as another element in this historical London tendency towards a rigorously materialist worldview.

Booth devotes a great deal of attention in his 'Religious Influences' series to the status and practice of religion throughout the city, and his considerations on south-east London are especially interesting. He was clearly alert, in the period of 'class conciliation' and bourgeois evangelism, to the class limitations of the religious effort in inner London. In his descriptions of south-east London published in 1902/3, he considers the 'worsening' of the situation in the area between the Borough and Blackfriars Road, and the problems of making religion felt in that area:

> There is in this part a great concentration of evil living and low conditions of life that strikes the imagination and leads almost irresistibly to sensational statement . . . the character of these places varies somewhat in detail, but in general it is lowness and wickedness here rather than poverty (quoted in O'Day and Englander 1993: 194).

Further South, he tells us, the church of St Saviours 'hardly pretends to grapple with local needs . . . what role can religion play in the cure of these evil conditions?' (quoted in O'Day and Englander 1993: 194). Of course, it goes almost without saying that Booth's judgmental speculations on the culture and experiences of south-east Londoners are very much of their time and should be approached, like Mayhew's, with caution. His work is useful, however, for its illustration of inner urban resistance – largely expressed at the level of implicit refusal rather than explicit critique – to the missionaries. For Jones, this impulse is not so much an expression of irrecoverable nihilistic despair as one of communal pride and class autonomy at a time when these things were under intense attack, and when church attendance signified abject poverty and the loss of self respect (1983: 196). Porter observes, in this connection, that

> Three surveys (1851, 1866 and 1903) document this popular paganism. East and south London had the nation's lowest church attendance. In working class inner city areas fewer than one in five attended a place of worship. London was no city of God (1994: 298).

There is thus one strand of submission, deference, institutionalization and, perhaps, *humility* – but also of possible social cohesion and widely-based collective consciousness – which never featured significantly in the cultural life of south-east London. In other words, the historical tendency towards a worldly materialism was never checked or softened by the profound communal embrace of a transcendental, non-worldly perspective.[14]

In an episode of *Only Fools and Horses* 'Del Boy' enters a church as if he is stepping onto another planet, for at no point do his mental universe and the meanings that he dimly takes to inhere in the church meet. He devises a scam to profit from an apparently weeping statue of the Virgin. White south-east London is represented here with some degree of accuracy, as an area with a spectacularly underdeveloped religious culture. And it can be argued that it is the guiding hand of Mammon, and not that of the Lord, which has by and large moved the successive generations of worker, entrepreneur and criminal in the area.

This view is supported by the work of Johnson (1996), on the question of class consciousness in the same period. Rejecting Jones's idea of a working-class 'culture of consolation', Johnson (1996) sees 'competitive individualism' as the primary factor working against the development of a stable corporate solidarity in London:

> The unrestricted competition in the London labour market, which had such a positive impact on the long-growth of the metropolitan economy, also had a profound effect on London working-class politics. Intense economic rivalry between individuals in the labour market induced, I would argue, a degree of competitive individualism among the workers of London which was a more powerful political influence than in other parts of the country . . . Londoners were remarkably anti-social. Their church attendance, their trade union and friendly society membership, their use of co-operative trading societies, even their turn out as voters in general elections, were all significantly lower than the national average . . . The institutional forms of industrial capitalism – employer's organizations and trade unions – had little place in the dynamic metropolitan setting (1996: 35).

Here then are the dimensions of some of those schemes of perception and patterns of practice within which working-class south-east Londoners entered the twentieth century, though it is plain that the various groupings have never been constituted as an homogenous mass. It is therefore untenable to posit the outlines of a definitive, all-encompassing *habitus*. Rather, it may be possible to summarize a number of key themes which, even in their unevenness, have structured particular sensibilities and orientations out of extraordinary processual histories. The spatial arena of this history is unique in this country, its primary characteristic being its constitution as an obscure, mysterious and darkly conceived other place close by the very heart of the metropolis.

This unique experience of simultaneous proximity to and exclusion from a great world city has generated a sensibility in which metropolitan arrogance and a kind of conservative, defensive assertiveness may be fused. The routine romanticization of 'East End' life has arguably left the south-east with a sense of underhistoricized, underglamorized but ultimately *authentic* Londonness. A proprietary attitude toward the city can therefore coexist with a kind of embittered isolationism, often as fractious towards other sections of the English working-class as it is to a more obviously antithetical bourgeois culture. I would suggest, then, that it is a largely implicit consciousness of these matters that lies at the heart of particular embodiments of (autonomous, larger-than-life) south-east London culture and identity. The majority of south-east Londoners are not, of course, underworld superstars like Charlie Richardson. But Charlie Richardson is a south-east Londoner, and it is instructive to look briefly at the south-east London cult of the gangster, for it both expresses many of the foregoing themes *and* provides Millwall and the area's more general masculinist subcultures with their particular mythic repertoire.

'Up the Elephant and Round the Castle': Teddy Boys, Gangsters and Masculine Mythology

The Teddy Boy phenomenon of the 1950s is regarded as the first and defining moment in British youth subculture, the first expression of a distinctively novel post-war 'teenage' impulse. However, Pearson demonstrates that the Teds represented something much more like a particular strain of cultural continuity than novelty (Pearson 1983: 22). Many of the constituent parts of their stylistic and behavioural repertoire were in evidence even before the war – a fact completely effaced in media constructions of the 'phenomenon'. The Teddy Boy first emerged from the 'slum neighbourhoods of London, in particular the Elephant and Castle in south-east London' (Pearson 1983: 22). That the area should be the focus of a moral panic in the media comes as no surprise – for this was but a further expression of its historical role in these matters. But what kind of place was this almost mythical 'Elephant and Castle' at the time of the Teds?

The actor Michael Caine (1992: 38), who grew up in the area, reminisces: 'The Elephant was not exactly a classy district. The streets were as rough and dangerous as it was possible to get without anybody actually declaring war.' Nobody ever said the whole phrase, 'Elephant and Castle': 'If you were asked where you came from, you only said "the Elephant", and if you could keep a reasonably straight face, this was usually enough to strike terror into anyone from outside the area' (Caine 1992). Continuing his characterization of life in the area in the late forties, Caine notes the infamous presence of some 'very vicious groups of criminals', the VIPs – London backslang for 'spivs'.[15] In Caine's rhetorical schematic the two types – 'Teds' (one of which he attempted to become) and 'vicious criminal gangs' are condensed into a single mode of representing the nature of the area as hard and tough, violent and dangerous, *criminal*. If Caine's memoirs remind us at this point of the centrality of issues relating to the dialectical complexities of reality and representation in these matters, they also demonstrate a very deep-rooted and widespread folk conception of life in the area, of the close detail of lived experience in a heavily mythologized urban landscape. In the twentieth century the bulk of this masculine mythology has both attended, and been significantly derived from, south-east London gangland culture.

Gilbert Kelland is a former head of Scotland Yards' CID. In 1951, as a newly promoted young sergeant, he was posted to Carter Street station in the Walworth Road, 'about half way between the Elephant and Castle and Camberwell Green in south-east London. The Walworth and Elephant and Castle were tough neighbourhoods, but they were good places to learn some facts about coppering' (Kelland 1993: 30). Kelland, whose Walworth Road is a little more benign than Caine's, still portrays the area as characterized by teeming markets in stolen goods and illicit gambling. He also notes the significance of the scrap-metal business, and was not surprised to find that a decade after his tenure at Carter Street 'it was in the Walworth area that the Richardson brothers became notorious criminals with extensive interests in the scrap metal business' (1993: 30).

All of this, as well as the more historical themes outlined earlier, coalesce in the emblematic figure of Charlie Richardson. The details of Richardsons' biography have been well documented,[16] and I will not rehearse them here. It is important to note, however, that his empire grew out of his scrap-metal business, an arena in which the dividing line between street-level trading and outright criminality was never clearly drawn. To this day Richardson portrays his past career as that of an energetic and adventurous businessman. Tough, ruthless, exacting and 'creative' in his business dealings, his severest contempt is reserved for those things sought by the sheepish common man: 'Caution and security stop people from really living' (Richardson 1992: 52). His larger-than-life and bellicose appetite for material success is a theme we are now familiar with. However, he combines it with two others – an inviolable masculine toughness and a still more intense sense of autonomy. His refusal to submit to what he saw as the humbling indignities of National Service is a case in point (1992: 102), when he did not – and this was a view shared by a good many of his peers – need the army to 'make a man' of him. For he was a man already, with allegiances only to himself, his immediate family and associates, and with a fierce hunger for material success. The extent to which his almost Nietzschean desire for an autonomy of self is a matter of temperament or culture is open to speculation. Yet it is clear that in his exaggerated and self-consciously archetypal self-representations, Richardson is expressing a south-east London value-system based on a demand for autonomy and the freedom to 'trade' that can be traced back to the eleventh century.

Richardson personifies a particular London *habitus*, or orientation towards material reality. He recognizes that his was not an especially spectacular gangsterism. James Morton, in his survey of London's' underworld, concurs:

> Until recently the East End villains have always had a much greater press coverage than their South London counterparts, but informed observers have always regarded the latter as more dangerous, perhaps because they have displayed a greater ability to keep their heads below the parapet. (Morton 1994: 95)

The Richardsons (brother Eddie was known in his youth as 'King of the Teds') neither sought nor achieved the level of public notoriety of the Kray brothers from east London, whose almost cinematically spectacularized careers brought them a much broader audience. While the Krays were being fêted by West End celebrities and living like film stars, the Richardsons were getting on with business in their dark, mysterious, *other* London.[17] It is from his embodiment of this south-east

London masculinist *habitus* that Charlie Richardson draws his power as an archetype. He represents the area in a particular cultural sphere, and he and the identificatory possibilities that inhere in his persona are, in their turn, situated within that repertoire of symbols through which definitions of what it means to be certain types of south-east-London *man* are understood.

Richardson's autobiography is a fascinatingly constructed mixture of condensed metaphor and explicit reflexivity which cannot easily be read in terms of the working-class restricted linguistic coding posited by Bernstein[18] (1979, 1990). This draws our attention to two things. First, that individuals in increasingly complex and highly differentiated societies are not always entirely confined in their communicative practices to the linguistic *habitus* of their class background;[19] and second, that Richardson's book was to an unknown extent co-authored, by Bob Long. Despite these ambiguities of narrative, it is clear that Richardson realized his success almost purely on the basis of *embodied* practice – it was built by his own hands and the force of his own personality. It is in this sense, of someone who both acquired and realized this particular set of orientations and desires experientially, and at the level of practice, that Richardson has become a genuinely emblematic figure for certain south-east Londoners.

In telling the story of the Brinks' Mat bullion robbery, Hogg *et al.* (1988) also provide an account of the culture of Richardson's gangland successors. By the 1980s, they note, an interesting phenomenon became apparent to detectives investigating the growth of the well organized armed robbery:

> An inordinate number of men convicted for the more professional type of robbery, and a number of others thought to be likely suspects, came from just one area – south-east London. (1988: 69)

The geographic and demographic peculiarities of the area, the authors feel, are of particular significance. For it was the largest unbroken tract of an entrenched white working-class left in the city, an unbroken sprawl of ungentrified, 'modest or run-down housing developments' stretching without interruption from the south side of the Thames to Kent and therefore entirely unleavened, presumably, by those pockets of bourgeois civilisation that characterize even the dourest regions north of the river. This is the context of a particular south-east London criminality, an obscure phenomenon which they seek to account for in the absence of a 'full sociological survey'. Using the assessments of those who policed the area, the core of the problem is seen to be the 'widespread disregard for law and order that has existed for centuries among certain families of dockers in the riverside Bermondsey[20] and Rotherhithe areas, where pilfering cargoes was once a way of life' (Hogg *et al.* 1998: 70).

This localized culture, then, is an example of a specific *habitus* at work through the centuries, and in particular a continuation of south-east London themes that have their origins in the period of Linebaughs' analysis of the central role of the riverside in historical class relations.[21] It is interesting that these police attempts to account for this localist underworld revolve entirely around the effects of historically continuous patterns of material culture, practical disposition and practice. It would appear that the detectives of the Metropolitan Police – whether or not they have read Bourdieu – are fully aware of the broad outlines and workings of the *habitus*, for it is the very cohesiveness of these communities, in fact, that is significant:

> Until the very recent dockland developments [the authors are writing in 1988] those ties remained virtually intact. The East End of London may have been decimated by the German air force in the second world war and the city planners afterwards, but in the South East one of Londons' largest working class communities, centred on the Old Kent Road, stayed put. (Hogg *et al.* 1988: 70)

These attempts to explain the phenomenon in material sociological terms are supplemented, in the same passage, by an awareness of a powerfully symbolic dimension to these matters:

> The Great Train robbery too had a part to play in the process – most of the robbers came from South East London. The heroic status they were to achieve in the eyes of many was nowhere more evident than on the streets where they grew up. Even though guns were not used on that occasion, armed robbery took on a romantic hue. (1988: 70)

These processes, of the cultural valorization of the gangster, and embodied dispositions and orientations derived from a dialectics of identity forged in particular material social realities, have clearly generated some fairly distinctive forms of working-class masculinity. This is confirmed by the 1987 statement of a Metropolitan Police 'senior flying squad officer':

> Some 60 per cent of all armed robberies in the country take place in London, and about three quarters of those which take place elsewhere are committed by Londoners. Proportionally, the chances are high that an armed robber is from South East London. (Hogg *et al.* 1988: 71)

The point, of course, is not to suggest that the area is swarming with volatile and dangerous armed criminals,[22] but rather to note the crucial possibility that the raw symbolic material central to the experience of localist working-class masculinities is of a particular sort in south-east London. Here, archetypal and highly celebrated versions of performative manliness are as likely to be flavoured by a no-nonsense and gangsterish inviolability as they are by a legacy and iconography of industrial–proletarian toughness.

This has important consequences in Millwallism, where performative manliness is characterized by something beyond mere toughness itself, and where an imperious, contemptuous and inviolable sense of (intra-working-class) cultural superiority pervades and sets up an expressive context in which rivals are constituted as a *joke* – for both their lack of toughness and/or metropolitan Londonness. These particular and historically grounded forms of social self-awareness – only tangentially related to the broader development of 'football hooliganism' – have preceded and determined the participation of Millwall fans in the latter domain, and in the more general practices of football culture.

Millwall and Some South-East London Archetypes: the Den of Thieves and the Raucous Dockland Music-Hall

The historical formations of class cultures in London, and especially the metropolitan social-dialectics outlined in the foregoing, have sedimented a powerful strain of combative local sensibility in the city's working-class populations. Local-patriotic and masculinist folk-taxonomies suffuse the interactive everyday life of the city, and are nowhere more firmly rooted – and articulated – than in south-east London. Elaborations of Millwallism are invariably situated in these broader networks of understanding, sentiment and attribution, and fans will often articulate the two as coterminous. Terry, a lifelong Millwall fan in his late twenties, exemplifies this tendency:

> Like, when you go to certain parts, when you go north London, east London, 'ave a look round an' you think 'nah, I wouldn't like to live over 'ere, its not home'. In south-east London they're on a different wavelength, they really are, from like, up North, or even on the other side of the river. Its like, we got *common sense* an' they aint, that's 'ow it really is. Its really 'ard to explain – but its there. There aint no gettin' away from it. An' they say all about the gangsters an' all that from south London, most of 'em live in south London, or in the suburbs, like, of Kent, like Welling, which is still in south-east London.

There is much that is implicit in Terry's statement about the defining characteristic of south-London people as 'common-sensical'. The reference is to understandings of specific, folk-taxonomic characteristics and qualities which are not necessarily held in the sphere of articulate reflection. Terry has a powerful sense of the uniqueness of his cultural background which may be very difficult to put into words. It does not derive from a fully programmatic and detailed system of classification but is rather located in the sphere of experience, of a commonly held and tacit sense of specific and embodied forms of cultural capital. This does not mean that these identifications do not find public articulation – as they clearly do in moments of cultural or violent conflict between sets of fans – but that they are experienced most powerfully as constitutive elements of the self rather than as explicit themes awaiting cognitive deliberation.

Terry's invocation of the south-London gangster tradition is, in this context, a metaphorical clue to the substantive content of this distinctive sphere of 'common sense'. Terry is a law-abiding family man, who, in all likelihood, will never come close to committing a serious crime. But this does not prevent him from emblematically summoning up the gangster as the representative of a particular strain of south-east London masculinity. The *traditional* gangster thus continues to function in the broader culture as an ambiguously folk-heroic ideal type. He is, first and foremost, personally inviolable and answers, in the main, to nobody. He is materially successful and able to provide the best for himself and his family. He has a deeply rooted sense of tradition and moral code – and, though he might be a 'complete *bastard*' – he looks after his own. Moreover his capacity for violence is matched by his guile, his practical intelligence and his metropolitan social alertness – his 'common sense'. He has, in an important sense, triumphed (whether materially or gesturally) over the apparent limitations of his class origins. He is his own man and *no one fucks with him* lightly. He is, ultimately, a force to be reckoned with, for he is potent, resourceful, sharp and experienced.

These themes are understood and are being implicitly drawn on by Terry as a specific kind of masculine aura, as characteristic of himself and his peers. It is for these reasons that the archetype of the gangster continues to resonate powerfully at Millwall amongst an overwhelmingly law-abiding interpretative community. And these interconnected themes of specific patterns of culture, of masculine autonomy but collective identification, are routinely spatialized by Millwall fans in connecting the character of the club with the culture of the area. Mick, a fan in his late thirties, makes this explicit:

> I sometimes think the big estates, the redevelopment, was a conscious attempt to try an' break it all up, move the people around, break up the culture of the area. But there you're into social policy . . . I don't think the area will ever change. Even the yuppies, they won't last. They all bought their houses in Dockhead, but they'll move out of the area, they'll go. You'll never change the area, I mean, Bermondsey, Deptford, you won't change 'em. Its like, the Bonamy Estate – before they knocked that down there was more armed robbers and villains coming from there than any other part of London. I dunno why, social deprivation I suppose, if people got nothin' they'll take what they want.

Mick's view of the unchangeability of the area emphasizes a particular conception of depth. This is a view which grants historically reproducible characteristics to places themselves. Bermondsey and Deptford may be physically altered, and are even subject to relatively high levels of social and demographic change, but they will never be places amenable to the creation of comfortable gentrified niches. The area has retained the unique and indelible stamp of its class history. There is a sense in such commentaries of south-east London as a distinctive region separated by the Thames from both the metropolitan centre *and* from the 'East End' – its rival in the historical contest over authentic Londonness. It is typical in Millwall and south-east London circles to encounter a concern to demonstrate that its masculine cultural formations have an edge lacked by their more widely celebrated and famous counterparts. The extremely violent nature of the intermittent encounters between Millwall and east London's West Ham[23] expresses, in this sense, a struggle for the physical supremacy of the capital, but also the right to be defined as the authentic representatives of a distinctive London manliness. Contrasting perceptions of gangster archetypes are relevant here. John, another local-patriotic Millwall diehard, feels that

> They're all fakers over there – the 'East End', all that 'loveable cockney' bollocks. An' this thing about the fuckin' Krays, an' its gone *on and on and on*, you know what I mean, like they're all loveable cockney rogues an' all that . . . you know, they've always 'ad this sort of – even the media – if you talk about the East End its where they all love the Queen mum an' it was bombed durin' the war. Whereas wiv us its like, 'they're all thieves an' gangsters over there', but wiv them its like 'oh, they might be thieves, but they've all got 'earts of gold an' they all 'ave nice street parties, they're not really bad lads', you know what I mean? Like, they keep sayin' about the Krays, 'you could always leave your door open, they looked after everyone', its all bollocks – the Richardsons lived round the corner from me, an' they were bastards an' everyone knew it, know what I mean? No one looks on 'em as sorta Robin Hood figures round 'ere.

There is a realism here, a lack of sentiment, a brusqueness and a kind of dourness. However, there is also a sense of real pride in a neglected and traduced identity and area, which characterizes the masculine formations from which much of Millwall's support is drawn. This is the social source of that peculiarly embittered and volatile passion with which its fans have become associated, and which has fused in recent decades with the events and processes around the club itself. These inform and give shape to that vernacular, expressive semantic field that structures the participation of individuals in Millwall's interpretative community.

But The Gangster is not the only masculine archetype at large in this semantic field. For his role as an exemplifying symbol is mirrored by a second ideal type, The Docker. *He* represents a more mainstream and perhaps general tradition of labouring proletarian masculinism. For he references a world of hard work, raw humour, extreme physical toughness and visceral pleasures. And though he is often an ambiguous and semi-criminal figure himself, his links are also with a world of honest industrial toil, with community and with the traditional virtues of endurance, commitment, loyalty, pride and a plain-speaking contempt for hubris and pretension. Despite the closure of the Surrey Docks and the demise of its specific occupational culture, he continues to exist as an archetypal, mythologized moral custodian of the football club and its traditions. He is as frequently and casually invoked in discussions on Millwall by fans and, as here, former players. Eamon Dunphy (1986) remembers the Den of the 1960s as a place with a distinctive occupation-based ambience:

> To us the Den was home, its wit always good for a laugh, its passion often worth a goal or two. If the game was boring the crowd would amuse itself by picking on some unfortunate player – home or away – whose every desperate lunge would draw roars of derision. Sometimes this unique gathering would parody itself. If the home team's efforts were particularly fruitless, mock passion would be conjured up on the terraces. Coming to this raucous dockland music hall, a smart manager might have decided to play to the audience. He might have decided to build a side likely to respond to the rough and ready atmosphere, a side that in turn might draw a response from the dockers on the terraces. (1987: 17)

This association of Millwall with the dockers and their culture is widespread and very close. Older fans have fond memories of this golden age of Millwall support, and above all remember the humour. David, who has supported the club since the 1950s, remembers :

> I used to like it, down at the old Den, and I also remember the old docker days, when there were still docks, and it was very funny. It wasn't all crude stuff either and you would actually detect a ripple. It was almost like 'pass it on', sort of thing, with sort of like a wave of laughter going around, so I used to feel part of that.

Although he has memories of a rather cruder oral culture than David suggests, Peter remembers the dockers as

> Incredibly funny and incredibly sociable. Its not a myth, there were lots of them. I regret the passing of the Surrey Docks, they added a lot of character to the area. They related to Millwall, Millwall was always known as 'the club in the heart of London's docklands'. I think the characteristic that I remember is the one that is totally and absolutely still there. Though on the surface it seemed violent, rough and the language was, according to some parts of the country, absolutely appalling . . . underneath it they were really good people, with very, very good values, values of family, values of loyalty. The club sort of bound them together, and a lot of this is left.

This may or not be an idealised version of the characteristic Millwall values. What is not in doubt is the extent to which many fans, in their formulations of what the club means to them, stress these themes of loyalty, of being bound together. This is the case across the spectrum of individual supporters, from the club chaplain to those who have had a direct hand in the development of the activities that led to the status of the Millwall fan as archetypal hooligan. In the next chapter I will examine – at the general/theoretical and empirical levels – the experiential sources of this preoccupation with forms of collective solidarity. We will see that, contrary to popular understanding, Millwall fandom is characterized not by 'cultural deprivation', 'underclass culture', 'anomie' or 'deviance' but by particular kinds of *values*. And although these are not the bourgeois values of sentimental humanism, they are values nonetheless, and an account of the ways in which they are embodied in the more general social orientations and practices in which Millwall is implicated is the essential next step to a fuller appreciation of what is at stake at the club.

Notes

1. 'People' should, of course, be in the plural here – London has always been a city of remarkable social diversity. My focus, however, is in general upon those broadly working-class settlements historically characteristic of the area under consideration. I am thinking of those white working-class communities which have, until relatively recently, been predominant within the area.
2. The term is, of course, problematic. For the purposes of an historical overview that begins in the twelfth century, it is a practically meaningless categorization. As E.P. Thompson repeatedly stressed, in his seminal work in this area, the term is a descriptive one which evades as much as it defines. Observing that classes must be regarded in terms of process rather than static, reified or final groupings, he says that a class is a 'very loosely defined body of people who share the same congeries of interests, social experiences, traditions and value-system, who have a disposition to behave as a class, to define themselves in their actions and in their consciousness in relation to other groups of people in class ways. But class is not a thing, it is a happening' (1963: 939). In the modern age, I would suggest, a vital impetus of class consciousness and dispositions thus conceived has been towards defining sovereign, embodied working-class identities and cultures in contradistinction to increasingly hegemonic bourgeois ones. This historically continuous (if uneven) tendency of class-based cultures

towards a kind of implicit, albeit often defensive, sovereignty cannot easily be matched by a continuity of terminology which can accurately define these developing processes. I choose to use the term metaphorically, and, despite its problematic nature and its status as one among many, primarily in the interests of thematic and linguistic consistency.

3. The complex multicultural nature of Early Modern London and its class cultures is routinely effaced in social histories of the city. Fryer (1984: 72), notes that many of the 10,000 or so black people thought to be living in Britain throughout the eighteenth century, for example, were at the centre of London culture and politics. Any account of class and culture in the modern period must be alert to this presence. Working-class London (the riverside districts in particular) was certainly not perceived at the time as monocultural: 'When one goes into Rotherhithe and Wapping, which places are chiefly inhabited by sailors, but that somewhat of the same language is spoken, a man would be apt to suspect himself in another country' John Fielding 1760, *A Brief Description of the Cities of London and Westminster*, in Linebaugh 1993: 135).
4. In *Oliver Twist*
5. The dynamics of an ongoing dialectics of social identity are complex and various, and it is clear that the latter cannot be usefully conceived of as definitively fixed and unchanging. Cultural identities are, as Hall (1990: 225) notes, a matter of "becoming" as well as "being" . . . Far from being eternally fixed in some essentialized past, they are subject to the continuous "play" of history, culture and power. Far from being grounded in a mere "recovery" of the past, which is waiting to be found, and which, when found, will secure our sense of ourselves into eternity, identities are the names we give to the different ways we are positioned by, and position ourselves within, the narratives of the past.' It is likely that the underlying workings of a particular *habitus* will orient groups towards those preferences for specific symbols and patterns of identification defined as 'traditional'.
6. Del Boy is the central figure in BBC TV's exceptionally popular *Only Fools and Horses* series. A rather spectacularized caricature embodying these themes, he is characterized by his skill in 'ducking and diving': pursuing a form of resolutely autonomous, marginal entrepreneurialism in which the boundaries between legal and illegal, crime and speculative endeavour, are always ambiguously defined. He lives in Peckham.

   Hobbs's account of 'ducking and diving' in East London describes a set of practices similarly grounded in the historical class formations of the area: 'Independence, internal solidarity, and pre-industrial characteristics combining to form a community that does not conform to either proletarian or bourgeois cultural stereotypes. The vital contradiction of this cultural inheritance is that it is essentially working-class, favouring an entrepreneurial style that is rooted in pre-industrial forms of bargaining and exchange' (1988: 101).

7. McMullan identifies five key areas in this growth and institutionalization: (1) wider structural opportunities for theft (2) a secrecy of operations (3) established criminal habitats (4) networks of criminal association, and (5) an elaborate black market for disposing of criminal goods (1984: 15).
8. *The Harry Roberts Song* and *Kill, Kill, Kill the Bill*, which have been in circulation at Millwall and other London Football grounds for the last few decades, are prime examples. The latter is a chant, the former a song which runs to the tune of *London Bridge is falling down*:

   Harry Roberts is our friend,
   Is our friend,
   Is our friend,
   Harry Roberts is our friend,
   He kills coppers !

   Let him out he'll kill some more,
   Kill some more,
   Kill some more,
   Let him out he'll kill some more,
   Harry Roberts !

9. The autobiographies of Frankie Fraser (1994) and Charlie Richardson (1992), for example, exemplify this orientation
10. Linebaugh (1993: 122–3) notes that the term 'proletarian' first appears in the 1660s to describe the lowest of the social low whose origins, as a group, were held to lie in the multinational, or 'deep sea', flotsam to which London – the great mercantile, maritime and slaving centre – was host. This early London proletariat was, Linebaugh repeatedly illustrates, a grouping of immense ethnic and cultural heterogeneity.
11. Peter Burke notes of this period 'the appearance of the entrepreneur as popular hero, a type apparently without any European parallel' (1977: 158). This peculiarity of London is confirmed by V.S. Pritchett (1986: 64), as acute an observer of historical themes in the life of the city as there has been: 'There is usually money at the bottom of the London liberties: there has been nothing abstract in the London view of the desirable life.'
12. Jones (1983), sees the latter third of the century as a period in which the dimensions and character of London working-class culture were reshaped. Following the defeat of Chartism, 'working people ceased to believe that they could shape society in their own image . . . Capitalism had become an immovable horizon.' This recognition of capitalism as the immovable frame of social action, and the acquiescence this generated, was reflected in the

capital in the formation of a parochial, defensive and overwhelmingly politically conservative 'culture of consolation' centred upon the Music Hall (1983: 237). Elsewhere, Jones (1971) notes that those dispositions of the London 'casual poor' which were to underpin the development of this conservatism emerged from a material reality that provided 'no focus for any growth of collective loyalty upon which a stable class-consciousness could be based' (1971: 344).

13. Fighting – in its codified as well as its informal manifestations – could scarcely have been more central to the cultural life of south-east London's working-class communities at this time. In the period of the professionalization of football in the latter part of the century, Thompson notes (1988: 295), the game faced stiff competition in the area: 'Locally, other sports might outrank soccer in their following: in the poorest parts of London, the East End and Southwark, professional boxing was the most consistently popular and accessible spectacle.' This centrality is exemplified by the folk-heroic status enjoyed in south-east London and beyond by Bermondsey featherweight Tom Causer. Bermondsey, in particular, was a locality in which 'good boxers lived in every other street. Between 1897 and 1914 it produced six British champions, which must surely be a record for a borough of 130,000 people, who all lived in an area of 1,500 acres' (Shipley 1983: 35). The six were Causer himself, Ben Jordan, Jack Goldswain, Jim Sullivan, Sid Smith and Curly Walker.
14. Pelling (1979: 20) notes 'Working-class religious commitment in the nineteenth century seems to have been most complete in isolated single-occupation districts, where a new sect could secure a high degree of identity with the whole community.' Elsewhere, he suggests that any generalized claims that the urban working classes were positively anti-religious are exaggerated 'except perhaps in relation to London' (1979: 27). Shipley (1979: 34), apropos the Bermondsey featherweight champion already mentioned, notes that 'the Causer family, like most London families, was not religious'.
15. The 'spiv' is an important iconic figure from the immediate post war era. As Hebdige (1974a: 5) observes, this London variant on the New York mafioso prototype, possessing a highly developed and Italianate-style consciousness more contemporary than that of the Teds was, along with his increasingly visible Jamaican 'hustler' equivalent, amongst the formative influences on that most metropolitan of all youth subcultures, Mod – primarily a phenomenon of south-east and east London.
16. Campbell (1994), Morton (1994) and by Richardson (1992) himself.
17. Hebdige (1974b) considers the contrast in his *The Kray Twins: A Study of a System of Closure.* For more recent accounts of the ongoing fascination with the Krays, see Jenks and Lorentzen (1997) and Sinclair (1997).

18. This is not the case with the autobiography of Frankie Fraser (1994), a former associate of Richardson. His story, as told to James Morton, is an almost entirely unreflexive account of a life spent in organized crime and prison. The long and remorseless catalogue of beatings inflicted upon him whilst in prison are the product of his extraordinary intransigence and sense of inviolability. Yet Fraser tells us little or nothing about their psychological sources – he simply details (in a striking echo of the Algerian sense of honour described by Bourdieu) his *enactment* of them. This hatred of policing and penal authority is an antiestablishmentarianism minus the politics, an autonomous, oppositional impulse defined implicitly in social embodiment rather than reflexively articulated. Born in Waterloo in 1923, he is the product of a London only a generation after Booth. Whilst he is clearly in many ways an exceptional figure, it is arguable that he embodies some of those dispositions and orientations taken by Pearson, for example, to be characteristic of particular kinds of nineteenth- century London *habitus*.
19. Bernstein (1979) notes that, as primary agents of socialization, it is families which predispose children towards particular realizations of linguistic code. He is unambiguous that families of either code-type (restricted and elaborated) exist empirically within each class. His more recent work, particularly (1990), attempts to detail, at a high level of complexity, precise relationships between social class, occupational structure and linguistic predisposition. Class background does not, it is clear, straightforwardly or unambiguously determine linguistic orientation.
20. See 'London's Meanest Manor?', *Time Out* no. 1252 (January 1995), in which Bermondsey's reputation for being the 'roughest place in the capital' is said to have existed since the Victorian era. Jacob's Island, 1920s bare-knuckle fighting, the Richardsons and Frankie Fraser, the Arif brothers, Millwall football club, contemporary boxing culture and racism are all invoked in a short and rather obvious article purporting to assess the current state of play in the area.
21. Linebaugh (1993: chapter 12) examines the importance of the docks, in particular in relation to struggles over customary practice, the redefinition of crime, and the extension of anti-working-class moralizing discourses to policing, legislative and economic policies throughout the late eighteenth and early nineteenth centuries.
22. Although this is not, apparently, the view of the US State Department. 'The Yanks aren't coming. At least not to Peckham, rated by US Government experts to be as dangerous as a Latin-American hell-hole. According to State Department mandarins you are as much at risk on Peckham Rye as in Guatemala, where the streets are stalked by death-squads . . . the State Department has "Red-Flagged" Peckham, Brixton and Lewisham . . . Red-Flagging means

American tourists should avoid at all costs, and is normally applied to some of the world's worst trouble spots tells an understandably indignant report in the *South London Press*, 5.1.96.

23. The intensity of this conflict has been fuelled and exacerbated, since the mid 1970s, by a death on each side and a series of extraordinarily violent encounters since. This vendetta, which continues to mobilize many otherwise 'retired' men once active in the hooligan formations of the 1970s, therefore has its own internal logic and momentum. Its broader cultural context, however, is one in which a struggle over the right to be regarded as the toughest and most authentic London region is primary. See King (1996) and the previous chapter for a compelling and largely accurate account of the detail of such conflicts, and for its acknowledgement, from a Chelsea perspective, of Millwall and West Ham as *the* forces to be reckoned with in the capital. King and Knight (1999) broadly supports this view, and also gives an historical overview of the Millwall–Chelsea rivalry.

–3–

The Social Sources of Millwallism: Embodiment and Locality in Working-Class Masculinity

> Britain has 'the lowest staying-on rates in Europe', the worst 'gap in attainment' between lowest and highest achievers of any comparable European or North American society and, most importantly for our purposes, the 'worst education' population of youth of a country that describes itself as being 'advanced'. The overwhelming point about figures of this kind is the way in which they underline the crucial, definitive 'conditions of existence' – the moral and cultural shallowness, and lack of alternative experience, which feeds into the tribal weekend rituals of the underclass soccer hooligan.
>
> Ian Taylor , 'English Football in the 1990s'

> It was with the rise of the bourgeoisie, particularly in the consciousness of its critical intellectuals, that not only the honour of the *ancien regime* and its hierarchical prototypes was debunked, but that an understanding of man and society emerged that would eventually liquidate *any* conception of honour.
>
> Peter Berger , 'On the Obsolescence of the Concept of Honour'

> *Fuck 'em all! fuck 'em all!* ,
> *United, West Ham, Liverpool,*
> *'Cos we are the Millwall and we are the best*
> *We are the Millwall SO FUCK ALL THE REST!*
> *Fuck 'em all!* . . .
>
> Millwall Song

In this chapter I will explore Millwall's social sources from a different direction. Where the previous chapter focused on the substantive detail of the local contexts out of which Millwallism emerged, this will look in a more general sense at the processes, experiences and tendencies in cultural orientation characteristic of the social backdrops against which *any* study of working-class participation in football culture should be set: in short, at how salient aspects of localized working-class cultural personality becomes embodied in boys and young men. This entails a return to the often neglected possibility that the transformations of personalities, manners and cultural forms inherent in what Norbert Elias (1982) called the *Civilising Process* have, in fact, been partial and uneven. That is to say that the post-Enlightenment historical tendency towards universal individuation according to the principles and practices of the bourgeois public sphere has met with varying degrees of resistance at a range of social locations. Of these, deeply sedimented orientations, sensibilities and forms of embodiment generated by working-class cultures appear to have been the most intractable, and have not simply evaporated in line with incrementally improving material conditions.

In the long historical march towards the establishment of a hegemonic liberal–individualist paradigm of personality formation and cultural practice, the kinds of particular, implicit counter-bourgeois cultural forms that characterize the kind of local working-class contexts out of which Millwallism emerges, have customarily been rendered barely visible. When visible at all, have been driven to the very margins of the public sphere,[1] where they occasionally appear as expressions of an inchoate and illiberal barbarism.

The *Millwall fan* is a significant and widely invoked referent in this context, representing as he does the 'unreconstructed', white working-class man. But if it is irresponsible to simply pass over the more spectacular anti-social manifestations of contemporary male culture as part of a mindless celebration of 'ladism', neither is it helpful to dismiss the apparent disengagement of many working-class young men from liberal–individualist definitions of social-being as mere 'cultural shallowness'.

It is in this context that I have developed a broad and schematic, theoretical model of the kinds of urban ecologies in which working-class masculinities are forged, aimed at delineating their most salient experiential bases.[2] In this way I connect the account of the particularities of south-east-London life to the ways in which fundamental orientations and perspectives derived from such urban–masculinist environments underpin cultural practice at Millwall. Most centrally, after Bourdieu, I explore the theme of the body as the primary site of social memory and cultural reproduction, and relate this to the persistence of the kind of non- (or counter-) bourgeois – and to some extent historically continuous – moral forms and patterns of class-based practice that make Millwallism possible.

This involves the intersection of three key themes. First, the dynamics of urban–masculine personality formation and sociality; second, the significant characteristics of their environmental/cultural contexts relating to the idea of 'community'; and third, the fusing of these into class specific forms of bodily culture and social consciousness. An awareness of these frequently overlooked interconnections is indispensable to a full appreciation of the social sources of Millwallism. It is also essential to the development of any anthropologically meaningful approach to working-class traditions of football supporting, structured as these have been by varieties of mechanical solidarity, humour, violence and toughness, and the working of all these into ritual and physical contests. Here a grasp of their experiential depth, rather than their 'cultural shallowness', is essential. With this in mind I link a theoretical position on these themes in working-class male embodiment with concrete examples, later in the chapter, of how Millwall fans draw upon and utilize their distinctive varieties of cultural and physical capital in confrontations with opposing fans.

The Body and Class in Modernity

Though it is a widely accepted truism that the primary significance of the transition to modernity in Europe lies in a decisive discontinuity with pre-modern cultures and ways of life (Giddens 1991: 17), the question of the extent to which liberal–individualist paradigms of the subject and cultural practice can be thought of as having accomplished a universal hegemony is, in fact, a complex one. Leaving explicit and formal articulations of political resistance aside, I suggested in the previous chapter that a critical but largely neglected sphere of working-class opposition to that transformation of culture and manners characteristic of the eighteenth century and beyond was in embodiment itself. It is, however, a possibility overlooked in much of the proliferating work on the body in recent social theory.

The most celebrated and influential contributor to this emerging field has been, of course, Foucault. Central to his project was a concern to map the relations between the body and the effects of power upon it (Foucault 1980b: 151). The body, in this view, is not merely given meaning by 'discourses' but is *wholly constituted by them* (Shilling 1993: 74). This extreme social constructionist conception of the body and agency makes one critical point:

> The development of modernity brought with it a transition in the social spaces occupied by discourses, which had a profound effect on the construction of individuals. This transition involved a change in the target of discourse, as the fleshy body gave way to the mind as a focus of concern. (Shilling 1993: 75)

It is not difficult to accept the disembodiment of consciousness as a decisive development in bourgeois, liberal–individualist culture, and Foucault's recognition of this is critically important. But the blanket application of the idea of the shift to the mind to a range of historical contexts is doubly problematic. First, it tends to elide the historical possibility that counter-hegemonic forms of embodiment may themselves be expressions of an inarticulate but not insignificant sphere of resistance and autonomy. It is important to remember that, as Linebaugh noted, the theme of the 'great confinement' in eighteenth-century Europe was accompanied by a counterposed one of 'excarceration' (Linebaugh 1993: 23) and patterns of sub-political refusal. The extraordinary passivity attributed by Foucault to his historical subjects thus expresses his overarching conception of the biological individual as an infinitely malleable and highly unstable social construct (Shilling 1993: 74).

This negation of the possibility of an ontologically rooted and corporealized agential depth expresses a broader difficulty inherent in Foucauldian analyses, that is the disappearance of the fleshy body, ostensibly from history but actually from the Foucauldian paradigm itself (Turner 1984: 48, Shilling 1991: 663). This constitutes one of the great ironies of contemporary social theory in that it demonstrates the central fact that this conception of the social world, for all its much vaunted radical potential, proceeds entirely according to disembodying, abstracting discursive principles, and thus itself represents a high-water mark in the historical development of liberal-individualism.[3]

Any attempt to reinstate the kinds of social class subjectivity exemplified by Millwallism as a primary sphere of social analysis, must, in this context and climate, proceed from a sense of the body as positioned in a dialectic between phenomenological experience and material social reality. It must also recognize the central possibility that the historical tendency towards the disembodiment of consciousness has not been registered evenly across social locations. I suggest that forms of embodiment generated and sustained by non-bourgeois cultural groupings have been characterized by rather different tendencies. These may be best approached, in the first instance, through a brief consideration of new conceptions of the individual integral to the development of modernity.[4] The primary tendency in this process was, of course, towards individualization, constructed as antithetical to the kinds of pre-modern, collectively experienced forms of social identity to which contemporary football culture is connected. Longer-term, gradual developments in a Europe-wide civilizing process (Elias 1982), which were centred on greater control over the expression of affect and less of a tendency to fluctuate between emotional extremes, can thus be seen to underpin the emergence of an ideal bourgeois individual, characterized by restraint, rationality and, critically, a fully *reflexive* way of 'dealing with himself' (Kuzmics 1987: 517).

But this new type of personality was not spread evenly across populations. At the core of the work of both Bourdieu and Bernstein is the suggestion of the possibility that differences in class cultures in Britain and France may be sufficiently profound to register at the level of cognition itself. But whilst Bernstein's analysis is confined to the sphere of language, Bourdieu makes an attempt to ground his examination of class-based social identities in a conception of embodiment. His formulation of the concept *bodily hexis* is an attempt to account for the ways in which the *habitus* inscribes social consciousness, meaning and identity in the body itself. In this sense, different classes and class fractions develop distinct orientations towards the body, resulting in the appearance of a variety of class-specific bodily forms. These differing bodily forms are, of course, valued differently, and are inextricably linked to the formation of capitalist social inequalities.

Bourdieu's view of the working class (or 'popular') relation to the body is that it is primarily instrumental. The male working-class body – rooted classically in a densely corporeal material reality – is seen as both a means to an occupational end and a vehicle for the experience of excitement and/or enjoyment.[5] Whilst the valued physical capital contained in this (preferably well-built) body expresses strength, speed and agility, that of the dominant or bourgeois class fractions is derived from a social world in which 'economic practice is generated more strongly by the presentation of the self' (Wilkes, quoted in Shilling 1993: 132). This kind of physical capital has a currency and exchange value in a variety of contexts in which social confidence and a kind of individuated mastery may be expressed in control over a range of psycho-social situations (there are clear parallels here with Bernstein, who demonstrates that bourgeois individuated personalities are especially fluent in decontextualized social situations).

The primary bodily characteristic of bourgeois class fractions is a distancing of the individual self from vulgar corporeality. On this point Bourdieu notes

> variations in objective and subjective distance from the world, with its material constraints and temporal urgencies. Like the aesthetic disposition which is one dimension of it, the distant, detached or casual disposition towards the world or other people . . . can only be considered in objective conditions of existence that are relatively freed from urgency. (1986: 376)

The social, economic and cultural conditions in which distinctive class cultures are forged and maintained are registered upon the body itself:

> Everything takes place as if the social conditionings linked to a social condition tended to inscribe the relation to the social world in a lasting, generalised relation to one's own body, presenting it to others, moving it, making space for it, which gives the body its social physiognomy. Bodily hexis, a basic dimension of the sense of social orientation, is a practical way of experiencing and expressing one's own sense of social value. (1986: 474)

The primary social orientation of the male working-class body, then, is not towards distance and the expression of a unique, precious self, but towards corporeal *presence* in a context of collective sociality. This is a phenomenon both generated and sustained by, and necessary in, a range of social environments. Work is one of these. And Bourdieu's ideas on the instrumental relationships between such bodily forms, 'necessity' and occupational cultures (Bourdieu 1986) is insightful and useful in developing a sense of the primary social themes structuring working-class masculinity. His work, however, only takes us part of the way towards understanding the pressures and dynamics that impinge upon the working-class boy from his early years, or that characterize the social contexts in which his orientations and dispositions develop and mature. These themes precede absorption into specific occupational cultures – where they continue to exist – and are played out in two important spheres: the street (or its contemporary equivalent) and school.

Physical Capital, Practical Culture: The Recursive Bases of Male Sociality

Two broad approaches add depth and detail to Bourdieu's general scheme. First, there is the British sociology relating to class, masculinity and the urban environment. Second, there are the more general approaches to the anthropology of manhood which bear directly on the issues under consideration here. A brief overview of representative contributions from both areas will help develop a picture of the kind of psycho-social forces that structure the experience of the working-class urban boy. Though this will obviously be schematic in nature, it will provide a focus on some of the detail of the contexts in which working-class boys (of the kind who grow up to participate in and maintain Millwallism) experience their socializations, and the impact of these specific kinds of environment upon the orientations of the bodily hexis.

The striking thing to emerge from these accounts is the endemic nature of violence – or at least the potential for it – in the social environment of the working-class boy. Humphries' (1984) examination of the street gang between the years 1889 and 1939 demonstrates the centrality of two spheres in the historical experience of boys and adolescents. The first relates to violent territoriality, and the second to the generation of contexts for the experience of physical excitement. Both are integral to the structuring of young masculinity, and form the basis of focal concerns – of 'tough' independence, the celebration of the ability of the group to outsmart and defeat an opposition, and to ritual displays of physical prowess (Humphries, 1984: 179).

Given the omnipresence of the informal 'gang' in young urban society, Humphries extends this characterization to cover virtually the whole of the young male working class, and insists that, at their centre, these informal collectives had the expression of independence or autonomy from parents and social institutions. The masculine working-class impulse towards autonomy is a characteristic of all the groups studied in the literature on the young urban male (Cohen and Robins 1978, Murphy *et al.* 1990, Willis 1988). An even more forceful theme, however, is the routine use of the body both to experience and to express high excitement, physical conflict and mastery over the immediately experienced social and material environment.

That these tendencies may not simply express a wayward pathology of 'youth-culture' is made clear by David Gilmore's (1990) cross-cultural analysis of the various ways in which manhood must necessarily be 'accomplished'. Manhood, though a primarily cultural institution, still exhibits intriguing cross-cultural similarities. The most significant of these is the sense that 'achievement' of manhood is a relatively precarious process that must be 'won against powerful odds'. Gilmore observes, in this sense,

> The recurrent notion that manhood is problematic, a critical threshold that boys must pass through testing, is found at all levels of sociocultural development regardless of what other roles are organized. (1990: 11)

Though there is no universal construction of manhood, Gilmore observes that most widespread by far is what he calls the *pressured* type, involving ritualized hardening and the achievement of the critical threshold through traumatic testing (1990: 12). These testing procedures broadly integrate men into social structures and organize masculinity across a range of cultures around three spheres: men must impregnate women, protect dependants, and provision kith and kin (Gilmore 1990: 223). There is a direct correlation, in Gilmore's view, between the level of hardship characterized by a material environment and the extent to which hardness plays a central role in the masculine cultural formation located therein.[6] Conceptions and models of manhood, therefore, express an adaptive, dialectical relationship inherent in material–cultural practice, and are especially significant in the defence of social-group boundaries.

In the context of contemporary Britain, the class dimensions of this are clear. That relative freedom from material and temporal urgency that Bourdieu takes to be characteristic of the various fractions of the middle-class, has generated 'manhood scripts' based upon distance from the corporeal, refinement and individuated cultivation. Historically, the more pressing demands of working-class life have generated very different masculine cultural formations. These formations, which continue to flourish in changing circumstances through the adaptive mechanism of the *habitus*, revolve around orientations and practices alien to the bourgeois imagination which, as a consequence, is only able to pathologize and interpret them as incipiently backward. If concepts such as honour, initiation into manhood and visceral collective pride – all of them in their ways central to the maintenance and reproduction of Millwallism – are likely to meet with derision in the liberal–bourgeois worldview, they literally remain matters of life and death elsewhere.[7]

Particularly pressing, as Connell (1983) and Thompson and Pleck (1987) suggest, is the critical necessity that young men's culture should distance maleness from the feminine. For working-class boys, however, practices aimed at securing this distance may be doubly intense when some of the forms of male identity expressed in bourgeois culture are themselves considered to be feminized. It is therefore necessary in this situation to express – via bodily and verbal forms – a distancing from both women *and* bourgeois men.[8] This is the point of origin of the ubiquitous ideal-type of the 'middle class wanker', who is held distant from working-class masculinity both by his perceived feminized cultivation and his alleged physical weakness. His lack, in other words, of manly pride. The role played by these conceptions of masculine honour remains important in working-class culture (Polk 1994: 187), and for the most part is beyond the capacity of 'respectable' observers to understand it, along with its connections with violence:[9]

> It is the observers in the criminal justice system . . . who, drawing upon middle- and upper-class values which have shaped legal norms, describe the disputes which lead to homicide as trivial in origin. For the working- or lower-class players in the homicide drama, the challenge to manhood is a matter of consequence. (Marvin Wolfgang [1958] quoted in Polk, 1994: 172)

A central characteristic of working-class-male culture within and without the sphere of football is, therefore, the continuing valency of (physiologically grounded) personal honour. Challenges to honour may be registered in an experiential sphere deeper than conscious reflection, and be met with striking immediacy and force.[10] In their turn, class differentials in conceptions of corporealized personal integrity will be reflected in identifiably different bodily forms. Class cultures bound up with a world in which economic practice is generated more strongly by the presentation of the self and a kind of reflexive distance from the corporeal will, on the whole, produce differently embodied men. The dispositions of working-class men, which may be carried by the *habitus*[11] into changed or improved material circumstances, must often still underpin an embodied and 'credible threat of violence' (Daly and Wilson 1988: 128). As we will see, it is the credibility of this threat which often forestalls actual violence, and thus plays a central role in the ritual contests between Millwall fans and others.

This kind of credibility is an essential component of a boy's cultivation of relative autonomy, and the two are combined and expressed in the overarching importance of personal integrity and a reputation. Specific cultural dynamics in working-class life serve to push the boy in the direction of developing these skills and qualities from a very early age. The use of public space as a context for collectively structured sociality is of primary significance here. And it is a commonplace to observe that boys, for the most part, control communal space at the expense of girls, and enjoy a far greater parental range of permission for activities outside the home (McDowell 1983, Ward 1977: 154).[12] The street (and other forms of public space) has, in addition, been of far more significance in the socialization of working-class children in general than it has for their middle-class counterparts, and such class differentials in the social use of public space in England[13] were well documented in the 1960s and 1970s.[14]

These characteristics of early-years working-class experience structure those particular orientations towards the social which Humphries (1984) noted as historically consistent. Urban public space has therefore structured, in historically consistent ways, the development of a vivid, collective, relatively autonomous and intensely corporeal sphere of public boyhood, in which a dynamic and shared relationship with the local ecology[15] is everything. The development of the personality here is, therefore, intimately fused with locality, and in ways that are unlikely to be paralleled among children from middle-class backgrounds, whose activities tend to be more controlled, overseen and domestic (Ward 1977: 33, and see Ball *et al.* 1995).

The arrival at a culturally middle-class school of children from a working-class background, and the social dissonances it engenders for them has, of course, been the central motif of Bernstein's entire oeuvre. This post-Durkheimian project has, as Jenks observes, been centrally concerned with a consideration of children as 'metaphors for the different forms of consciousness within different realizations of solidarity' (Jenks 1996: 59). And it is in the sphere of education that tensions between these forms of consciousness and the cultural worlds that they express are perhaps most acute. The general historical–processual context of this tension concerns the transition to modernity, and those changing conceptions of the subject and personality already mentioned. The shift is discernible in changing pedagogic forms. The change from 'closed' to 'open' curricula can in this sense be understood as signifying the move from one kind of moral form to another, where control becomes 'more personalised, children are confronted as individuals and there is a reduced appeal to shared loyalties' (Jenks 1996: 80).

As I have noted, these transformations have been only unevenly accomplished. For if this model of the school as an individually constraining and panopticizing institution is familiar from Foucault, then the extent to which definitions of identity and patterns of culture may be intensively struggled over by working-class schoolboys gives the lie to the Foucauldian tendency to frame such subjects as inevitably pacified and recast. This recurring point of tension between forms of (implicit) class awareness expresses a more or less continual historical struggle over embodied definitions, and shows little sign of abating.

Patterns of working-class cultural practice brought by boys to the school are often antithetical to the stated aims of education, and may be used as resources in a protracted and attritional struggle over identifications and behaviour (Willis 1988). Though there may be little by way of explicit critique in this process, these struggles are organized around competing forms of embodiment and cultural orientation. Fighting – both actual and ritual/symbolic – and the constancy of violence represent a central structuring principle in the development of the primarily white[16] adolescent masculinity surveyed by Willis, and define a context for masculine hubris, dramatic display and the solidarity of the group (Willis 1988: 34).

The internal dynamics of the group itself may be extremely violent, for violence and 'pisstaking' are inextricably linked, and each are involved in the central sphere of *having a laff* (Willis 1988: 29). This, as Humphries (1984: chapter 5), suggests, is itself a continuous historical theme, and alerts us to the significance of a ludic dimension in this kind of boys' culture. These forms of play express a holistic fusing of the physical and the verbal in collective sociality, and are characteristic of the implicit struggles over definitions that are central to British education and the informal public life of the collective. Indeed, there is evidence (Apte 1985, Back 1996, Hewitt 1986) to suggest that humour in the form of 'pisstaking' and the 'wind-up' is the primary organizing principle of initiation, inclusion and status among working-class boys, of men in occupational settings (Roy 1960, Vaught and Smith 1980) and, by extension, of Millwallism. As such, it may be used more routinely than actual violence, which in this sense has the appearance of a vital resource often held in reserve. Internally, then, it is clear that the working-class peer group defines itself as a group that *plays* (Back 1996).[17]

This sense of play – of challenge, counter-challenge and the undermining of challenge – underscores the integrative maintenance of the group and, it should be noted, forms the ground upon which virtually all subcultural contestation/football-hooliganistic behaviour is based. It is a sphere of embodied, holistic (bodily/verbal) practice in which the individual experiences social humour as a fundamental, recursive dimension of mechanical solidarity. The critical conceptual focus in analysing these cultural currents must be on practical logic and the implications of habitual embodiment, for cultural knowledge in non-bourgeois spheres is, as noted, more often expressed in action than in cognitive declaration[18] (Bloch 1991, Hastrup 1995). Humour in this context is less a discursive practice belonging to the explicate world than an expression of embodied knowledge and the 'inarticulate mind', where language is not the only store of cultural knowledge (Hastrup, 1995: 182).

It is difficult to imagine that all of this does not generate the development of specific forms of embodiment. The boy must clearly develop both his mental and physical toughness if he is to participate successfully in the life of the collective, and his body is bound to both absorb and reflect the peculiar intensity of this sociality. Those categorized as 'soft' or 'incapable' automatically become targets, and it is therefore a matter of high priority for the boy to develop a style of comportment and demeanour which implicitly suggests that he knows how to 'look after himself', and to give appropriate demonstrations of such. Tolson (1977) suggests that the working-class boy 'enters adolescence, expressing himself not so much in an inner, compulsive struggle for achievement, as through a collective toughness, a masculine "performance"' (1977: 40). The centrality of the performative is obviously critical, as it is imperative that the boy equips himself with a bodily orientation, an exterior personality, which can be quickly and unambiguously *read* by his audience of peers – and potential adversaries.

The context for this broadly communicative exterior personality is one of Bernsteinian metaphoric condensation. Just as the restricted code tends to orient the working-class boy towards a positional, collective expressivity organized around a commonality of linguistic forms and symbols, the communicative use of the body is predicated upon the implicit meanings of particular stances, postures and gestures. The grounded, unambiguously inhabited male working-class body is the most basic, naturalized expression of this tendency towards implicit communication in a collectively structured and interpreted social environment.[19]

It is precisely this embeddedness that orients 'restricted' groups towards the ritual expression of shared meanings, and the ritual and symbolic forms developed around English football culture exemplify this. The lingering appeal of ritual and ritual forms among working-class groupings thus becomes an expression of a deeply held predisposition towards collective and metaphorically dense communicative forms in an age more broadly characterized in the West by a large-scale movement *away* from ritual.[20] This capacity for the manipulation of, and responsiveness to, condensed symbols – and nowhere more meaningfully than in the sphere of the body – permeates the expressive practices of Millwallism.

Good Fun With Bad Emotions: Bodily Culture and Millwallism

It is impossible to overestimate the extent to which both the expressive shape of Millwallism and the capacity to participate in it appropriately are grounded in the modes of culturally specific male embodiment discussed above. The one implies the other. An examination of the empirical characteristics of those modes is therefore an indispensable next step to understanding Millwallism as an intensely corporeal phenomenon.

The masculine *presence*[21] tends, in its non-bourgeois variants, to be expressed through a grounded and unambiguous corporeality. The body is never effaced, or sublimated to a sense of the self as a disembodied or abstract psychic personality. The working-class man as ritually manifest at Millwall tends in this sense to be clearly present in his body, and is oriented towards the communication of a sense of full and certain occupation of the space around it[22] – and a preparedness to command it if necessary. The contingent and always potentially hostile nature of life at street level in the urban working-class environment places a premium on this particular kind of physical capital. The centrality of the performative means that the embodied presence must at least appear to be fully prepared to meet with that contingency and be unperturbed by its possibility.

Basic stance, posture and movement must therefore be able to communicate assurance, imperturbability and an unostentatious and alert preparedness, in addition to those qualities of power, strength and resourcefulness central to the historically shaped occupational physicality of working-class experience. The communicative economy of masculine embodiment thus proceeds from a basic demonstration of the body as fully present and self-containedly prepared. Its collective and performative underpinnings mean that communication, which occurs primarily in terms of visual cues, is unambiguously directed outward and intended to be read as such.

> A group of eight fans, mostly in their mid to late thirties, are walking to Millwall's stadium on a matchday. Most walk with some variation of the 'bowl': a well recognized London term denoting a motion characterized by a slightly exaggerated, lolling sideward motion coming mainly from the shoulders. When the back is straight, the chest is open (with hands swinging at sides or in pockets) and the body moves through space with purpose, direction, certainty and assurance, then one is said to be 'bowling along'.[23]

They are *bowling* with differing degrees of emphasis. Most are not especially exaggerated, the movements not spectacularly large or broad and it would be a mistake to think of the important communicative techniques here as being primarily bold or over dramatic. There is a nuance here, a suggestiveness about much of the movement which does not conform smoothly to a schema of working class (i.e. strong/crude/gross in terms of movement). And while the signals that the body sends are quickly identifiable in their social context, such movement is well able to transcend the prosaic and literal. In the case of Londoners, this may relate to what Hebdige (1974a) has characterized as a metropolitan consciousness of complexity.

In this connection it is interesting to observe the clothes the men are wearing. They are unfussy, unspectacular, simple and, for the most part, informally elegant. The customary stylistic attitude of the majority of younger London football fans (now disseminated throughout the country) is in this way broadly categorizable as post-mod or 'Casual' (Giulianotti 1993) – that is unambiguously masculine, overwhelmingly normatively guided, formally and stylistically uncluttered, attentive to detail, and sharp. The style is conspicuous for its lack of subcultural spectacle,[24] expressing an orientation to implicitly structured canons of taste and self-presentation. Changing trends in fashion may inflect this with differing emphases and nuances over time, but they tend not to undermine the basic guiding principles. The stylistic norm at Millwall, then, is resolutely restrained, non-individualistic and often, but by no means always, subtly elegant ('casual/smart'), the product of a milieu that combines close proximity to a highly sophisticated metropolitan culture with a working-class disdain for individuated exhibitionism.

Belonging to the metropolis is thus symbolized not by ostentatious display, but by a kind of knowing understatement. This latter, whilst most obviously expressed at the sartorial level, may also play a role in a kind of movement not always categorizable as being simply derived from an overt manual physicality. The perception that you can always 'tell' a Millwall fan in a provincial city, repeated by a number of men with whom I have discussed Millwall, must be closely bound up with this kind of collectively understood physical expressivity .

Forms of movement may therefore express the density and complexity of metropolitan experience in subtle and difficult to interpret ways, and I wish only to register such a possibility here. The men walking to the ground in our example are not, of course, entirely uniform in their movement. But it is the commonalities that are significant. Most common of all is an impression of purposeful, directed and assured forward movement. Even when understated, the *bowl* is, in its individual applications, unambiguously demonstrative of a capacity to cope at the physical level with the varying demands of the urban working-class environment. In older men it speaks of an accumulation of the right kind of physical capital, of a prolonged negotiation with and mastery of urban social contingency. The masculine presence is never effaced but is asserted, not merely in a crudely material corporeality but in a symbolically condensed communicative presentation of the self. The *bowl*, mediated by nuanced individualizations of expression, is a representation of accumulated urban experience in movement, of the possession of highly prized physical capital *and* of a preparedness to accumulate more.

As the basis of a distinctive ritual bodily culture, there is little doubt that this constitutes a vital – and integral – modality of expressive communicative action. Serious and intense football supporting, at Millwall as elsewhere, has the capacity to animate and express the whole being, so that verbal and physical expression may not be meaningfully disassociated. The interpretative community at Millwall may not, in short, be theoretically reduced to a 'discursive formation', a limited concept in the analysis of what is a cultural grouping overwhelmingly oriented towards implicit oral and mimetic forms.

This physicality of expression is most characteristic of moments of extreme affective engagement with unfolding events. Played out in the ritual space of the stadium, on and off the field of play, the ritualized nature of participation imparts a high degree of formality to ostensibly individualized movement and gesture. This extends to the space around the stadium in the build-up and aftermath of a game, where the forms of stance and comportment receive heightened and subtly dramatized expression. In the pre-match promenade before a game, where groups and individuals circulate, and static groups form to socialize, informal communicative embodiment has the unspoken performative effect of establishing a visual environment centred on shared modes of presence and physical capital. The *bowl* may be more amplified into a fuller swagger, the general air of physical certainty, composure and capability heightened. All of this is conveyed and read at the level of practical awareness, and so the semantic field upon which the ritual event will be played out is established in advance of entry into the stadium proper. This is the first point of non-discursive participation, a ritual preparation and demonstration of the baseline of involvement: 'I am Millwall. I belong here. I know the ropes.'

Inside the stadium, and with the game underway, a loosely formalized repertoire of expression becomes apparent. The physical aspects of this combine customary forms of movement with newer styles dictated by the physical limitations imposed by all-seater stadiums. Most characteristic is an explosive upward movement out of the seat stimulated by celebration or, more frequently, by anger or encouragement. The upward motion is accompanied by the throwing of either or both arms into the air and the impassioned use of the clenched fist of anger, the open hand of urgent encouragement, the pointed finger of accusation, or the rounded motion of the wanker sign. Although the scope for movement is more limited in the all-seated space of Millwall's new stadium, jumping and dancing in celebration continue, as does the practice, in moments of highest intensity, of the basic static posture of standing feet apart with extended arms, and open hands raised to the sky in the primary gesture of heavenly glorification (Speigel and Machotka 1974).

In its most dramatic moments, ritual participation involves the whole body in unified expression. Especially important and widespread at Millwall are the intensely physical moments of impassioned urgency and vituperative contempt (for opposition players, their fans, referees and, often, Millwall players themselves) summoned up in a kind of ballet of bad emotions and physical tension.[25] Here threat, menace and spite (at varying levels of playfulness) are more characteristic than enactments of uncritical support and benign celebratory joy. The peculiar atmosphere long associated with Millwall derives from these forms of communicative practice, which are capable of generating a theatricalized spectacle of extraordinary affective intensity. At its furthest reaches, the primary mode of participation is of a visceral intensity and physical articulacy which mark it off from the other spheres of social life, while simultaneously drawing on the particular forms of embodiment that make it possible. The Millwall ritual is, therefore, specific kinds of south-east London *habitus* symbolically condensed and writ large. Commitments and feelings of this order are clearly inexplicable in terms of the internal workings of a football club, for they have deeply rooted social and psychological sources. It is the latter which structure participation and underpin the power of Millwall as both symbol and site of this highly charged activity.

Locality, Social Memory and Boundary

The intensity of the working-class localism and regionalism for which football is an arena of expression tends to startle neutral observers. But for the participants in Millwallism, the very experience of the self may be intimately connected to the kinds of deep and pervasive social experiences inimical to modern universalism. This is especially true of relationships between self and place, and it is hardly necessary to engage in any romanticization of a 'golden age' of working-class community in order to demonstrate those empirical factors that have generated the ontological significance of locality and neighbourhood in working-class life. Willmott's broad characterization of class–community types echoes the Gemeinschaft/Gesellschaft distinction, contrasting the specific/interactive/affective with the general/associational/instrumental:

> The first set (of characteristics) might be described as the 'traditional' bases of solidarity and local interaction: long residence, having kin locally and being relatively constrained by the lack of private transport. These characteristics have been more common in working class districts than others. They are the ones which, without deliberate effort from residents, help to encourage the growth of local relationships and loyalties.
>
> The second set depends by contrast on the disposition and action of people themselves: the application of social skills in making friends nearby, and the readiness to do so; the creation of local campaigns against actual or potential external threats; the existence of many local organizations. Such means, it is clear, have in the past been more often used by middle-class people, and have therefore been more important in middle-class areas than others. (Willmott 1986: 97)

Willmott's schema is no simple ideal-type. It is based on a detailed analysis of social networks, and recognizes well the shifting complexities of 'traditional' working-class localities, considering their often unstable demographies and internal divisions (Bourke 1994) as well as any unproblematic, spontaneous conflation of place and community. What it does, however, is draw our attention towards three critical themes in the historical development of working-class community and attachment to place: *Territorial Identity*, *Class Awareness* and *Continuity*.

We have already observed the pronounced territorialism of working-class boys and men. However, a sense of mutual affinity and identification based upon shared space can extend across sectors of a population and generate a high degree of consensus about the informal boundaries of locality. As Seabrook observes, neighbourhoods are often defined by the people who live in them and may have little to do with ward boundaries or other administrative conveniences (Seabrook 1984: 2).

Research in the area of neighbourhood cognition supports this (Herbert and Raine 1976), and favours a conception of neighbourhood as a mentally constructed interaction. It follows that the concept of local community is, as with other definitions of the term, inherently relational (Cohen 1989: 12). That is to say that neighbourhoods, communities and folk identities (as well as linguistic communities, ethnicities, nationalities etc) may be significantly organized around a sense of distinctiveness in juxtaposition to others. Communities and their boundaries – spatial, metaphorical, rhetorical – may therefore exist in the minds of people rather than as being objectively apparent. This sense of belonging, especially for those closely grounded to the local and specific, is far from being merely declarative :

> As one goes 'down' the scale so the 'objective' referents of the boundary become less and less clear, until they may be quite invisible to those outside. But also as you go 'down' this scale, they become more important to their members for they relate to increasingly intimate areas of their lives or refer to more substantial areas of their identities . . . At this level, community is more than oratorical abstraction: it hinges crucially on consciousness. (Cohen 1989: 13)

In this respect, it is important to consider the gendered nature of intensive association with, and investment in, localized identities. If the long-recognized patterns of kin-derived matrifocality central to working-class life (Gorer 1955) now appear to be far less secure than they once were (Oakley and Rajan 1991) their practice remains largely confined to the private sphere (Rose 1993a). The continued masculine domination of public space in working-class areas mirrors growing trends towards an increasingly marked dependence upon and isolation within home and immediate vicinity amongst women, especially those caring for children (McDowell 1983, Oakley and Rajan 1991). Though the deepest structures of the working-class neighbourhood have historically been maintained by women,[26] the profound separation of men's and women's lives generated by the late-nineteenth-century restructuring of economic and class relations (Jones 1983, Rose 1993b) continues to frame forms of working-class sociality, and the public sphere of the urban neighbourhood remains primarily male. However, it is possible that the fetishism of male space is underpinned at the still deeper level of personality formation. This precedes and perhaps significantly moulds the kinds of intensely masculine urban sociality examined earlier.

Differences in the identity formation of girls and boys – under the conditions of overwhelmingly female child-rearing environments – may in themselves be most acute in relation to boundaries:

> Women and men, then, grow up with personalities affected by different boundary experiences, differently constructed and experienced inner worlds, and preoccupations with different relational issues. This early experience forms an important ground for the female sense of self as connected to the world and the male sense of self as separate, distinct, even disconnected . . . Thus, the boy's construction of self in opposition to unity with the mother, his construction of identity as differentiation from the other, sets a hostile and combative dualism at the heart of both the community men construct and

> the masculinist world view by means of which they understand their lives . . . The construction of the self in opposition to another who threatens one's very being reverberates throughout the construction of both class society and the masculinist worldview. (Hartsock quoted in Massey, 1994: 170)

It is clear that this 'construction of the self' can also reverberate through notions of place as a source of belonging, identity and security. A visit to practically any important football game in England provides empirical examples of the relationships between this relative plasticity of the male personality and its potentially deep interweaving with both the sense of specific place and the schemes of embodiment and symbolism that express it. This fusing of self and place, the experiential and the symbolic, is perhaps the central process in the development of locally inflected working-class masculinities. It is the source of that 'fierce local pride' (Willmott 1986: 94) in a viscerally experienced communal identity seldom encountered in middle-class culture.

The full affective force of these social orientations can be observed in heightened and concentrated form when two sets of fiercely localist football fans face one another at an important game. It is this juxtaposition – of forms of embodiment, traditions, identities, reputations and attributed qualities – which structures such contests.[27] Regional rivalries (e.g. north–south, east London–south-east London), historical feuds and the significance of particular games determine the intensity of these conflicts. What is at stake, in the current context of increasingly rare actual violence, is the assertion of the supremacy of identity. And it is from this primary impulse that the hostile, sometimes playful subcultural rivalry that is so characteristic of British football is derived.

Particular contests have their own frames of reference, and come replete with a commonly understood (though differently nuanced) expressive repertoire of insult and counter-insult, threat and counter-threat, claim and counter-claim. All of these are grounded in locally inflected versions of the foregoing general themes, but most particularly (where locally identified clubs are concerned) in specific patterns of social memory and folk-taxonomic 'mappings' of the social world. Many of the Millwall fans who have, historically, shown a marked capacity for bearing grudges participate with particular relish and zeal in the dramas of rivalry set up by important games. Two examples illustrate how these aspects of masculine experience come together around particular games, and accounts of visits to Crystal Palace and Everton are structured around brief explications of the expressive semantic field generated by Millwall fans as communicative contexts of participation. I will analyse the songs, chants and forms of bodily expression that form the core of this field later, but I introduce them here to substantiate the preceding arguments about folk-taxonomies and juxtapositional rivalries.

Crystal Palace *v.* Millwall, 22.10.95

A bright autumn Sunday afternoon in suburban south-east London. The winners will go to the top of the Endsleigh first division, adding spice to an always fiercely contested derby. The 6,000 vocal and impassioned Millwall fans present divide their time between glorifying themselves, ridiculing their counterparts and abusing with cries of 'Judas! Judas!' the player Andy Roberts, who has recently transferred to Palace from Millwall.

The home fans are quiet and subdued, as is often the way when a concentrated group of away supporters energetically sets up its own expressive semantic field – or 'feeling space' (Canetti 1962: 39) – on enemy territory. At times, the noise and clamour in the Millwall part of the ground is overwhelming. Repeated and increasingly feverish airings of the self-referential praise anthems *No One Likes Us*, *Fuck 'em All,* and *Let 'em Come*[28] alternate with no less than four differently tuned variations on the word *Millwall.* The highest moments of intensity are generated by intermittent and spontaneous invocations of the drone-like *Lion's Roar*.

However, these anthems of assertion and supremacy are matched in frequency and intensity of rendition, by songs and chants directed outward, away from the Millwall section of the ground. Two in particular characterize the day, and are chanted with enormous venom throughout the game:

Palace, Palace, who the fuck are Palace?
Palace, Palace, who the fuck are Palace?[29]

The second is an ironic and spiteful borrowing of Manchester United's

Ooh aah, Eric Cantona, Ooh aah, Eric Cantona . . .[30]

Another song (sharing the ubiquitous 'Go West' tune) is spitefully aimed at Palace players and fans alike:

You're shit! and you know you are, You're shit! and you know you are . . .

Three other frequently rendered songs vary the theme. All run to the tune of 'Bread of Heaven':

Who the fuckin'
Who the fuckin'
Who the fuckin' 'ell are you?
Who the fuckin' 'ell are you?

You're the scum of,
You're the scum of,
You're the scum of South London,
You're the scum of South London.

You're supposed to,
You're supposed to,
You're supposed to be at 'ome,
You're supposed to be at 'ome.

All of this is conveyed by a massed chorus of several thousand voices, lifted still higher when Millwall score a second goal to win 2–1. Celebrations are accompanied by incursions onto the field of play, fireworks, minor confrontations with police and officials, and general hilarity. The Millwall section is a pandemonius swirl of sound and movement, of screams and songs, shouts and dances, shakings and arms raised, as if in supplication, to the heavens. This is the most expansive and deeply felt assertion of Millwallism of the season. Outside after the game there are bodies swelling with pride and pleasure and exuding a celebratory swagger verging on menace. But on this occasion, there is no violence, nor need of it. The point of Millwall's superiority has been sufficiently and ritually made on this occasion, without recourse to anything significant in the way of physical confrontation.

This is because the contest of identity for which the game is, in part, a context, has been played out and won at the level of collective expression. The first and most important determinant of the character of the semantic field set up around this game by Millwall fans is the fact that this is an important local derby in which Millwall fans are concerned with demonstrating superiority in the context of a localized social semantics. The contrastive field could be characterized as revolving around opposing, ideal-type taxonomic sets:

Millwall as	**Crystal Palace** as
Inner-Urban	Suburban
Working-Class	Middle-Class
Strong	Weak
Virile	Effete
Passionate	Dispassionate
Volatile	Pacified
Dangerous	Harmless

The expressive activities of the Collective Imaginary on this occasion revolve very heavily around these kinds of oppositions, which speak clearly of the dismissive contempt for Crystal Palace, and of the meanings that are taken to inhere in its fan culture. This is achieved, as we saw, by means of two mechanisms. First, the congregational summoning-up of *Millwall* via invocations of the *Lion's Roar*, *No One Likes Us*, *Fuck 'em All* etc. Once established as a domain of celebratory group assertion, the semantic expressive field is maintained by a cyclical and contrastive opposition of celebration and denigration: *We are the Millwall and we are the best/Who the fucking hell are you?*, *We are, we are MILLWALL/Palace, Palace, who the fuck are Palace?*

The ritual manipulation of these binary contrasts represents the condensed articulation of an implicit folk-taxonomic understanding of the identities involved. The full dimensions of these taxonomic sets, held in the practical sense of participants, are referenced by these simple oppositions rather than laid out and elaborated in full. One act of direct expressive contrast is sufficient to trigger the commonly understood chain of complex associations. All of this is deeply grounded in the informal cultural–ecological maps of south London known to participants on both sides. And the extra-footballing theme of the day, fully backed up by the distinctive modes of corporeality that contextualize expression, was clear: *Millwall rule south London.*

Everton *v*. Millwall, 4.10.95

Two weeks previous around 800 almost exclusively male fans, who were no less vocally committed, had travelled to Liverpool for a Coca Cola evening cup-tie against Everton. This was an important fixture: first, because Everton are Premiership opposition, and second, because Liverpool is a locus which tends to bring out a contemptuously anti-'scouse' regionalism in visiting fans. The desire to assert the supremacy of the Millwall identity was, therefore, an urgent one, structuring the evening's activities.

If the semantic field generated by the Millwall fans on this occasion is centred on an abusive and antagonistic hostility, the home fans are notable for a quietude bordering on indifference, for this is a far less important game for them. The general tenor of the evening is thus one of a placid home crowd enduring the sustained abuse and rancour of Millwallism at its most confrontational.

Viscerally expressive versions of the centrepieces – *No One Likes Us*, *Let 'em Come*, the *'Roar'* etc. – are accompanied by the full panoply of gestural insult and challenge: *wanker*, *fuck off*, *sit on this* hand signs; arms extended and hands motioning back and forth in classic *come and have a go* style. These are accompanied by vicious looks and sarcastic sneers, and that solid, planted and assured comportment which conveys inviolability and menace in the same moment of muscular tension.

Invocations and expressions of identity differ in two important ways from the local derby conditions in the game against Crystal Palace. First, they celebrate south-east Londonness, and Londonness more generally. Second, they spitefully ridicule and undermine a contrasted provincialism from a perspective of metropolitan superiority. Thus:

Maybe it's because I'm a Londoner,
That I love London town,
Maybe it's because I'm a Londoner,
That I think of 'er wherever I go, whoah,
I get a funny feelin' inside a me (spunk!),
Just walkin' up an' down,
Maybe it's because I'm a Londoner,
That I love London town (get off me sister!).

is alternated, with still more pronouncedly antiphonal elements, with

Oh South London (oh South London),
Is won-der-ful (is won-der-ful),
Oh South London is won-der-ful,
It's full of tits, fanny and Millwall,[31]
South London is won-der-ful.

The counter-motion, which employs the same ('When the Saints Go Marching In') tune, could scarcely be more abusive:

Oh Merseyside (oh Merseyside),
Is full of shit! (is full of shit!),
Oh Merseyside is full of shit!,
It's full of SHIT, SHIT AND MORE SHIT!
Merseyside is full of shit!.

There is one song in the repertoire, however, which is intended to be even more abusive and contemptuous. Used only once, as if in recognition of its extraordinary capacity to outrage and offend, it encapsulates all of the bitter regional rivalry and contempt characteristic of this juxtapositive drama. The tune is 'She'll Be Coming Round the Mountain':

I would rather be a paki than a scouse,
I would rather be a paki than a scouse,
I would rather be a paki, rather be a paki, rather be a paki
Than a scouse! [32]

Wild celebrations accompany what is destined to become for Millwall fans a famous 4–2 victory. The exhilarated and gloating Millwall fans are shepherded out of the ground and away from the home support under extremely tight police supervision. There is no violence in the environs of the ground.

The most significant aspect of the Everton game for present purposes lies in its demonstration of the fact that the polarizing of identities may be rather differently inflected according to context. Against Everton at Goodison Park, where the supremacy of Millwallism's toughness and virility is less taken for granted as the contest was played out in a 'hard' northern city and not a prosperous south-London suburb, the semantic field within which Millwallism is embodied is constructed through the folk-taxonomic hierarchy of cultural forms and identities:

Millwall as	**Everton** as
Metropolitan southern, 'Cockney'	Provincial northern, 'Scouser'
Witty	Stupid
Sharp	Dull
Hostile	Docile
Passionate	Dispassionate

The contrast of regional masculinities is set up, in this case, by the appearance in Liverpool of a smaller but perhaps more expressively hostile and physically ready group of Millwall fans. Carrying the most combative and hostile strain of Millwallism to Liverpool on a cold winter's night is not for the faint of heart. Tight police organization notwithstanding, this was a game with the potential to spill over into physical confrontation.

The participation of the majority of those present was grounded in a communicative base of physical inviolability and south-east London truculence. However, the chains of taxonomic association are triggered in precisely the same ritualized ways. One contrast is as good as another for this purpose, whether, *Maybe its because I'm a Londoner, I would rather be a Paki than a Scouse, Oh south London, Is won-der-full, Oh Merseyside, is full-of-shit*, or *South London, la la la/ In your Liverpool slums*.[33] These venomously expressed contrasts, it should be noted, are remarkable for the spectacular absence of any hint of general class solidarity. The contest is between versions of regional class identity in which the 'metropolitan'/ 'northern provincial' couplet is absolutely paramount, and structures the entire event. In this context, popular conceptions of the economic and infrastructural problems characteristic of the city of Liverpool become fair game in the struggle to abuse, hurt, and undermine the juxtaposed other. This evening's repertoire includes moments specifically intended to highlight this theme: *Does the social know you're here?, Sign on, sign on, One job between ya* and *Sing when you're stealing, you only sing when you're stealing* each receive an airing. The contrast connects ideas about the superiority of metropolitan working-class culture with the historical themes of south/north and plenty/poverty, sophistication/

backwardness. These associations draw heavily on the idea of the primacy of 'all the old cockney things' (chapter five) in the sphere of competitive working-class identity – resourcefulness and guile, wit and style, *Londonness*. Thus are the poor ridiculed for their poverty and the unemployed for their helplessness – as dumb northerners.

These kinds of spectacle, familiar to all close watchers of the game's culture, are clearly rooted in the ontological concerns of class-specific English masculinities. All of the elements surveyed here – collective pride, traditionally conceived manly honour, the capacity for violence and often harshly ludic sensibilities – inform and structure such activities on the basis of their activation in rituals of embodiment. The next three chapters trace the empirical connections between the distinctive social forms discussed throughout Part One and the experiential content and character of Millwallism at both the individual and collective levels. This entails, as far as developing a holistic picture of what Millwallism actually is at its furthest experiential reaches is concerned, the examination of the key processes of *symbolization* and *practical mastery*.

Notes

1. With the exceptions, perhaps, of the bastardizing caricatures of situation comedy, serial drama and advertising.
2. These basic themes are, of course, inflected, nuanced and mediated by local specifities derived, most importantly, from region and ethnicity where these intersect with class. Though cultural settings may differ, however, my suggestion is that these primary themes will characterize most, if not all, communities in which public and class-based socialities are framed by the principles and practices of practical consciousness and embodied local identity.
3. As Terence Turner observes, apropos Foucault, 'the severance of the body's social roots, its de-materialisation as a figment of discourse, and its reification as a transcendental individual combine to promote a general tendency towards the psychologisation of discourses on the body. In all of these respects, there is a substitution of "the body" conceived as a set of individual psychological or sensuous responses and needs for the body as a material process of social interaction. This substitution betrays much of the contemporary discourse on the body as an expression of the individualistic social ideology of the middle-class professional intellectuals who have developed it as an alternative to class and other socially based political and intellectual perspectives' (1994: 29).

4. The transformation of social forms according to the principles and requirements of capitalism, protestantism and bourgeois individualism is by now well understood (e.g. Elias 1992, Weber 1985), and has been examined in considerable historical detail in a wide range of by now classic works (Hill 1969, Malcolmson 1973, Thomas 1971, Thompson 1967, Wrightson 1982) and more recent (Hutton 1996, Linebaugh 1991, Mason 1994) accounts. All of these – and many more like them – stress the centrality of the application of the principles of instrumental rationalism and Puritan-derived manners to the social sphere, as integral to the cultural and economic requirements of the emergence and subsequent stabilization of Capitalism.
5. This is an idea supported by the work of Crawford (1987: 102) who, in a United States context, analyses the resistance of working-class people to the dissemination of new ideologies of health consciousness and individual personal fulfilment: 'For most non-professional and non-managerial wage workers, self-direction and continuous striving are not the usual job requirements, nor are rewards for such efforts plentiful . . . Demands for bodily controls during *time off* are likely to be regarded as an invasion of time reserved for enjoyment. There is no need to recreate the self for the "competitive edge", no need to run marathons in order to demonstrate a capacity for endurance . . . There is no value in denying gratification. "Enjoy it, shoot. You only go around once."'
6. Gilmore (1990: 224) asserts that 'manhood ideologies are adaptations to environments, not simple mental projections or psychic fantasies writ large. The harsher the environment and the scarcer the resources, the more manhood is stressed as inspiration and goal. This correlation could not be more clear, concrete or compelling.'
7. It is clear that these themes continue to structure the social development of many young men in working-class communities. Street-level urban ecologies may begin to assume the aspect, in this sense, of some of the 'traditional' forms of social organization examined by Gilmore (1990) and McCarthy (1994). The latter develops a heuristic model of trans-historical 'Warrior values' centred on four broad themes entirely appropriate here: *Physical Courage, Endurance, Strength and Skill*, and *Honour*. All of these are characteristic of the kinds of informal testing practice which, in lieu of formalized alternatives, tend to be generated spontaneously by young men in complex societies. Much of the behaviour subsumed under the rubric of *football hooliganism* is an expression of these (testing, hardening) processes, and thus represents a heightened collective context for the smaller-scale practices integral to street-based male sociality.
8. 'Men especially', Bourdieu observes in this connection (1986: 382), 'are forbidden every sort of "pretension" in matters of culture, language or clothing. This is not only because asethetic refinement, particularly as regards clothing

or cosmetics, is reserved for women by a representation, more strict than in any other class, of the sexual division of labour and sexual morality; or because it is more or less clearly related with dispositions and manners seen as characteristic of the bourgeoisie or of those who are willing to submit to bourgeois demands so as to win acceptance, of which the "toadies", "lick spittles" and "pansies" of everyday invective represent the limit. It is also because surrender to demands simultaneously perceived as feminine and bourgeois appears as the dual repudiation of virility, a twofold submission which ordinary language, naturally conceiving all domination the logic and lexicon of sexual domination, is predisposed to express.'

9. Polk proceeds from the central fact that in Australia any given murder is most likely to be committed by a man from a *lower* or *working-class* background. His examination of homicide cases and statistics is concerned with identifying that *something* that is 'behind the apparently inconsequential event which generates the heated response which results in lethal violence' (1994: 168). At the source of this *something* are confrontations over honour and reputation, displaying the two fundamental characteristics that they take place in *public* and *collective* spaces and contexts.

   Polk, in general, supports Gilmore's view of *manhood ideologies* as adaptions to specific social and material environments: 'physical prowess and aggression no longer become necessary for the economically advantaged male to assure his competence . . . males who are well integrated into roles of economic success are able to ground their masculinity through methods other than physical confrontations and violence (1994: 186ff.).
10. This is because the practical–logical conception of honour combines the qualities of assertiveness and potency. The rules of honour, as Bourdieu (1979: 113) records them, run according to the particular logic of challenge and riposte – a challenge both validates an individual's honour by recognizing him as worthy of the challenge, and serves as a provocation to reply. Inability to reply to and counter the challenge results in a loss of honour: 'Evil lies in pusillanimity, in suffering the offence without demanding amends.'
11. Hobbs (1988: 120) notes that 'Working-class communities, despite de-industrialisation, often cling to a muscular or highly specialised imagery in order to define essences perceived as essential for the maintenance of internal hierarchies.' The continued existence of this muscularity may, however, be a little less conscious and a little more fundamental to working-class culture – where resources and status still have to be competed for – than this 'clinging' implies. Hobbs himself seems to acknowledge this when he characterizes violence as a consistent theme of childhood and 'an essential tool in structuring [the] identities' of his male subjects. These themes suggest fundamental and habitual patterns of culture – the social conditions for which have, as yet, to disappear.

12. No consideration of these activities should underestimate the importance of football – as a participant and spectator sport – in these contexts. Mays (1954) is an early, and exemplary, account of the absolute centrality of the game for working-class boys in Liverpool. See also Cohen and Robins (1978) for an integrated, rather than football-focused, account of the pervasive significance of the game among boys in north London.
13. Classic American accounts such as those of Cohen (1955) and Suttles (1972) confirm the relevance of these themes in different cultural contexts. Gender segmentation and local patriotism characterize the kind of peer-centered public sociality in which, contra the middle-class tendency, 'The family is not the world' (Cohen 1955: 73).
14. Newson and Newson's (1970, 1971, 1976) extensive longitudinal study of urban childhood is of particular importance. Their findings were condensed into a series of seven key propositions by Mercer (1976):
    (1) The working-class child lives in a more crowded environment – more siblings and less space.
    (2) The play of the working-class child must perforce take place in the street or other communal areas and *not* on the home territory.
    (3) The working-class child is therefore more likely to come into contact with all sorts and a greater number of children.
    (4) The working-class child's choice of friends is not guided by the parents, as all children play on communal areas.
    (5) For the same reason the play of the working-class child is not generally supervized by adults.
    (6) The working-class parent is reluctant to interfere in children's play, because this may lead to conflict with other parents who are also neighbours.
    (7) Conflict with neighbours is less easily tolerated in the working class environment because of the greater propinquity of families, and the fact that working-class parents could not help but come into contact with the offended neighbours and meanwhile the children would have made up anyway.
15. In this context Opie and Opie (1969: 15), in their account of children's games, reference the unique urban–ecological opportunities afforded to south-east-London children by the legacy of the blitzkrieg: 'Ironically the bombing of London was a blessing to the youthful generations that followed. "We live facing a bombsite where boys throw stones, light fires, make camps and roast potatoes", writes one 11 year old'. The bomb site was an important space of ludic danger, excitement and violence for south-London boys as late as the 1970s. Many of those who would go on to participate in practices and events surrounding the development of the Millwall myth are likely to have had much

of their grounding here. For, along with the scrapyard, it was the most representative and iconic south-east-London space in the decades following the war.

16. Willis's assertion (1988) is that such practices revolve around an informal rejection of the middle-class mores of the school, and is therefore implicitly political. For black pupils, this culture of resistance will largely be differently framed and expressed because of the realities of racism in education and beyond (see, for example, Carby 1982: 184). In terms of the bodily hexis, it is obvious at the level of common sense that forms of black-male embodiment may have had a similarly significant impact upon white peers as is the case in the sphere of language (see Back 1996, Hewitt 1986). The adoption of forms of posture, gesture and movement (in *dance),* derived from the broader aesthetic dimensions of Soul, Reggae and Hip Hop cultures – most clearly in the context of the globalisation and ascendancy of black popular culture and its imagery – is the obvious primary vehicle of this. See, in addition to the above, Hebdige (1979).
17. Drawing on Bateson's (1978) theory of the meta-communicative transformations of meaning made possible by play, Back suggests that 'comments, practices and actions that are invested with non-play meanings are subverted and inverted by collusion. Through playing, a negotiated alteration of meaning takes place that dislocates practice from "what it stands for" in wider usage . . . In operating this kind of ("duelling") play the sensitive lines of significance are policed . . . The tension in this kind of early and late adolescent play is centred around the issue of whether these acts mean what they stand for or not. Duelling play is a process whereby young people test out the boundaries of interpersonal relationships . . . They not only mark the boundaries of tolerance within dyadic friendships but they also mark those who are included in the peer group' (Back 1996: 74).
18. This is not the 'inarticulacy' of *cultural deprivation*, but a mode of consciousness widespread among groups for whom the distant and de-corporealized reflexive self has not been the primary organizing principle of cultural and economic practice. In this respect Hastrup (1995: 184) explores a duality of communicative forms among Egyptian Bedouins who 'Often sing or punctuate their discourse with poetry, thus switching from one discourse to another. The switch is not possible in all circumstances; poetry can be used only within an intimate social context. There are strict social barriers, mostly gender-specific, to the use of the poetic mode. It belongs to a realm of secrecy that cannot and should not be betrayed. "Poetry is, in so many ways, the discourse of opposition to the system and of defiance of those who represent it: it is antistructure just as it is antimorality" (Abu-Lughod 1986: 1993). As such it can not be part of the articulate understanding of social life. It belongs to a

separate register, and belongs to an estranged vocabulary' (Reference in original).

If *humour* is substituted for the poetic, clear parallels can be drawn with the forms of masculine sociality under consideration here. Humour exists not only to organize and maintain the group, not only as a vehicle for negotiating relationships within it, but as an internally communicative moral form expressive of the deepest cultural orientations of the collective. This is a sphere in which cool articulacy and individual reflection carry little weight. Intimacy, as the following account makes clear, is understood as shared experience rather than personal confession: 'When you go out wiv ya mates you just go out, 'ave a beer an' get on wiv it. I think if you spoke to 'em about personal things, ya mates, I think it would go in one ear and out the other. You'd get right coated [abused, ridiculed] if ya talk about something personal, they'll slaughter ya, take the piss.' (Lee H. – fieldnotes)

19. Mary Douglas (1973) attempts to apply Bernstein's schema to the body and ritual in an important work whose profound implications have been insufficiently connected to the British class context. Hargreaves's (1993: 162) account of the aims and objectives of 'progressive' physical education is a useful exception. Following Bernstein's (1975) characterization of progressivist pedagogy as an 'integrated code', Hargreaves examines relationships between schooling, the body and class, and observes that the 'loosening of the subject's boundaries, of the time and space framework of the lesson and the greater informality therein, is a method for developing in the individual child the qualities of flexibility and adaptability, the ability to explore and solve problems independently, and to co-operate with others – qualities which are seen as required for competent occupational role performance among the new middle class. This model of physical education functions so that body management symbolizes individual responsibility as the basis of a harmonious social order.'
20. 'The causes of anti-ritualism in middle-class American and European communities would appear to be a predictable result of a process of *socialization* in which the child never internalises a pattern of social statuses and never experiences authoritative control which exalts the self-evident property of a social system to command obedience. Symbols of solidarity and hierarchy have not been part of his education' (Douglas 1973: 55).
21. Berger (1972: pp.46–7) famously suggests that 'A man's presence is dependent upon the promise of power which he embodies. If the promise is large and credible his presence is striking. If it is small or incredible, he is found to have little presence . . . A man's presence suggests what he is able to do to you or for you. His presence may be fabricated . . . but the pretence is always towards a power which he exercises on others.'

22. Connell (1983: 19): 'To be an adult male is distinctly to occupy space, to have a physical presence in the world.'
23. This example of performative embodiment is taken from my fieldnotes. Bourdieu (1979: 70) is alert to the importance of such a comportment, and his comments are relevant. He notes, in relation to the Kabyle of north Africa, that 'The manly man who goes straight to his target, without detours, is also a man who refuses twisted and devious looks, words, gestures and blows. He stands up straight and looks straight into the face of the person he approaches or wishes to welcome. Ever on the alert, because ever threatened, he misses nothing of what happens around him.'
24. I would suggest, in this respect, that the kind of orientations examined by Hewitt, in an area of south-east London, come closer to representing a norm in white, urban masculine youth milieux than any manifestation of subcultural spectacularity. He notes that while some elements in 'mod' style did occasionally inflect their dress, the young subjects of his analysis 'eschewed visible youth styles, and regarded as spurious the interpretive social gloss placed on such styles by their users and by popular sociological commentators' (Hewitt 1986: 25) .
25. The rendering of songs is an intensely physical and felt experience, not easily accomplished unless the whole being is thrown into the activity. The bodily and expressive orientations which generated this repertoire and sustain its reproduction are, as Bourdieu observes (1991: 86ff.), class specific: 'In the case of the lower classes, articulatory style is quite clearly part of a relation to the body that is dominated by the refusal of "airs and graces") i.e. the refusal of stylisation and the imposition of form) and by the valorisation of virility – one aspect of a more general disposition to appreciate what is "natural". Labov is no doubt right when he ascribes the resistance of male speakers in New York to the imposition of the legitimate language to the fact that they associate the idea of virility with their way of speaking or, more precisely, their way of using the mouth and throat when speaking.' Bourdieu therefore locates the primary impulse of 'popular' male speech as a refusal of that 'conspicuous distance from the things of the body' expressed in bourgeois articulatory styles. The relaxing of articulatory tension in the muscles of the throat represents a style of speaking, or singing and chanting, absolutely contradistinctive to models of restrained articulacy expressive of the disembodied mental personality, or autonomous cognitive ego. The opening of the throat and whole-body involvement characteristic of the expressive culture at Millwall are exemplary instances of this.
26. The work of Gavron (1966), Oakley (1974) and Pahl (1980) demonstrates the historically continuous burden of domestic and familial responsibility shouldered by women, and working-class women above all. More recent

studies connected to debates around 'community care' (Green 1988, Parker 1990) highlight the persistence of this gendered sphere of responsibility for the maintenance of the primary structures of communal existence.

27. Moerman (1974) suggests that ethnic identity for the Lue of Thailand is an experiential category activated only in material social interaction with juxtaposed tribal groupings. The Lue generate a full, explicate account of who and what they are only in this context. Whilst to claim that Millwall fans constitute an ethnic grouping would be to push even this line of ethnomethodological interpretation a little far, it is clear that some of the fullest and most tangible experience of *being Millwall* derives from similar experiences of juxtaposition. This is achieved not merely by the physical concentration of an otherwise diffuse group of people, but by the internal logic and practice of ritual itself. See Chapter Six for a detailed examination of ritual contests and 'taxonomic sets'.
28. 'Let 'em Come', as recorded by Roy Green, is Millwall's 'official' anthem. It is played, as these songs usually are, before home games, as a ritualized curtain raiser. Crowd versions restrict themselves to the 'Let 'em Come' chorus, but the central verse should be noted for its specific symbolic imagery:

    Let 'em come, let 'em come, let 'em all come,
    Let 'em all come down to the Den,
    Let 'em come, let 'em come, let 'em come,
    We'll only 'ave to beat 'em again,
    We're the best team in London – no! the best team of all,
    Everybody knows us, we're called MILLWALL,
    Let 'em come, let 'em come, let 'em come,
    Let 'em all come down to the Den.

    It's Saturday in Cold Blow Lane,
    We've all come down to cheer,
    We've 'ad our jellied eels,
    And our glass of beer,
    Come rain or shine, all the time, our families we'll bring,
    And as the Lion's run on the pitch, everyone will sing,

    Let 'em come . . .

29. An adaptation of the Smokie/Roy 'Chubby' Brown 'comic' re-recording of 'Living Next Door to Alice', which was riding high in the charts at the time.
30. This chant was used here with double intent. First Eric Cantona had recently assaulted a Crystal Palace fan during a game, and this was being recognized as simply a good and praiseworthy thing to do. The second is more implicit, drawing attention to the fact that Palace fans are the sort of (honour-deficient)

people who *could* be assaulted by footballers. As Bob R. (see Chapter Five) said, 'If Cantona 'ad done that at Millwall, 'e'd a been *lynched*. There woulda bin *murders* – they would've ended up closin' the club down!.'

31. These sexual – and sexist – references serve a double purpose. They identify the interpretive fan community as definitively male (and therefore beyond feminization) in a celebration of virility. They also possess the additional capacity to confront and offend liberal sensibilities. This latter is a central orientation of the Millwall-carnivalesque.
32. Back *et al.* (1996: 56) note the ways in which racial epithets are combined with club identities to produce 'complex racially-exclusive representations of group identity'. The extreme malice in this song derives, of course, from the overturning of prevailing hierarchies of 'ethnicity' internal to football culture: even the 'paki' is preferable to the 'scouse'. These insults draw on both an acknowledgement of the historically racist tone of Merseyside football culture, and a shared understanding of racial categories. The key to understanding this song lies in 'its stigmatised racist categories and a racially exclusive notion of who a "normal" fan is and what s/he looks like. Once again we see a banality, a "taken for granted" quality of racism within football culture' (Back *at al.* 1996: 56).
33. A popular piece with London (and other) fans, sung to the tune of 'In my Liverpool Home', runs :

    In your Liverpool slums,
    In your Liverpool slums,
    You look in the dustbin for something to eat,
    You find a dead rat and you think its a treat,
    In your Liverpool slums . . .

    The latter two songs here reference the folk-taxonomic association of Liverpool with small-time thievery and scally, or 'noddy' culture. The first two acknowledge the city's long-term unemployment problem.

Part II

–4–

'The Lion Roars': A Window onto the Collective

> Even as the television audience demands the presentation of sports as a form of spectacle, however, the widespread resentment of star athletes among followers of sport – a resentment directed against the inflated salaries negotiated by their agents and against their willingness to become hucksters, promoters and celebrities – indicates the persistence of a need to believe that sport represents something more than entertainment, something that, though neither life nor death in itself, retains some lingering capacity to dramatise and clarify those experiences.
>
> Christopher Lasch, *The Culture of Narcissism*

> Us and our ancestors have made this club what it is, and even if they're [the club] not, we are proud of what we the Millwall supporters are, and we want to celebrate all the previous glories, victories and might have beens, before they attempt to change us once and for all.
>
> Editorial, *The Lion Roars*

> Yours, pointlessly, on the windswept plastic seats for another year.
>
> Bernie Kaestner, *The Lion Roars*

In this and the following chapter I examine the ways in which the symbolic life of the club is internally organized and experienced by its interpretative community of fans. An interpretative analysis of written material from the longest established and most widely circulated of the Millwall fanzines, *The Lion Roars* (*TLR*), is followed by a consideration of more detailed interview-based accounts. I will demonstrate connections between the frameworks of meaning drawn on by fans in articulating their commitment to the club with those broader themes in social embodiment already discussed and I will reflect on the extent to which it is meaningful to think of the identity of the *Millwall Fan* as being one of potentially genuine ontological depth in a footballing age that is apparently characterized by an intensifying commercialization and free-floating consumer choice.

One means of assessing the kind of identifications and issues that circulate among Millwall supporters is afforded by the open-forum letters pages of the fanzines. As we saw in Chapter Two, the 'fanzine' phenomenon of the late 1980s represented something novel in English football culture, and generated a fixed and stable space for written, discursive reflection on the experiences and meanings of specific fan-formations. This decisive break with the previously hegemonic matchday 'programme' – containing the *official* view of a club's corporate controllers – was marked by both a more formalized rational–critical voice, *and* the opening up of a sphere of folk-taxonomic contest and surreal self-inspection and elaboration. This literary turn meant that well-established staples of embodied and enacted ludic–competitive fan culture came, for the first time, to be written down. The contemporary football fanzine is, therefore, of particular sociological significance, for it offers probably the only objectively available place in which these embodied–recursive cultural forms are subject to discursive representation and dissection *from the inside*. Thus *The Lion Roars* warrants serious discussion and analysis, as an important sociological end in itself, and as an interpretative and empirically testable entry into the substantive issues around which discussions of Millwallism are organized.

Although *TLR* is not the only fanzine in circulation at Millwall (others being *No One Likes Us* and, less frequently, *Some One Likes Us)* it is by far the most widely circulated and regularly consulted. It is as visibly read and discussed throughout the stadium and its environs on matchdays as the official match-day programme, and large numbers of fans buy and draw on both for discussion and enjoyment. Better presented and more comprehensive and balanced than its, frankly, crazed and marginal counterparts at Millwall, *TLR* has a monthly circulation of approximately 4,000, and is widely available in newsagents throughout south-east London and Kent. The following material is derived from an examination of its correspondence pages, and covers the period from the end of the 1992/3 season (the last at the 'old Den'), until the end of 1995/6.

The range and nature of published pieces is wide, from the considered to the brusque, and from the concrete suggestion to the bizarrely comedic. The correspondence, however, provides a vital window onto the intrepretive community and makes it possible to delineate the kinds of discussion the collective has with itself about just what it is to support Millwall. Particular and salient themes crop up with a high degree of regularity, and these are important in that they reveal the explicit constructions and articulations of some of the minutiae of fandom and its sometimes divergent meanings. For a number of reasons, these letters cannot be regarded as fully representative of Millwall fandom. They are drawn from an *edited* magazine, and thus express the views of that minority who choose to write letters, and who may tend to write such letters when they want to complain. Given the limitations imposed by these considerations, the correspondence can nevertheless be treated as a broad indicator of themes and issues circulating amongst fans. Of course, the content of a given issue will reflect specific events as well as general trends in the life of the club, and letters may therefore be sorted into a series of somewhat arbitrary categories. This is because correspondents often explicitly address more than one issue in a letter, or address an issue in which a number of themes intersect. Therefore, I have categorized them in terms of the primary, though no means always exclusive, burden of the correspondence.

The largest category (21.6 percent), which I will not examine here, is the miscellaneous collection of the anecdotal, the comedic, the bizarre and the incomprehensible. The next is *Millwallism* itself (19.7 per cent), or expressions of what Millwall means and how people feel about and understand their fandom and their expectations/demands. In recent seasons the discussions of the latter have focused on the move from the old ground to the New London Stadium, or 'New Den'. The watershed in the culture of the club marked by this move has been widely experienced as being negative and culturally attenuating. The other numerically significant categories are criticisms of the board of directors, administration and general organization (11.3 per cent), criticism of the manager and team (11.3 per cent), media coverage of the club and fans (7.8 per cent), the selling of players (7.5 per cent), the pricing of entrance to the new stadium (7.3 per cent) and race and racism (5.6 per cent). The remaining categories are letters from fans of other teams (4.0 per cent), positive analyses of manager and team performance (1.8 per cent) and calls to 'get behind' the team (1.3 per cent).

The analysis, for the most part, is restricted to letters that address extra-footballing themes impinging on meaning and identity, on Millwallism, on race and on media reputation. These discussions about the metaphysical core of Millwallism were precipitated, in their pervasive sense of a cultural crisis, by the fact of the club's moving to a new purpose-built stadium in 1993, and the examination of these correspondences is preceded and contextualized by a short ethnographic description of the last day at the Den.

Leaving Home: Millwallism and the New Era

Millwall v. *Bristol Rovers, 8.5.93*

The last game at what will soon become the 'old' Den, and the definitive end of an era. The future is uncertain, but today sees a great gathering of the Millwall clans come to say goodbye to their most special place; a large and expressively complex crowd unsure of its feelings and responses, whether exuberant or morose, jubilant or melancholy, raucous or reflective. The train stations and pubs are disgorging the constituents of the crowd earlier than usual today, and the swelling numbers making their way under the darkened tunnels, past the shattered scrap-yards, around the empty boom-time housing developments and through the narrow terraced streets around the ground are buzzing with anticipation and anxiety. Past the scarf-and-hat traders and the hot-dog stalls, their pall of fetid onions hanging, as always, in the air and blending with beery exhalations in the exemplary smell of the forming collective. The moving numbers swell and thicken, coalesce and swing into Cold Blow Lane for – it hardly seems possible – the last time. This close to the ground the crowd – of all ages but overwhelmingly white, overwhelmingly male – becomes a compressed mass, its coming together marked by the growls, the roars and the movements which say: *we are Millwall.*

Through the antique turnstyles with their rusting mechanisms, past the police search, up, at a snails pace, the impossibly narrow steps, and into an arena literally bursting with vitality and emotion. Millwall fans will seldom, if ever in the coming all-seated era, watch their team play in these conditions again. The terraces are packed and swaying, and it is an effort to secure and retain a sure footing: the body is heaved, swayed, crushed. There is delirium in the sensory environment of guttural noise, cascading song and swarming movement. Again, the smell of hot-dogs, onions and beer, but now, also, the sight of the green field of play. The field of play upon which folk-heroic and embodiments of Millwallism like Pat Neary and Barry Kitchener, Harry Cripps and Terry Hurlock, Keith Weller and Teddy Sheringham plied their trade for the club. They, and the rest, all seem to be here. Some in spirit and others, like Cripps and Kitchener, in the flesh, walking the perimeter of the field before kick-off, offering their salutes to the crowd and taking theirs in turn. As they complete their circuit of the field, hundreds of blue and white balloons are released into the sky from the centre circle.

The game itself is an irrelevance, its main purpose to contextualize the songs and chants, dances and gesticulations, expletive anger and wild-eyed laughter that have so characterized the historical occupation and use of this place. But beside the general clamour and the lion's roars there are other, less spectacular things happening. Small knots of men, watchful and pensive, working together at coming to terms with their last experience of the Den. The utterly novel and unreal atmosphere appears to teeter on a point between manic hilarity and pathos as we await the end of the game. In expressive terms, the former predominates, and seems to fill the space of the stadium with anarchic zest: the ball is kicked in to the crowd, but does not emerge. General hilarity ensues. Time appears to stand still as the referee appeals for its return. All around people are laughing, singing, watching, waiting, utterly absorbed not in the game but in the activities – the existence – of the crowd itself. The ball is retained by its captors but soon, in an erratic and shapeless game, its replacement describes its own high arc onto the terraces. This happens six times, on two occasions for extended periods of over a minute. The club seems to be running out of balls! Each incidence in this bizarre pantomime heightens and intensifies the feeling of the exceptionality of the event and the crowd's uncertainties about its precise nature. The precarious appearance on the roof of the stand high above the 'half-way'[1] enclosure of a man in a lion-suit does little to clarify matters, but does enhance the atmosphere of pervasive surreality. Greeted uproariously by those in the crowd able to see him, he is quickly established as the visual focus of proceedings. The increasingly meaningless game begins to drag, thanks largely to the time consumed by the stealing of the balls, and the final whistle is greeted with palpable relief.

The field of play is immediately flooded with hundreds, and then thousands, of people. Most of them appear to have one thing, primarily, in mind: the liberation of a piece of turf from the playing field. The area is alive with neo-agricultural motion, as individuals break up and remove sections of an appropriate size to be carried home. Elsewhere people are dismantling sections of terracing, fencing and crowd barriers, fixtures and fittings of every description, advertising hoardings and anything else that can be removed as a material souvenir of this place. This is conducted for the most part in a quiet and methodical manner, and, following the exuberant storming of the pitch minutes earlier, the scene takes on an aspect of eerie calm. This hiatus is filled with many hundreds of fans circulating around the pitch clutching their trophies. The singing has stopped. On the terraces stand bewildered knots of older men, some of them in tears, heads shaking, lips pursed. Euphoria abated, those on the pitch and those still on the terraces fall into a listless milling-about. There is nothing left to do or to say, and yet it appears that nobody wants to leave. The air is thick with disbelief and resignation; the sense of anti-climax and loss is almost unbearable.

It is late afternoon, and the darkening sky threatens rain. The moist air is enriched with the scent of newly disturbed soil and grass. Three-quarters of an hour after the game, the ground is still full of the apparently mesmerized, and the police move in and begin to clear the field. This is not well received, and a small number of individuals protest by throwing turf at the encroaching officers. Within moments a full-scale confrontation has developed, and the atmosphere erupts. The sky is black with chunks of flying grass and dissolving soil. The unprepared police have little option but to retreat from the field under the onslaught. Soon the former intensity of the proceedings is re-ignited, and the thing develops a momentum of its own. A crowd of four-hundred or so converge on the epicentre of the confrontation and, having driven the police from the field, pursue them up the terracing in a scene of extraordinary hilarity. Still the turf continues to fly, and before long a number of officers are pinned against the back wall of the terrace under the relentless hail.

Reinforcements arrive and the police move quickly down the terrace and on to the pitch. Their tormentors retreat, continuing the bombardment as they fall back onto the Cold Blow Lane terrace. The police, seeking to press home their advantage, advance onto the terrace in pursuit. There is a standoff between the two groups as the atmosphere sours for the first time, chants of *kill, kill, kill the bill* and *no one likes us* defining the transition. But there is little real malice in the air, and after a tense five minutes the remaining crowd allows itself to be moved on without violent response, and the stadium quickly empties. The sun has re-emerged. The streets, pubs, kebab-houses and stations around the ground are soon filled with subdued fans clutching mementoes deriving from the virtual destruction of the Den. Strung out along the New Cross Road, as far as the eye can see, are the legions trooping home with the material fragments of their most special place. The most characteristic – and incongruous – image in this bizarre procession is the determined tread of men and boys each staggering, arms full, under the weight of several rolls of heavy turf. In this manner the crowd wends its way from the environs of the Den, to spend a long summer presumably contemplating the uncertain future of Millwall fandom.

* * *

For the final *TLR* issue of the 1992/3 season (no. 42 – 'RIP The Den'), the editors included a special section devoted to reminiscences on Millwall's old 'home', and speculations about the impending move to the new ground. The general tenor of the contributions is resigned, the inevitability of the move underpinned by a foreboding sense of what may be lost. All the letters, as in this example from Roy Green, refer to the uniqueness of the Den and its peculiar atmosphere:

> My earliest memory of the Den was way back in 1936. I was too young to have any interest in football, but my dad took me to the speedway in New Cross. I wondered what the huge construction was next door and asked my dad, who was a Policeman. He replied 'you don't want to go there, that's Millwall's football ground, not a very nice place'. Like any child, this obviously aroused my curiosity and I went along at the first opportunity I got. I wonder how many people could turn round and realise that, that is why they support Millwall – the forbidden! My funniest memory and one that just proves that whilst the language might not have been the same, but it didn't just start with Peter Beardsley and Paul Birch, was when Fulham were at the Den in the FA Cup in the sixties. Johnny Haines was their big star. He got a right good kicking, I can't remember who from but it spurred the crowd into voice, 'who's that hobbling down the pitch? Johnny, Johnny. Who's that hobbling down the pitch? Johnny, Johnny Haynes'. Haynes tried to wave at the crowd but it just spurred them on some more, he had a bad game. It makes you wonder with all those seats whether the atmosphere will be lost, because that is the real spirit of the club and if that was lost so would the club.

Mervyn Payne (*TLR* 42) is equally ambivalent about the change:

> Of course it'll be nice to have a smart, all-purpose, all-seater ground, but no-one will forget the sordid novelty of the Den. How many times have you heard the opposing manager expressing his delight at coming away from the Den with a point?

There are clear anxieties here about the likelihood, in this new setting, of fans being unable to reproduce this atmosphere in the new setting, of the Den itself as

Figure 1 The ritualization process: fans preparing for the last ever game at their Den. Photograph used with the kind permission of Millwall Football Club

a sacralized symbolic marker and site of identity, memory and spontaneously historicized experience. Particularly significant are the connections drawn between the space of the stadium itself as a historical repository and symbolic arena of collective identification, and the practices, propensities and attitudes of participants themselves. David Jones (*TLR* 42) observes that:

> I always thought of the Den as being different from other grounds, a seething cauldron of passion that made the Den such an unpopular place for visiting teams . . . I celebrated my 21st birthday seeing Millwall go top of Division One after beating Queens Park Rangers, and when we left the ground, someone had put a hand-written poster in their front-room window saying "Millwall, Top of the League – Fuck 'em All'. Here's one supporter who doesn't want to move, the new ground will be too expensive for me, I doubt if I'll be a regular anymore. I suppose I'm a victim of change.

A number of the letters are centrally concerned with the idea of continuity in a more broadly existential sense. Steve Chance, who is more positive about the move, connects the change of stadium with changes in the broader cultural context:

> In the last few years, the Den has lost some of its atmosphere, the family enclosure hasn't helped as it prevents you walking from the Cold Blow to the North Terrace, and only club members stand up the Ilderton End, so I'm quite looking forward to the change. In the 60s a load of our supporters would go to work every Saturday morning, then go straight down the pub and finally to the Den to cheer Millwall on, but those days are now long gone and so, soon, sadly will the Den. Here's to a new ground, and a new future.

The moment of a close fit between the occupation of the Den and particular patterns of social and cultural organization has passed. Social change and changes in the space and use of the stadium mirror one another. The vibrancy and cohesion of the past have receded on both fronts, to the extent that this writer is prepared to positively embrace a new context. The implication is clear: *atmosphere*, *spontaneity* and *community* are already becoming increasingly fragile and tenuous, both at Millwall and beyond, and a shift to the new space will symbolize and more effectively express the new conditions.

The key motif, here as elsewhere, is the contemporary dynamic toward the perception of an increasing rupture of cultural and ontological continuity. Historical working-class preferences for continuity, stability, cohesion and relatively bounded identifications are having to negotiate these broader changes wherever they are met. The ontologization of place[2] represented by the sacralization of the stadium itself is thus connected to more general understandings of the intersections between materially situated biography and identity. 'Mark' is particularly anxious about the loss of the Den, almost a constituent part of himself:

> I mean, I know that come next August I'll be sitting in my ridiculously over-priced plastic seat in our shiny new ground, but, it is just that I can't imagine it, its just that it doesn't seem real to me. That a place that is such a central part of my life is no longer going to be there. Think of it like this, you know when you're going through Lewisham and you see a pile of rubble, you think 'bloody hell, there used to be an Odeon there, I used to go there as a kid', well every time in the future that you walk anywhere near Cold Blow Lane where the Den used to be, it will be like that, but a million times more so. (*TLR* 42)

For Reggie Spooner, the psychological and affective dissonances inherent in these discontinuities in the built environment are underpinned by more personal and troubling concerns:

> We all need something constant in our lives. Wives, girlfriends, lovers, even mothers will come and eventually go, but whether you went once a year or week in week out, you know the Den, Millwall will always be there. Football clubs don't die. However, things are going to change, a move whether it be a few hundred yards or a few hundred miles, is a move. Maybe it will be for the better but a constant in many lives will be broken, and once broken its much easier to break again. (*TLR* 42)

This elegiac vision of the possible consequences of change on Millwall culture derives from what many regard as a decisive turning point in the history of the club. This enforced break with the past, with a particular cultural tradition rooted in a specific place, initiated a period of soul searching and gloom amongst many fans concerned to somehow keep alive the central elements of the culture. This is one of the primary contemporary contexts in which any consideration of football fandom in general, and Millwallism in particular, must be set. In a sense, if the seasons following the relocation of the club were characterized by this sense of crisis, they also forced participants to explicitly articulate the often implicit central principles of the Millwall way and to consciously bring them to bear on the new situation. It is the impact of this transition upon customary supporting traditions which has preoccupied fans throughout this period, and it is widely reflected in the letters pages.

The central Millwall values, of pride, passion, commitment, ruthless gallows humour and expressive volatility are widely held to be suffering in the transition to the age of the all-seater, heavily panopticized stadium. The first casualty has been the previously overarching experience of the crowd as an organic and volatile mass, responding in spontaneously ritualized ways to events on the field of play and conveyed, throughout the stadium, through *atmosphere*. This has traditionally been twinned at Millwall with the practice of *intimidation*, characterized by the interactive play of song, chant, comment and expressive bodily forms. These have proven difficult to sustain in the customary ways under the new conditions.

Considerations of these matters on the correspondence pages of *TLR* highlight the ways in which individuals understand what it means to support Millwall.

'There is no atmosphere,' writes T.Scott,

> no laughter, no piss taking. I'm only 24, but able to remember some great moments at the Den, like slagging off Garth Crooks when he played for Stoke, slagging off John Jackson when he was at Orient (remember the milkman chants) . . . And more recently there is the slagging off of David Speedie, Robert Fleck, Glenn Hoddle, Paul Birch,[3] and last but not least, the funniest slagging I ever took part in at The Den, our old mate Tony Norman . . . So come on Millwall fans, I know a lot of us don't like the new ground, or the way we've been treated by Burr[4] and his cowboy friends. But let's at least make it hard for visiting players to settle, by giving them hell, and not our own boys. It's worked in the past and it will work again. (*TLR* 46: 27)

The attempt on the part of club authorities, police and stewards to suppress and control expressively volatile and/or abusive behaviour throughout the ground is regarded by many fans as symptomatic of the new consumerization of football, a process with potentially serious implications for customary practices. Michael Kelly, responding to the banning of a fan from the ground without charge or proven criminal offence, asks

> So where will it stop? Could it be that he's a victim of the political correctness which is sweeping football, up and down the country? Middle class families are welcome through the turnstiles, anybody else – let's get rid of them. Don't sing, don't shout, don't stand up, and so on. (*TLR* 65: 26)

External pressures working against the continuation of customary practices mesh with the psycho-social limitations imposed on individual expression by the move to a separated, numbered, atomizing seating arrangement. This facilitates against the crowd mobilizing itself and finding its voice, in rhythm with the ebb and flow of the game in the unforced and spontaneous ways which obtained previously. Canetti (1962: 39) illuminates this critical moment in the life of the football crowd with exemplary clarity:

> The discharge must come sometime. Without it, it would be impossible to say that there really was a crowd. The outcry which used to be heard at public executions when the head of the malefactor was held up by the executioner, and the outcry heard today at sporting occasions, are the *voice* of the crowd. But the outcry must be spontaneous. Rehearsed and regularly repeated shouts are no proof that the crowd has achieved a life of its own. They may lead to it, but they may also be only external, like the drill of a military unit. Contrasted with them, the spontaneous and never quite predictable outcry

> of a crowd is unmistakable, and its effect enormous. It can express emotions of any kind; *which* emotions often matters less than their strength and variety and the freedom of their sequence. It is they which give the crowd its 'feeling space'.

The achievement of this moment has been made more difficult by the transition to the new arena. There has without doubt been a reduction in the intensity of the atmosphere at run-of-the-mill-games, a point reiterated by many correspondents. This is a significant problem, given the centrality to the Millwall experience of atmosphere and intimidation. But the panopticizing (Foucault 1977) of the stadium – which is at times successfully resisted and triumphantly overcome – is not entirely responsible for this reduction in the level of passion. For in addition, a perceived lack of commitment and pride on the part of players and management has set up a kind of circular drama of dissatisfaction that verges on crisis amongst the collective.[5] Both of these broad strands have contributed to an atmosphere of gloom, disaffection and pessimism settling around the club, and bringing to the fore intensive discussions of exactly what Millwall is and should be.

These discussions invariably proceed from an acknowledgement of Millwallism as consisting primarily in a durable set of core values and expectations. Ground zero here is the requirement for players to demonstrate pride in representing the club and 'give 100 per cent'. As with the idea of *atmosphere,* the symbolically dense concept of *100 per cent* carries a heavy burden of meaning in discussions and expressions of the Millwall creed. An essentially romantic notion in the post-Bosman[6] and consumerist football age, *100 per cent* derives from the belief that a player should seek to embody the spirit of the club and its followers. 'Flip' is clear about these requirements:

> Being a Millwall supporter for over thirty years now, I have seen some players who were very proud to pull on a Millwall shirt and give 100%, and growl at the opposition, and to make them know that they have been in a game. Players like Kitch, Cripps, and of course Hurlock, they were players that all had the supporters talking after each match, even if we lost you knew they gave their all with their blood, sweat and tears, but today's lot look like they just want to turn up, grab their money, and run. (*TLR* 51: 28)

Barry Kitchener, Harry Cripps[7] and Terry Hurlock are thus invoked in the manner of symbols, as embodiments of the classical Millwall virtues. This use of the contributions of such iconic player-symbols to foreground traditional concerns and highlight their relative contemporary absence is a recurring theme in accounts of the central perspectives of Millwallism, and of attempts to identify the causes of their apparent attenuation. For 'Terry', the cultural and footballing rejuvenation of the club lies in reestablishing the tradition represented by figures such as Hurlock:[8]

Figure 2 A Millwall cult figure of the 1970s, Barry Kitchener retains close links with the club. Photograph used with the kind permission of Millwall Football Club

Figure 3 Millwallism embodied: Harry Cripps in his 1970s prime. Photograph used with the kind permission of Millwall Football Club

> In my opinion, if a player isn't Millwall through and through get rid of him, it's as simple as that. Terry Hurlock gave 100% for Millwall. I loved him and we need more players like him with fight in them as well as skill, and Hurlock in my opinion had those two things to make Millwall winners. Find more determined players like Terry and Millwall will go places. Straight to the premier . . . determination is what playing for Millwall is all about – chase every ball, go into every tackle, no bottling out like some I've seen this year. Millwall fans expect players to play for ninety minutes week in week out. There's no surrender in a game as far as Millwall's concerned, we expect everyone in a Millwall shirt to fight for every ball and tackle hard, that's what the Lion stands for. (*TLR* 65: 29)

This is not exactly the stuff of 'new' football fashionability, and fans' insistence on pride and commitment over spectacle has been integral to the informal project of maintaining, safeguarding and revitalizing the club's association with a highly specific identity. Nothing is more usefully illustrative of the dimensions of this identity than the tension between the idea of folk–cultural 'ownership' of Millwall and developments in the contemporary football market.

'Millwall Through and Through': Identity, Boundary and a *Blood Tradition*

The attempt to apply to the club the marketing principles that have been so successful in the Premiership has consistently foundered on the fundamental numerical limitation of appeal that the Millwall identity imposes. The fear that Millwall will 'lose its identity' (or at least have it radically transformed) in the manner of Arsenal, Manchester United or Newcastle United has been countered by the closeness of this association, and a widespread refusal to bow to new consumerist practices, such as buying tickets in advance of matchdays and sitting in allocated seats.[9] In this kind of way fans assert a conception of Millwall that is essentially metaphorical, and that this is a category that cannot be reduced to a material institution, the control of specific administrative personnel or novel sets of business practices. Millwall, in this sense, defines an interpretative community unevenly pushing against the new strictures and continuing to make the brand name virtually unsaleable in the new markets. It is, first and foremost, a matter of belonging. The impassioned argument of Bob McRee (*TLR* 64: 29) indicates this:

> We are Millwall, and not much will change. As ever the money, ordinary players, ever dwindling resources, and scarce reserves. When you swear the oath of allegiance to the Millwall flag, take the badge and become a supporter, those are the conditions that you sign up to. We always live in hope, but proper Millwall people know that's all it is – hope! This is not being negative, it is stark realism, and I urge everyone at MFC and its supporters to get their feet on the ground . . . Little did the non-Millwall rooted directors

> understand that supporting Millwall is a blood tradition, you are either born into a Millwall circumstance, or you are not. There are no neutrals where Millwall is concerned, and I know of very few real converts to the faith. Other people have always been put off joining us. So to talk of producing another 5,000 out of the oven, was always pure fantasy.

It is important to note that this broad concept of a 'blood tradition' works here as an extended metaphor for long-standing patterns of familial lineage *and* affiliation through local residence. This is important in two main respects; first, although it is true that 'converts' are few, they do exist, as I demonstrate in the following chapter; and second, because elective association with the club often proceeds on local, rather than familial ties. That is, some boys and young men do find their way to the club in the absence of patrilineal precedent. This is most obviously the case with Millwall's small minority of black fans, who tend to forge attachments with the club on the basis of affective localism. And the very existence of such fans, tenuous as their position often appears to be, indicates a degree of negotiability around the boundaries of inclusion in Millwallism. This I discuss below.

I would suggest that the notion of 'blood' as used by Bob McRee is intended to reference the important sphere of *authenticity*, established on either of the two bases, or combinations thereof. There is no doubt that the cultural significance of being born into or otherwise emerging from a 'Millwall situation' is considerable, and it underpins an apparent and widespread preoccupation with a 'metaphysics of belonging' (Gilroy 1993: 23). This desire to maintain the integrity of Millwallism is manifested in discussions of authenticity ('Millwall through and through'). And it is allied to a generalized secondary preoccupation with the boundaries of inclusion and exclusion, an aspect of the masculine boundary-drawing processes characteristic of working-class culture. This centres on three broad themes: first, there is the widely diffused and for the most part unchallenged understanding of Millwall as coterminous with 'hegemonic masculinity' (Seidler 1994); second, there is an overwhelmingly implicit association of Millwall with particular embodiments and communicative aesthetics of class, which is understood and acknowledged as an experiential rather than economistic category; and third, the connection of these central elements of Millwallism to a sense of broader, situated social identities in ways that are frequently, though unevenly, racialized. I will focus here on the second and third points and their interconnections.

Discursive and explicit assertions of class identity in the correspondence pages of *TLR* are rare. The experience of class in south-east London does not necessarily lend itself, as we saw in Chapter Two, to a manipulation of the symbols of corporate solidarity. Practical–logical and embodied working-class awareness, antithetical as it often is to logocentric and abstracted evaluations of personal experience and orientation, may be conveyed in ways that are oblique or metaphorically dense. Thus does Robert Thompson (*TLR* 71: 28) implicitly position himself in class terms, when questioning the authenticity of an individual who

> wasn't even a proper Millwall supporter, he was from Surrey, where the fuck is Surrey? You may disagree but I think all that lot from Surrey are a right bunch of 'wanky suburbans'.[10]

At the more mature end of the spectrum Bob Oliver, in the course of protesting about ticket prices, asks whether the board

> think we're all rich Yuppies or something? . . . They seem to treat us supporters like mindless unintelligent imbeciles. Well, we're bloody well not. Sooner or later, even the most loyal supporters like me are going to be tempted to tell them to stuff it, and refuse to go anymore, until someone genuine takes over. (*TLR* 65: 28)

The call for a genuine administration to put the club back on course has a significance beyond the sphere of mere business practice. It references, in a different way, the idea of authenticity at Millwall as being intimately bound up with non-instrumental, working-class patterns of commitment to the club itself as a repository of specific meanings and values. In a similar, though more explicit vein, P. Williams writes that

> Ever since we were founded by the workers of Morton's jam factory on the Isle of Dogs, Millwall Football Club have been renowned for their genuine working class values and strong working class traditions. These are simply not working class prices. (*TLR* 48: 30)

Again the insistence is on values framed in terms of class. The move to the new stadium and the new marketing represents, in this sense, not merely a steep hike in prices but a devaluation and traducing of a working-class 'tradition' itself. This often unspoken identification of the club with traditionally conceived class-cultural contexts marks the major boundary of inclusion. In large measure, to *be Millwall* is to adhere to this vision of values, to express or support the expression of pride, commitment and non-instrumental loyalty on the one hand, and manly toughness, plain speaking and a vernacular lack of pretension on the other. The connections with the broader culture are plain, and these connections set broad boundaries of belonging and participation.

However, this insistence upon a class-derived traditionalist ethos should not be taken as an expression of any simple cultural homogeneity.[11] Rather, the key symbols around which this interpretive community is organized sustain an umbrella of identifications beneath which a significant degree of individual, socio-economic and attitudinal diversity may exist. Not all Millwall supporters are the same, but most adhere and respond, at some level, and out of widely coincidental biographical experiences, to a common sphere of symbolic constructions and understandings. It is participation in this affective and expressive maintenance in both informal–social and collective ritual contexts which circumscribes both belonging and the broad (and occasionally negotiable) location of the boundary itself.

The maintenance of such a boundary is, therefore, an expression of that 'public doing' (Jenkins 1996: 196) which this way of thinking about 'community' itself represents. Based upon active public construction, the interpretive community at Millwall is, as in the formulation of Cohen (1989: 20), an aggregative rather than deeply integrative phenomenon. Individual differences are held in abeyance, in the moment of ritual participation, by the convergence generated by these communally shared symbols.

The ways in which this informally maintained boundary may be understood and articulated in racialized terms is arguably more complex, and certainly more ambiguous, than in its intersection with class. As with everything else at Millwall, the approach to the issue of race is complicated by the existence of a pre-constituted and widely diffused attributive schema and sphere of understanding which is circulated in the popular media and public consciousness. Here, the primary image is linked to a geographically inaccurate but convenient association of the club with the ostensibly far-right-inclined Millwall ward in Tower Hamlets. This sees the Den (old and new stadiums alike) as a hotbed of organized racist and neo-fascist activity with firm roots in a late-1970s socio-political context. Though the links between concerted far-right activity and contemporary football culture have been revealed, at Millwall as elsewhere, as opportunistic and instrumental rather than organic or significant (Back *et al.* 1996: 58), this imagery remains deeply rooted and widely accepted.

However, this imagery misrepresents the nature of the problem in ways that obscure the complex realities of relationships between Millwallism, identity and race, and which are inter-related matters which the current wave of anti-racist moralizing discourses aimed at combating racism in the culture of the game do little to apprehend or account for.[12] The easy demonizing of Millwall fans, in this sphere as elsewhere, serves to obscure the sometimes paradoxical role played by race in constructions of Millwallism. Something of the depth of these paradoxes, which persistently elude the liberal tendency towards a moralizing over-simplification in these matters, can be glimpsed in the recent comments of the black superstar Ian Wright. As an Arsenal player, he experienced an eventful and frequently bitter public relationship with Millwall fans, having been raucously vilified in a succession of closely contested games throughout the 1990s.[13] Yet in an interview in *Total Sport* (Febuary 1997), Wright spoke of his jealousy of former colleague Mark Bright's short spell at Millwall:

> When you put that shirt on, you are living Ian Wright's dream of pulling on a Millwall shirt. If you look at how Millwall fans expect their forwards to play and how I love to play, then I'm a Millwall player. I've had so much stick. They would love me. I give my all and I score goals. It's the team I first watched and no matter what we've had in the past, no-one can take away my love for Millwall.

A south-east Londoner himself, Wright, the black footballing icon, thus expresses a love for Millwall which seems capable of somehow transcending or displacing his experience of often racially framed abuse. His blackness, in short, seems not to constitute an impediment to his view of himself as a potentially emblematic Millwall player. His avowed understanding of the core values of Millwallism feed directly into his self-definition as being Millwall through-and-through. This indicates a potential space of belonging[14] for black men predicated on the adherence to and expression of these central orientations. And discussions of race at Millwall therefore highlight in their turn the ways in which that belonging, as well as the complexities of racist expression, are understood.

Racist Expression and the Carnivalesque

As we saw in Chapter One, the 1977 *Panorama* special on Millwall fans presented a televisually compelling and spectacular portrait of a violent, hyper-masculine and *racist* subculture. An interview with Martin Webster, the deputy leader of the National Front during the period of its most heightened media profile and electoral success, was used to advance the claim that football grounds were being targeted as foci for far-right activism. The programme thereby strengthened in the public consciousness the apparent link between the perennially unsettling imagery of football mob violence and politically organized racist practice.

Two aspects of these kinds of understandings are of particular significance here. First, and as already noted, Millwall football club became the specific and fixed exemplar of a general political moment.[15] Second, it is worth noting the ease with which these links are routinely imputed and generalized (via the 'racist/hooligan' couplet)[16] on the basis of often scant empirical evidence. This ease indicates widespread anxieties, notably from liberal and leftist as well as populist–right viewpoints, around manifestations of politically unfocused working-class physicality: the white male body, and its characteristic forms of expressive vigour, are framed and understood as incipiently fascistic.[17] It is this very distancing of vulgar corporeality and physical expressivity from the liberal imagination which tends to drive the initiative in these matters to the right and into a space where working-class masculine vitality can, at least notionally, be fascistically celebrated. Hoberman's account of the consequences of the Marxist 'renunciation of the body' (1984: 119) is relevant here. The failed Soviet attempt, for example, to impose an artificial, rationalist 'proletarian culture' upon essentially folkish and non-rationalist populations is contrasted with the ascendancy of a Nazi ideology and ritual culture premised significantly on a 'cultic exaltation of sport' (Hoberman 1984: 118). Control over the male body is contrasted with its glorification. The image of a bronzed and vigorous Mussolini, stripped to the waist and ready for sportive action has no equivalent among the disembodied intellectualism of socialist leaderships. The right's attempts, in Britain, to colonize youthful football hooliganism and the national game are played out on old and familiar ground, while a lack of interest in the body has been a consistent theme, until very recently, in leftist and liberal intellectual culture. The extremely limited and still waning impact of the interventions of the far right underlines the historical folly of conceding the field, and the (ostensibly) widely accepted, if relatively belated, arrival of concerted anti-racist counter-argumentation within the culture of the game confirms this.

These counter-arguments are in circulation at Millwall as elsewhere, and set up a tension between explicit anti-racist perspectives and a still widely diffused though diminishing tendency towards a casual vernacular of racist expression.[18] However, this tension rarely surfaces at the level of interaction during a game, and it remains rare for racist expression to be openly challenged. A long-lasting conspiracy of silence within the stadium, arising perhaps out of fear or a tendency to adhere to specific notions of white authenticity and Millwallism, was mirrored on the pages of *TLR*. A coherent anti-racist editorial stance did not occur until a series of exchanges in letters appeared just before the fiftieth issue. In one of these, which anticipated animated exchanges on the subject of race in subsequent editions, M. Coyne expresses his disgust at the racist chanting of 'some fans', and asks

> What about the black supporters we have, imagine how they must feel when a crowd around them are shouting racist abuse at a player. Despite all this, they still come back because they love Millwall, just like any of us. (*TLR* 46: 29)

'Jamie' (*TLR* 51: 30) is equally alarmed:

> Judging by the amount of racist abuse that goes on around me in the South Stand upper tier, something drastic has to be done . . . I realise that taking a firm anti-fascist stance is about as popular as a West Ham fan in a boozer down the Old Kent Road, but it has to be done. The majority of Millwall fans are not BNP dickheads, as the gutter press would have everyone believe, and its about time we proved it. (*TLR* 51: 30)

Jamie's analysis provides an important clue to the orientations underlying the resistance to the development of a 'firm anti-fascist stance' at Millwall. Many of the central perspectives of Millwallism are both implacably opposed to liberal culture, and are organized around the expression and embodiment of that opposition, in which anti-fascist 'stances' are associated with leftist local authorities and liberal progressivism in general. If, as I have argued, Millwallism is best understood as an expression of a defensive but culturally entrenched opposition to bourgeois cultural hegemony, then a certain reluctance to embrace 'right-thinking' moral perspectives is one of its central characteristics. Some correspondents to *TLR* are unambiguous on this point. Time and again racism is framed in a context of politically incorrect expressivity, and related to the Millwall sense of humour and the 'piss take'. A 'Lions fan' reminisces on his highlights of the 1980s:

> I've never felt so good on a Monday night as after that Chelsea cup game. Even now if I'm particularly pissed off and penniless I close my eyes and visualise Speedie taking that penalty. Coming out of that game some black bloke fainted in the crush getting through that one poxy stupid gate. Immediately a group of other (white) Millwall supporters shouted for order while they tried to lift the unconscious geezer to his feet. He could literally have been trampled to death in half a minute. Even so it was hard to keep him upright, he seemed to weigh more than Ken Bates' head. Then I heard one if the lifters offer an explanation – 'its his bloody knob innit?'.
>
> Then there was an 80s match at the Den (can't remember who we were playing) with a group of thumbheads at the front of the terracing (nearest to Ilderton Road end) shouting out some racist stuff while about eight rows back, three youngish black guys were rolling their eyes in mock terror and pissing themselves laughing. These two incidents always come to mind when I hear shit in the news about all the 'fascists' at Millwall – yeah, its always there but its always a bit of a bad joke – just like Jimmy Hill really. (*TLR* 51: 28)

An adherence to the values of Millwallism – in this case expressed by physical fearlessness and ruthlessly grotesque humour – is considered in this account to encompass a depth and complexity of experience inaccessible to the stereotyping crudities of media portrayals.[19] One of the central pleasures of this lies, as we have seen, in participating in the generation of the *intimidatory* Millwall atmosphere. For many participants, racist expression is intimately bound up with the prevailing dynamics of hostile partisan fervour and vulgar orality which underpin intimidation, and arguments about racism tend to be completely subsumed under these categories. The correspondence pages of *TLR* represent, therefore, a crucial place where fans can account for and comment on the patterns of expressive racism for which Millwall provides a public context. The thoughts of Gethin Davies (*TLR* 49: 29) illustrate these points:

> In the last few issues there have been the predictable pompous letters about how disgusting racism at the Den is, how do you think ET[20] feels, etc. To be entirely honest

> I don't really care. There are far worse manifestations of racial prejudice than singing 'Dayo' chants at a football match, and a few monkey chants hardly means that black people aren't wanted at the Den. What does worry me though, is why these chants have become so widespread? I don't think its so much that people hate blacks its just that the other songs are so crap!
>
> Imagine the situation of a tricky, powerful, ageing ex-England international juggling the ball and waving his arms about to confuse Rhino and Father Ken moving towards our penalty area while our defenders back off. Now you can either shout 'Oi!, do something 'wall, get into him' which merely flusters our own players or you can attempt to make the maestro in question panic. If it is Paul Walsh you can boo or hiss, if it is Mark Chamberlain you can . . . er . . . boo or hiss. Monkey chants, unlike booing, are an easy way of making players feel that they specifically are being singled out for abuse. As for the claim that it has no effect – I have just seen Mark Chamberlain trying to 'put one over on the racists' by running continuously and consistently losing possession, once on the by-line with two players unmarked at the far post. Having said all that, I don't like monkey chants. The reason people join in is because no-one takes the piss in any other way . . . Roll on Ian Wright. Remember, he's a cheat, he's arrogant, his song is ludicrous, he's loved by the media, he's adored by the FA, he plays for Arsenal . . . The fact that he's black needn't come into it! (*TLR* 49: 29)

It is worth examining in detail some of the mixed messages inherent in this account. Most obviously, it articulates the widely held view that racist expression is not racism *per se*, but an aspect of expressive practice aimed at intimidating and humiliating opposition players. The blackness of the player, like Paul Birch's hairdo, Peter Shilton's tabloid-led public demonization as a wife-beater, Peter Beardsley's facial characteristics or Ian Wright's iconic notoriety, is seen as a target at which to direct abuse. This abuse is intended to be hostile, threatening, unsettling and hurtful rather than politely humorous. It is designed to be offensive to individual dignity and liberal sensibilities alike, and Millwall fans are famous for it. It is one of the defining practices of Millwallism, and, given this, our correspondent reacts with horror at its apparent decline. The account is typical in its refusal to accept connections between ritualized racist expression and the wider social dynamics that structure racism in general, locating the primary significance of these practices in a sense of carnivalesque mischief (Bakhtin 1965). The deliberate affront to polite sensibility represented by this rather dark sense of carnival at Millwall is an important theme which runs parallel in matters of race, to the informal monitoring of and preoccupation with cultural authenticity already noted. A brief examination of the Millwall version of the carnivalesque, given its centrality in the explanatory accounts of participants, will illustrate the genuinely complex nature of continuing racist expression.

The relatively recent renewal of interest in Mikhail Bakhtin's particular conception of the carnivalesque is reflected in a tendency towards constructing

British football as a vehicle for its expression. Richard Giulianottti's (1996) work on Scottish international-football fandom is the most interesting example to date. Giulianotti focuses on carnival as an expression of fans' 'authorized transgression', the ritualized collapse or inversion of social boundaries and the integration of socially diverse groupings and individuals under the rubric of 'Scotland fan' (1996: 80). These activities, central to the ritual and symbolic forms of Scottish fans, constitute a benign and internationally popular sphere of carnival, with fans making up for their countries' formerly poor reputation by enacting a sense of informal and high-spirited cultural ambassadorship. In accounting theoretically for the central impulses of this fan culture, Giulianotti draws on Stuart Hall's reading of Bakhtin:

> The 'carnivalesque' includes the language of the market place – curses, profanities, oaths, colloquialisms which disrupt the privileged order of polite utterance – rituals, games, and performances, in which the genital zones, the 'material body lower strata', and all that belongs to them are exalted and the formal, polite forms of conduct and discourse dethroned; popular festive forms in which, for example king or slaveholder is set aside and the fool or slave temporarily 'rules', and other occasions when the grotesque image of the body and its functions subvert the models of decorous behaviour and classical ideals. (Hall 1993: 6)

Giulianotti feeds these ideas into his portrait of an alcohol-fuelled and raucous, benign and jovial Scottish fandom, but passes over two important areas of analysis: the extent to which such 'Bakhtinian' practices significantly constitute a stream of historical and cultural continuity[21] in the class-dialectics of social identity and modernity; and the possibility that certain manifestations of the carnivalesque may be less benign than others. At Millwall, the symbolic and gestural possibilities of a grotesque realism – the essential principle of which is 'degradation' (Bakhtin 1965: 19) – tend to be channelled in a negative direction, not always especially playful, and clearly contemptuous of 'polite forms of conduct' or its contemporary variant, *political correctness.*[22]

The attenuated version of carnival that often obtains may above all be used to convey a wilfully unpleasant offensiveness and an all-out attack on any form of hubris, pretension or liberal ideology. This potential for viciousness has, over the years, been frequently unleashed upon black players. Three interconnected but perhaps analytically distinguishable strains of racist expression may therefore run concurrently at Millwall. First, we will abuse you out of contempt for your blackness. Second, we will abuse you because it is fun, it upsets you and it puts you off your game. And third, we will abuse you because it offends liberal sensibilities. Those choosing to participate in this sphere may locate their priorities within each or all of these aspects, ritually connecting with and drawing upon those wider repertoires of racist sentiment and expression – complex and otherwise which continue to characterize much of white working-class life in the region. (Back 1996, Hewitt 1986)

On the whole, then, this is not the romanticized carnival of literary theory and cultural studies, overturning prevailing social classifications with playful zest. For there is not the merest hint in this of any utopian impulse. Rather, what is at stake is the expression, in attenuated, deromanticized and largely implicit forms, of counter-bourgeois social-being as a manifestation of customary embodiment and grotesque–realist sensibility. The impulse is ultimately towards the confirmation of boundaries as opposed to their dissolution, and the symbolic affront to multicultural–liberal sentiment and bourgeois-expressive orthodoxy is accompanied by a specific, integrative and normalizing rationale that repeats that ideal-type Millwallism is (with few exceptions) white and male and, (with no exceptions) hegemonic–masculine and working class. As Dentith observes:

> It is hard to accede to a version of carnival which stresses its capacity to invert hierarchies and undermine boundaries, without at the same time recalling that many carnival and carnival-like degradations clearly functioned to reinforce communal and hierarchic norms. (1995: 75)

The culture of broad, casual and socially embedded expressive racism that continues to linger, in a clearly reduced form, at Millwall must therefore be located within a context of a specific kind of carnivalesque embodiment and a set of ritual practices that manifest and celebrate it. These I will explore further in Chapter Six, but for now I wish to stress two broad points. The first is that racist expression has a genuinely carnivalesque dimension in the sense outlined, and second, that the boundaries of belonging are more fluid (within a very narrow range of possibilities) than definitively and immovably racialized. It is an indication of the complexity of these matters that the apparently contradictory views expressed in the following letters to *TLR* can both be contained within the limits of a vigorously embraced Millwallism:

> The reasons why it [racist chanting] won't go away are simple, abusive chanting is designed to put opposing players off their game. If somebody is black it makes an obvious target. Your article said it doesn't work. Well it doesn't with everybody but we can all remember the two excellent games that Ian Wright had last year and I'm sure the Millwall faithful will give him enough barracking to make it three excellent games in the cup! Much better to be politically incorrect than lose! The other main points you made are also wrong, people don't get stabbed at bus stops for being Scottish but they do for being gay as well as black – and that would rule out 99%[23] of Millwall songs. When will we have the anti-homophobic campaign or the 'let's be nice to scousers' week? Surely coming to Millwall *should* be unsettling? Just because we've left the Den we don't need to leave our traditions behind. ('Alan', *TLR* 49: 29)

> As a black Millwall fan, what can i say? arsenal 0 Millwall 2. ian wright[24] can fuck off – there's only one Tony Witter. ian wright claims Millwall fans are racist. Just ask Tony Witter what he thinks, ian wright is a tosser. It was the most exciting night of my life, and i was glad to see the many black Millwall fans that were there. The team played 100% out of their skins. All credit to Mick McCarthy. I had Millwall fans hugging me, shaking my hand, jumping up and down with delight – on this great night of glory. Tell me, does colour really matter? We are called the Millwall Blackskins – congratulations Millwall. (Trevor Little, *TLR* 62: 30)

'No One Likes Us: Do We Care?

The twinned themes of 'organized' racism and violent disorder represent the central elements of the Millwall media myth. Sensationalized accounts of the activities of Millwall fans invariably connect the two, in a cycle of often empirically dubious eternal recurrence. The somewhat infamous, and representative, anthem *No One Likes Us* was developed in the early 1980s out of a collective need to somehow engage with and comment upon this uncontrollable process of negative myth-icization. This song functions as a refusal of this distorting myth and as a celebration of the authentic Millwall identity known only to insiders. The accompanying melody is based on Rod Stewart's 'Sailing' :

> *No one likes us, no one likes us, no one likes us,*
> *We don't care,*
> *We are Millwall, super Millwall, we are Millwall,*
> *From the Den.*

This is now by far the most frequently and resolutely rendered song in the informal Millwall canon, and is widely acknowledged as the supporters' theme tune. Though its powerful role in the ritualized assertion of identity, however stirringly performed, is not without a degree of ambiguity, as the expression of blithe contempt for and lack of interest in the myth conceals the extent to which many fans *do* care, and care passionately, about matters of reputation and public perception. The picture here is complicated not only by internal divergencies of opinion about the valency and appropriateness of Millwall's mythic status, but by the frequently paradoxical or ambiguous responses of individuals themselves. It is tempting to frame these differing responses, of celebration or denial of the reputation, in a hooliganistic/law-abiding framework or, more broadly, in working-class terms of rough/respectable. However, the same Millwall heart may harbour urges towards both, and the two may not be so neatly separated at the experiential level. As a general principle, however, there have been clear signs in recent years of a growing anger at, and contestation of, the sheer inaccuracy, condescension and injustice inherent in the eternally recurring Millwall archetype. Outlaw glamour is one thing, the experience of living a reviled and wildly exaggerated public identity is quite another. Fuelled by the perennial themes of aggrieved injustice and a folk-pariah status, Millwall fans from across the spectrum are now taking their public image more seriously than ever before. It is possible to read these concerns as expressions of a broader shift towards, if not respectability, then at least a kind of cultural maturation.[25]

A preoccupation with the injustices of the media suffuses the *TLR*'s correspondence pages, and this can be especially acute where the routine charges of racism are concerned. Steve Davis writes:

> I, along with undoubtedly thousands of other Millwall supporters, was incensed by the comments of Sun reporter, and I use the term in the loosest possible sense, Stephen Howard, in the issue 10/9/93 after our draw with Derby. With absolutely no connection to football the Wapping Wonder told an estimated 1.5 million readers just how Millwall FC had single handedly voted in the BNP into the Millwall ward. Well, normally this rag wouldn't have us down as having the intelligence to tie our shoe laces unaided[26] let alone enter the hot bed of national politics. (*TLR* 46: 30)

This anger is provoked by the entirely spurious attribution of extra-footballing political significance to the club, and the high-handed and unanswerable context of its articulation. These are the kind of charges against which Millwall fans have little or no redress in the public sphere, where they circulate as virtually unchallengeable social facts. It is the recurring inevitability of these affronts which exerts such a pressure on Millwallism, whether in the form of pure and unfounded fabrications, as in this example, or in the fantastical over-elaborations of actual events. The latter category is often the more damaging, as any manifestation of disorder, however slight, is made to fit neatly into the historical 'roll-call of shame'. This well-established media tactic, which now has an ongoing accumulative momentum and internal logic of its own, is one of the banes of Millwall fans' lives. One important line of internal defence against it is to draw attention to disparities between the coverage of Millwall fans' misdemeanours and those of other clubs.

The 'Pressman incident', one amongst many, will serve as an illustration. In October 1995, during a game at the New Den against Sheffield Wednesday, a lone fan took the field to remonstrate with Wednesday's goalkeeper Kevin Pressman. His intervention was met by universal condemnation and a deafening crescendo of jeers, boos and calls to 'get off the fucking pitch!' The displeasure and lack of support for this gesture from the overwhelming majority of the crowd could not have been more pronounced or unambiguous. The following day's (26.10.95) newspaper coverage was characterized by banner headlines screaming 'YOU'RE A DEAD MAN: Millwall Yob Threatens Keeper' (the *Sun*) and 'Shame of Millwall

Fans' (*Daily Mail*). This level of disingenuity appalled even the most jaundiced media watchers among the Millwall faithful. Michael Saunders is a good example:

> As a lifelong Millwall fan, I had thought that I could no longer be shocked or surprised at the amount of exaggeration or rubbish the press write about Millwall. I should have known better. One moron runs on the pitch, makes ridiculous threats, and is then escorted off the pitch. Although there is no excuse for this type of behaviour, had this incident occurred at any other ground in the country it would be barely worth a mention. Where Millwall are concerned though, a different set of rules apply. In the case of Millwall, you're talking banner headlines and as much bad publicity for the club as the press can muster, taking events out of all context. There has been little mention of the fact that virtually the whole ground booed this idiot off the pitch, and even David Pleat [Wednesday's manager] was reported as making light of the incident . . .
>
> Of course there are a minority of trouble makers at Millwall, just as there at most football clubs. The press would point to Millwall's past reputation, but this is a reputation that has been developed by the media, with the help of a minority of hooligans. If all clubs were reported in the same manner as Millwall, there would be many clubs with equally bad reputations, some of them amongst the most fashionable in the country. (*TLR* 71: 29)

This is a relatively straightforward example of unacceptable behaviour and perceived media injustice about which a clearly unambiguous stance is taken by both correspondent and collective. A much more complex picture emerges out of responses to a more serious disturbance at the infamous First Division play-off game against Derby County on 18 May 1994. The visually dramatic, though comparatively tame, events of that evening were reported as if they signalled the advent of the apocalypse: 'MILLWAR' (*Daily Star* and *Daily Mirror*) and 'SOMEONE WILL DIE AT THE DEN' (*Daily Mirror*) exemplify the tone of the following day's reportage. Opinion on the correspondence pages of *TLR*, as elsewhere, settled around a debate between those accepting Millwall fans' culpability, and those expressing outrage at the sensationalist nature of the coverage. These responses highlight an area of profound disagreement about some of the central impulses of Millwallism.

Mike Degan, in an extended critique of BBC Radio Derby's coverage of the game, challenges the unnamed commentators' opinions:

> Quote: 'The Millwall area has a twisted history of politics and violence', 'It is a poor aggressive area that thrives on defeat' – What evidence has the commentator based these facts upon? Does this man know anything about the political or economic status of Millwall fans? I doubt it very much! If he did, he would also realise that many of the fans now live in the suburbs of South-east London and North West Kent. The apparent belief that Millwall FC has anything to do with the BNP victory in east London, displays

> his complete ignorance about the area. Furthermore, is poverty synonymous with violence? . . .
>
> There were 15,000 Millwall supporters at the game, of whom approximately 50 'supposed' fans caused trouble. These are the people who deserved condemnation, not the club, the area, or the real fans. If the commentator cannot contain his personal contempt, bigotry or emotions, then he would appear not to be fit to commentate for BBC Radio Derby. There can be no excuses for this deplorable standard of broadcasting. I expect an explanation and full apology to myself and Millwall FC. (*TLR* 56: 29)

This is the acute and respectable voice of Millwallism, accepting the culpability of a hooligan minority by suggesting that such behaviour is a marginal aberration with no basis in the broader culture. On the other hand the account of Ray Wild, whilst critical of the 'scum' element at Millwall, nevertheless tacitly acknowledges the connections between the *mindless minority* and rather broader patterns of response and expression:

> To see these scum, who go under the name of a 'Millwall supporter' cause havoc again, has sickened and upset me . . . However, there are ways in which we can help. Firstly, it amazes me that when a person is ejected from the ground by the police or someone runs on to the pitch, most of the supporters sing 'No one likes us', which, to an outsider, seems that we are condoning their behaviour. We should be applauding the fact that someone who is blackening the name of Millwall, is being ejected or arrested . . . Secondly, for the life of me, I cannot understand why we are so anti-police. We should be applauding them, pointing out trouble makers and cheering every time someone is ejected or arrested for causing trouble or running onto the pitch. (*TLR* 55: 27)

A number of the letters written in the aftermath of the Derby game express similar sentiments. They illuminate an aspect of Millwall fandom that it is easily neglected in an atmosphere characterized by the hegemony of a communicative idiom premised on expressive raucousness, for these correspondents are clearly not identifying with the atmosphere of gangsterish inviolability or proletarian toughness that is central to many fans' involvement. But Ray Wild's comments draw attention to a deep ambiguity in Millwall culture, which centres on the question of why are there times when it seems as if *everybody* in the stadium is singing *No One Likes Us*? Is it merely a responsive anthem of defiance? Is it really the case that a traumatic relationship with the media disguises the essential similarity of Millwall fandom with most other clubs, including some of the 'most fashionable in the country'? Can a neat division, in the affective heat of the ritual moment (*No One Likes Us!!*), always be made between the assertion of an injured and traduced but law-abiding respectability and the enormous experiential benefits to be derived from absorption in one of the most viscerally powerful repertoires of counter-bourgeois imagery and expression available anywhere in British popular culture?

Figure 4 Keith 'Rhino' Stevens, last of the great '100% Millwall' players? Photograph used with the kind permission of Millwall Football Club

Might the same heart be able to contain, harbour and express, in successive moments, such apparently opposed dispositions towards affectively restrained respectability *and* the exultation of *being* Millwall? An examination of some more detailed interview accounts, in which participants speak about their perceptions of the relationship between the sense of self and the experiential symbol of *Millwall*, may help us to decide. I will therefore now attempt to get closer still to the experiential heart of Millwallism, to the ways in which this process of *symbolization*, or the extra-discursive, deeply personal and ontologically significant fusion of the symbol and the self, takes place.

Notes

1. This is the vernacular term for the long side-terrace at the old Den.
2. We saw in the last chapter the significance place can hold in the development of individual and group identity in working-class cultural formations. In this sense, the disruption of continuity represented by the change of stadium may be thought of as a destabilizing of the capacity for collective memorialization and the experience of social identity itself. Halbwachs (1980: 137) stresses the relationship between the symbolic content of the material environment and ontological security in social orientation. See also Werlen (1993, chapter 7) for a useful discussion of these ideas. The destruction of The Den, the primary material symbol of Millwallism, has had potentially devastating and yet to be fully worked through effects on the morale of the culture.
3. Though there are many examples, the 'Paul Birch incident' is the most frequently cited and celebrated example of the pleasures and effectiveness of abuse in recent Millwall history. During his period at Aston Villa, Birch took the field at the Den in the 1990/1 season in a peroxide, elaborately coiffured, mid-length hairdo. His every intervention in a disastrous game was met by deafening catcalls, whistles and screams of derision. He soon became afraid to receive the ball and was substituted at half-time. This was an especially effective example of abuse directed at players thought to be demonstrating effeteness and/or pretension. This technique combines an undermining of hubris with an essentially homophobic attack on (emasculating) physical over-elaboration. It represents, into the bargain, a ritual confirmation of the kind of normative, hegemonic–masculine canon of self-presentation central to the Millwall creed.
4. Reg Burr, an almost universally disliked figure for much of his tenure, was at this time club chairman.

5. This has exacerbated an already well-recognized tendency towards critical intolerance among Millwall fans. When pundit Jim Rosenthal talks of Millwall's fans as 'London's most critical' (*The Match*, London Weekend Television 22.10.95) he draws on widespread folk-conceptions of a capacity for vitriol and abusive impatience characteristic of fans' responses towards even their own team. It is, of course, the players themselves who must bear the brunt of these peculiarities. Central defender Tony Witter, interviewed in the club newspaper (*Life with the Lions*, January 1996: 4) feels that 'QPR fans are very quiet and it is often mistaken for a relaxed atmosphere, whereas Millwall fans let you know what's what and never hide their emotions.' Dave Sinclair, after having left the club and signed for Dundee United with apparent relief, has a starker view: 'The fans are absolutely crazy. If you had a bad result, you felt they'd lynch you if they had the chance' (in *TLR* 86: 6).
6. A 1995 test case under European law which established the freedom of movement of professional footballers. Resulting legislation loosened player's contractual obligations, facilitating rapid turnover of personnel and minimizing the likelihood of individual players forming long-term affective ties with clubs.
7. Harry Cripps's iconic status as perhaps the primary embodiment of Millwallism was highlighted and confirmed by the response to his untimely death at the age of 56 in 1996. M. Milligate (*TLR* 74: 26) remembers him as 'the heart and soul of a solid defence during the 60s/70s when the opposition could only dream of winning at the Den. He wore the Lion on his shirt with such pride.' Former manager Benny Fenton felt that 'As a person, a player and a man, he had everything. He was the heart and soul of the club' (*TLR* 73: 1). On the following page Steve Chance declared that 'Other than Terry Hurlock in his first stint at the club, no other player has better epitomised the Millwall spirit than Harry. He stood for, and represented, what Millwall meant during his time at the club. It is so sad that only one current player (I need not tell you who), can compare. I fear that spirit is lost forever.' The player referred to here is Keith 'Rhino' Stevens, possibly the last of the powerfully emblematic 'Millwall through and through' players in the Cripps/Hurlock tradition.
8. This desire for a return to traditional Millwall values was, interestingly, acknowledged by the administrators brought in to stabilize the club following the financial crisis of Febuary 1997 when debts of ten million pounds were announced. David Buchler, senior partner in the firm of Buchler–Philips, explained to the *Evening Standard* (10.2.97) the rationale behind the reappointment of manager John Docherty, under whom Millwall had enjoyed their greatest successes in the late-1980s: 'If Millwall are to survive, they will need fighters. I am a fighter and so is John Docherty. He has been here before, he understands the Millwall culture. He's the right man for the job.' It is also no

accident that Keith Stevens, nearing the end of his playing career, was appointed in the same moment as reserve team coach.

9. The New London Stadium has a capacity of 20,000, 4,000 of which is allocated to away supporters. In some of the sections of the ground allocated to Millwall fans, any game attracting more than 10,000 people is attended by chaos generated, primarily, by the insistence of many fans on sitting where, and with whom, they like, regardless of the ticket numbering system. The apparent impossibility of forcing compliance upon recalcitrant fans has been tacitly accepted by the club authorities, and stewards may be regularly observed advising ticket-bearing latecomers to fill whatever empty spaces they can find.
10. This should not be taken to mean that all those living in the southern suburbs are 'middle-class wankers'. The writer is specific about the significance of Surrey. The Kentish suburbs are a different matter. Areas such as Eltham, Downham, Welling or Sidcup, though technically suburban, may therefore be held in a different category on account of the different inner/outer migration-flows and class compositions of their populations.
11. Overwhelmingly white, overwhelmingly male, the Millwall fan-base is at the time of writing drawn from a range of relatively heterogeneous social locations. In addition to geographic dispersal, this part of London is characterized by a wide range of entrepreneurial and occupational activity. Successful self-employed businessmen, at one end of the spectrum, share stadium space with the unemployed at the other. Although it is well beyond the scope of this work to quantify these socio-economic categories, it should be borne in mind that the cartoon media image of the New Den as populated by the scum of the underclass is wide of the mark. Indeed, one of the more interesting features of Millwallism, and south-east London masculine culture in general, is the potential for the coexistence of (working-class) *habitus*-derived forms of social identity and orientation, with ostensibly embourgeoisified material conditions.
12. The authors of the Commission for Racial Equality's *Alive and Still Kicking* report (Back *et al.* 1996 : 58) point out that moralizing approaches are doomed to limited success because they rely on a 'moralism that does little to understand the social configurations of racism . . . Limiting our understanding of racism to the racist 'folk demon' may help to sustain moral support for the campaign but will do little to identify and tackle the forms of banal racism which still haunt our national game both within its institutions and amongst its loyal fans.' Such folk demonizing has an invariable tendency, as we saw in Chapter Two, to settle itself around Millwall, so often the symbolic focus of moralizing liberal anxieties.
13. The most powerfully intense moment in these vilifications was, however, not racialized. During an FA Cup game at the New Den at a time when the always

fraught public relationship between Wright and Millwall fans was at its most acrimonius, the massed ranks of the latter focused their contempt through an adaptation of the Arsenal chant 'Ian Wright!-Wright!-Wright!'. The player was visibly shaken by the vituperative ferocity of ten-thousand voices chanting 'Ian Wank!-Wank!-Wank!' to mark his every intervention. He was substituted well before the end of the game. Whether this underplaying of the racial possibilities of ritual abuse represented an acknowledgement of its potentially motivating effects on Wright's combative temperament, a feeling that his stature and notoriety required something more specific and targeted, or was a concession to the prevailing unacceptability of collective racist expression, is open to speculation. The heightened atmosphere of the game was precipitated by Wright's description of Millwall fans as 'racist yobs' some days before the game. The *News of the World*'s correspondent (8.1.95) felt that Wright had 'only himself to blame', and observed that this was a game Arsenal 'did well to survive. On an ordinary day, Millwall at the Den is by no means a cakewalk, never mind when the atmosphere has been turned white hot by Wright's rantings. The savage taunting of the Millwall fans hit new heights when Wright wasted Arsenal's best two chances'.

14. Back *et al.* (1996: 53) are absolutely correct in their assessment that this space is most frequently available for black men around the 'hooligan formations': 'The involvement of black supporters within these groups is related to a shared experience of local communities, codes of masculinity and toughness. Indeed, the networks associated with "hooliganism" are often far more "multicultural" than the wider population of "respectable" fans'.
15. It is important to note that this moment, though easily exaggerated, was real. My own involvement in the late 1970s anti-fascist counter-demonstrations is relevant here. On two occasions in south London I encountered a group of hard-core Millwall fans known to me thorugh my experiences with the club, supporting National Front marches. The group numbered perhaps 15–20 young men. This was at a time when the broader hooligan formations travelling the length and breadth of the country in support of Millwall numbered approximately 200–400, depending on the game. The picture is further complicated by the presence, within this, of an active and significant black minority of approximately fifteen fans drawn primarily – and like Ian Wright – from the Brockley area. These rough historical estimates illustrate an apparent paradox: a clear, but numerically modest, uptake in National Front ideology and activity in the period of that movement's highest popularity. Though the cultural context for this was clearly a widespread and expressive casual racism, defining the club as a hotbed of neo-fascist activism is a different matter. It is the former, given the complete collapse of the latter throughtout the 1980s, that continues to characterize the club and is of primary interest.

16. Back *et al.* (1996: 58) note that football institutions' reluctance to meaningfully engage with widely diffused, complexly articulated racism at games helps retain a focus on an oversimplifed and empirically dubious racist/hooligan steroetype – an appropriately marginal object for moral crusading. The authors highlight (1996: 53) the dubiousness of this equation: 'Within the context of the English game, in both Premier and Nationwide leagues, the public expressions of racism are not typically being perpetrated by those fans associated with "hooliganism".'
17. Hoberman's account of the consequences of the Marxist 'renunciation of the body' (1984: 119) is relevant.
18. Back *et al.* (1996: 57) arguments are borne out by my own observations here: 'There are changes occurring which mean there are fewer racist expressions by fans. We have found a combination of change and continuity with regard to fan racism. While overt and crude forms of racist practice are in decline, complexly articulated forms of racist activity remain, even though they may not be universally expressed. This is in part the product of the impact of all seater stadiums, the "Let's Kick Racism" campaign and shifts within the moral landscape of grounds.'
19. This account provides a glimpse of the complexities involved in itself. The first example demonstrates how stereotypes about black masculinity (in relation here to racialized sexual mythologies) may be played with while ultimately leaving them in place. The second is quite different; here the 'mock terror' of the black fans in their confrontation with the racist is used to demonstrate their access to a kind of cultural *knowing* as a basis of inclusion.
20. Etienne Verveer, a black Dutch player pursuing a fitful career with Millwall at this time.
21. See Mason (1994) for an account of the ways in which Rabelaisian obscenity and lewdness were – via the double entendre and veiled sexuality in the music hall, for example – complexly woven into the ambiguous dialectics of working-class 'respectability' in the nineteenth century. This demonstrates the persistence of pre-bourgeois orientations and perspectives, and indicates, during the climactic years of the bourgeois cultural revolution, their smuggling into working-class cultures in ways that have persisted ever since. The concept of embourgeoisement is insufficiently subtle for grasping the nature and forms of these complex processes of embodied cultural resistance. Grotesque realism – expressed in obscenity, profanity, lewdness and the occasional and ritualized loosening of modern restraints on affect and physical expression – can thus be conceptualized as existing at a range of levels and in more entrenched ways than the notion of its 'repression' suggests. To experience a Millwall crowd in full, belligerent and vituperative flight is to hear a sometimes disconcerting echo of the historical bitternesses characteristic of these cultural

transformations. It is vital, impassioned, and at times viscerally moving, but it is hardly colourful in the current popular sense. Carefree Latins banging drums – or, indeed, kilted Scotsmen blowing bagpipes – it is not.

22. Back *et al.* (1996) note, as we have seen, the effective – and indeed epistemological – limitations of moral anti-racism in situations of *complexly* racialized expression. But there are signs that the tendencies towards ideological over-simplification, therapeutic individualism (Gilroy 1987: chapter 4) and political miscalculation set in motion in this area over the last twenty years by municipal anti-racism have actively helped lead to problematic and unintended consequences. The excoriation of insufficiently 'progressive' working-class groups in London by cadres of correct-thinking middle-class activists (Morgan 1993) has triggered alarm bells in the folk-memories of many of those whose predecessors knew well enough the firm smack of missionary authority – see Chapter Two. Cohen (1996: 194) notes, as an outcome of this frequently misguided zealotry, the 'pariah' status experienced by some white working-class groups 'excluded from due political processes'. If Cohen's view of some of the aggrieved responses to these developments is on the sceptical side, Hewitt (1996) is clear that the widespread undermining and driving underground of white claims to pride in cultural identity *per se* has been a disaster, and instrumental to the emergence and consolidation of new forms of distorted and aggressive white nativism. Though the extent of the latter at Millwall is difficult to quantify – and easy, probably, to overestimate – it is without doubt characteristic of the orientations of a significant minority of fans.
23. This is a wildly over-exaggerated estimate of the amount of explicitly homophobic material in the repertoire. Such expression is always targeted at specific players (as in the 'Paul Birch Incident'), invariably in the form of whistles, cat-calls, screams, jeers and whoops. Few homophobic songs have received airings in recent seasons, though one in particular was popular until the early 90s. Reserved for well-known players, and sung to the tune of 'Glory, Glory Hallelujah!', it ran, as in this example against Manchester United:

    Robson takes it up the arsehole,
    Robson takes it up the arsehole,
    Robson takes it up the arsehole,
    'Cos he's just a northern cunt !

24. It now a convention in the pages of *TLR* to deny despised opponents the dignity of capitals: ian wright, west ham and crystal palace, for example, are always rendered in lower case. Tony Witter, who is black, has been accorded minor cult status at Millwall. At the time of writing he remains far more popular than the majority of white players, and is seldom if ever seriously barracked.

25. Millwall fans in general appear to have significantly 'grown out' of routine hooliganism. With the exception of long-standing vendettas with the likes of West Ham and Chelsea, it has been rare in the 1990s for Millwall to mobilize a serious 'firm'. This appears to be not merely the result of external policing and preventative measures. There is a widespread feeling that Millwall have nothing further – having virtually written the book in the years when it really counted – left to prove on the terrain of hooligan culture. The relative destabilizing of affective involvement characteristic of the new consumerist arrangements and the general sense of disappointment that this has engendered at Millwall may also be a factor.
26. The summoning up of a particular kind of cartoon moronism is a staple of the genre of Millwall patronization. The technique and tone are employed in absolutely representative fashion by Geoffrey Phillips (*Evening Standard*, 8.5.96): 'Disappointment can be a powerful emotion. Imagine the feelings of Millwall fans on Sunday as the Ipswich crowd pointed out their predicament (relegation from Division One) in that amusingly graphic way in which rival sets of football fans communicate. Millwall's supporters should, of course, have kept their tempers. They should have taken a deep breath and counted slowly up to 100. We must all resist the temptation to point out that some of them would still be there now, trying to remember what comes after 49.' I will have more to say about events surrounding the Ipswich game in Chapter Six.

–5–

Being Millwall: Symbol, Sociality and Commitment

> When you get yer Arsenals an' ya Tottenhams, you get all the singin' an' all that but they're not, like, so much a family. Everyone at Millwall knows everyone, an', its not a family club, its like – how can I put it? – its like ya brothers, *you look after ya brothers.*
>
> Terry M.

> You only have to follow the Lions on their travels to understand the deep working-class passion that runs deep among Millwall supporters. As you approach an away ground on a cold winter's evening, it is easy to see why we're Lions through and through. The distant echo of police sirens and the unmistakeable 'Lion's Roar' confirm your reason for travelling, and further cement your love affair with the rampant blue Lion.
>
> Neal Bradley, *The Lion Roars*

> Commitment to a proposition or a symbol of any kind entails a relationship between symbol and person that transcends language. Commitment is both more and less than a semantic process, for the symbol to which one is commited does not only represent. In the relation of commitment, the symbol blends with experience; it is more likely to appear as a feeling that can be described than as a content that can be deciphered. It is a relation of meaningfulness, not only of meaning.
>
> Peter Stromberg, *Symbols of Community*

The written material drawn on in the previous chapter highlights the scope and nature of those themes and issues that characterize the explicit life of the interpretive community at Millwall. While such articulations are usefully indicative of the broad dimensions of the semantic field upon which the set of cultural imperatives represented by Millwallism are played out, they should not be taken to represent its core. Millwallism is not primarily a discursive phenomenon. Rather, it is a context for experiential relationships centred upon the activation of specific modes of expressive being. Analysis of explicit linguistic forms or objective material symbols is unlikely to reveal the essence of these relationships. In this chapter I will therefore focus on the ways in which eight individuals experience *being* Millwall as a deeply personal relationship of commitment, and as a dynamic and experiential process of symbolization as opposed, for the most part, to an adherence to a set of external, disembodied symbols. The absorption of individuals into this medium of social practice proceeds from two fundamental cultural imperatives: first, from the collective defence, assertion and celebration of a specific and experientially heightened sense of identity; second, from a dialectical maintenance of the broader structures of feeling and response within which that identity is grounded, highlighted and pressurized as they currently are by apparently accelerating forces of disintegrating social change. The latter is manifest in a widespread preoccupation with tradition, cultural transmission and what I will call the spine of history .

Millwallism, centred as it is in a sphere of experiential symbolization, should therefore be approached in terms of practical process and the active use of *commitment*,[1] which makes possible a moment of almost physical merger with a symbol. In this moment the symbol is transformed from a mere object of thought into an experience, in which the participant literally 'finds himself' in the activated symbol and state of altered perception to which this activation gives rise:

> A relationship of commitment occurs when the symbol and the self are, at least momentarily, merged. Such a relationship always therefore entails the possibility of self-transformation, because it enables the self to be seen in terms of the symbol it has collapsed into . . . Such a relationship entails a bond of sentiment between the person and the symbol which has come to partake of the significance of the self. It is the existence of this bond of sentiment, I would hold, that constitutes what has been called an 'inner' relationship between believer and symbol. (Stromberg 1986: 52)

This bond, or transformative experience of *being* Millwall, is at the heart of the process of match-day ritualization. I will examine this in detail in the next chapter. Its significance on a lower level of intensity is that personal relationships with Millwall the symbol have a crucial role to play in the structuring of everyday accounts of engagements with Millwallism the social phenomenon. When committed fans talk about the bases of their commitments and feelings for the club they are clearly not talking about something that is external to themselves. They speak, rather, about something that is a constituent part of themselves.[2]

Eight Fans 1997

Though the eight men whose accounts I present here differ widely in terms of temperament, opinion and current social location, the majority have a commitment to Millwall rooted in an apparent attachment to particular, local social forms. Some of them may, ostensibly, have little 'in common' with one another beyond their commitment to Millwall, yet for most there are similarities in what appear to be deeply entrenched patterns of thought. Stromberg, drawing heavily on Bourdieu, discerns that the members of a community are veritably constituted by their attachment to certain social forms, and that these 'cultivated dispositions' represent embedded understandings which may be 'manifested as extraordinarily consistent patterns of conception in the believer's thought, patterns of which the believer is not aware' (Stromberg 1986: 65). He concludes this line of reasoning with the observation that such a pattern could be called a 'posture', a stance in experience, and that it may even be useful to think of such a pattern not as a phenomenon of the mind, but of something that operates on a more basic level than the mind because it organizes the mind (1986: 65).

I would argue that these understandings and communicative dispositions, moreover, are potentially situated in a pre-conscious sphere of experience all the more deeply entrenched potentially in those socialized early into (working-class) structures of a practical consciousness that lean toward context and positionality, inference and implication. Thus the particular modalities of consciousness and agency characteristic of Millwallism become embodied, and it is a shared grounding in these enduring structures of consciousness and feeling which frame and direct the participation of the majority of individuals, and which converge, differentially, upon the common symbol of *Millwall*. It is the solidity of these distinctively regional and working-class patterns of culture which allows, as we shall see, a minority of fans from beyond the *blood tradition* to understand and engage with Millwallism as a coherent cultural institution with a very specific kind of appeal.

Six of the eight men presented here were born into self-defined working-class contexts in south-east London. Two, who were both born well outside the capital, define their backgrounds as middle class. Three are self-employed, and four are homeowners. All are white, as are the overwhelming majority of Millwall fans. Beyond these broadly identifiable and empirically supportable characteristics (of class origin, gender and ethnicity), a detailed picture of the socio-economic and demographic composition of the active Millwall fan-base is difficult to achieve; a detailed analysis of the lives of some seven- or eight-thousand people has been beyond the scope of the current work. In my selection of twenty-five formal interviews and the condensed representativeness of the eight presented here, I have drawn on prolonged observation of Millwall and its fan-base, and its changing demographics. Five of the interviewees live in inner south-east London, and three beyond it. Six out of the eight began life there. This, if anything, is an underestimate of the extent of the displaced nature of the broad fan-base, for in the broader sample of twenty-five interviews, twelve respondents lived in inner south-east London, and fifteen in the suburbs and beyond. In the absence of a statistical breakdown of the fan-base, I work with an assumption derived from close observation over many years and the informal accounts of a large number of fans that at least half, and probably more, do not reside in the inner area.[3]

Three of the eight are, as I have noted, self-employed, in approximate line with the broader sample of twenty-five, where nine fitted this description. The eight cases mirror the broader sample in other important respects. Twenty-one were self defined as working class, and four as middle class; thirteen were homeowners; twenty one saw their participation in Millwallism as being connected to the *blood tradition*, four as based on *elective association*.

The eight cases below, the extended sample of twenty-five and, I suggest, the broader Millwall fan-base, exhibit a range of interesting socio-economic characteristics for adherents to such an unambiguously *working-class* cultural institution. The relatively high levels of homeownership, self-employment and geographical mobility indicate something of the complexity of contemporary experience, but are also connected to the historically significant themes of autonomy and non-corporatism discussed in Chapter Two. If the details of social experience and practice in the region are as complex and resistant to easy categorization as they ever were, the commitment to locating them within a local frame of 'working-class' culture and identity – in this case, of *being Millwall* – appears to have an intransigent continuity of its own. The eight fans are:

1. Keith is in his late twenties. He was born and raised in a middle-class family in Sussex. He is at present studying for a degree and rents a housing-association flat in Peckham in inner south-east London. He has no familial connection with this part of the capital, and thinks he will probably move on in the future. He went with friends to his first Millwall game in 1991, and is electively associated with the club, having had no awareness of or connection with its blood tradition prior to his first match.
2. John is in his mid-thirties. He was born and raised off the Old Kent Road in a classical working-class context, very close to the old Den. He rents a council flat in Camberwell in inner south-east London. He is committed to remaining in the area following a brief sojourn in the suburbs as a younger man, and currently works as a printer. Steeped in the blood tradition, he was taken to his first Millwall game by his father in the late 1960s. He now attends games with his son on a regular basis.
3. Mick is in his late thirties. He was born and raised in what he calls 'a right old-fashioned working-class' family in Deptford and now lives nearby in New Cross in inner south-east London. He is a homeowner and envisages staying in the area, to which he has a deep emotional commitment. He works as a black-cab driver. He was taken to his first Millwall game by his father in the mid 1960s and identifies with Millwall on the basis of the blood tradition. He has two daughters, who are 'not all that interested' in Millwall despite repeated visits.
4. Paul is in his mid-forties. He was born and raised in a working-class family in New Cross, to which he retains a powerful emotional attachment. He now owns

a house in Dagenham, Essex (following his parents' move to the Isle of Dogs in east London when he was a teenager), where he works as a motor mechanic. He was taken to his first Millwall game by his father and uncles in the early 1960s. He maintains his sense of the blood tradition, despite living in an area closely associated and 'caked up' with West Ham fans, by keeping season-tickets for himself and his son.

5. Terry is in his mid-twenties. He was born and raised in a working-class family in Eltham on the outer southern fringes of the capital – an area he 'loves' and defines as 'part of south London' – where he now owns a house. He is employed as a youth- and community-worker in Lewisham. Though he was not absorbed into the blood tradition inter-generationally, he 'grew up in a Millwall area' and went to his first Millwall game with his older brother and friends in the late 1970s.
6. Bob is in his early sixties. He was born into a what he describes as a 'big, old-fashioned' working-class family and raised at the Elephant and Castle in inner south-east London. He lives in private rented accommodation nearby, off the Old Kent Road, but would move out 'like a shot' to the Kentish suburbs had he the resources to do so. He is now retired, having built up a successful haulage-contraction company. He went with friends to his first Millwall game in the late 1940s. He has three sons, two of whom actively support Millwall.
7. David is in his late forties. He was born and raised in a working-class home in New Cross in inner south-east London, an area which, he says, 'made me what I am', but to which he would not return to live 'under any circumstances'. He now owns a large house in Tonbridge, Kent. He is a career diplomat in the Foreign Office. He was taken by his grandfather to his first Millwall game in the late 1950s, and adheres to the blood tradition to the extent of taking both his daughters to games – one of whom 'loves it down there, absolutely loves it' – despite their otherwise marked social-cultural and geographical distance from the area.
8. Martin is in his mid-thirties. He was born and raised in a middle-class family in the Home Counties. He holds a degree in history, and is currently employed as a motorcycle courier. He rents a private flat in Bermondsey in inner south-east London, an area on behalf of which he is something of an advocate and where he plans to stay: 'where else could you live?' He is electively associated with Millwall, having attended his first game with friends in 1989.

In their own ways, all of these men have very strong feelings about Millwall. Although their biographies – and to some extent their social experiences – are far from uniform, they were all inclined to talk about the club and their relationships to it in deeply serious and personal terms. Indeed, most of them give the impression that there are few things more important *to* talk about.

'These Colours Didn't Run': Sticking Together and the Social Bases of Participation

Togetherness

Given the relatively small size of the club's fan-base, participation in supporting Millwall is always measured on a human scale that is fundamentally inimical to the anonymous and impersonal. Time and again fans stress a preference for collective experience which, while occasionally capable of a transcendental affective power, is closely known and bounded. Paul's pride in Millwall, which his move to Essex has done nothing to diminish, is palpable and connected to its status as 'a *real* club, y'know . . . Millwall supporters are real people.' He loves this sense of intimacy, uniqueness and authenticity which he associates with the club:

> People say 'who d'you support ?' and I say 'Millwall' and, it's like, great to be an outsider, great not to be a glory hunter, like wiv a Newcastle or a Man United. It's great to be a minority. Its great, I love it . . . I dunno what it is, I've gone over Millwall like, 'an it makes the 'airs on the back a ya neck stand up.

But this is not any minority. It is Millwall, where glory is hardly sought beyond participation itself, and where smallness of scale is accompanied by a kind of notoriety that transforms it into a positive source of strength.

John explicitly situates this strength in the fact that although 'we might never be in the Premiership, we've got that, sort of, Premiership support – everyone knows 'oo we are'. John brims with pride as he discusses these matters of reputation:

> We get drawn against Bury in the cup an' its like 'who the fuck are they?' but they *know* who we are. They know we're all gonna come up there, an' we all know that when they 'ave the draw, an' that ball comes out the bag, people cringe when they see our name. An' its like 'oh no, not again' . . . One bloke at work is an Arsenal supporter, an' this time when it came round again 'e went 'oh fuckin' 'ell, not you lot again', and, its like, they don't think we're gonna beat 'em, it's. . .'e might be goin' to see Arsenal in the European Cup but 'es *never* gonna be in a group of six- or seven-thousand geezers all screamin' their 'eads off like that!'

If John's account of the uniqueness of being Millwall is significantly connected to the functioning of the Millwall archetype, which both amplifies the smallest misdemeanour *and* circulates that sense of being different of which fans are so proud, it also expresses a self-definition and way of feeling underpinned by social sources characteristic of the area.

Though he claims only to have been involved in limited defensive violence when following Millwall and is not 'that way inclined', John's voice is reminiscent of many of those who laid the groundwork upon which the Millwall myth was built. A sense of the distinctiveness of his local culture and the strength he and his peers were able to draw from it is at the centre of Mick's account of the golden years of the 1970s:

> When you went to away games you didn't 'ave to wear colours, you knew who everyone was an' everyone knew the different areas, an' when you drank down the Old Kent Road, or in Bermondsey, or wherever, everyone still knew one another. I mean, when you useta go away games an' there'd be trouble or whatever, you might be terrified, you might wanna run but you couldn't run 'cos everyone knew ya, so you stood. An' although there was less numbers of ya, an' you was as terrified as the other mob, the fact that you didn't run worried the other crowd. It'd normally be the other lot that run because they didn't 'ave that trust an' reliability that we 'ad. So I think that was a strength, especially in them sorta days, when their was confrontation an' that. You knew people was gonna stand wiv ya, you knew the faces, you knew the fellas from Bermondsey, or the Walworth, or Peckham, or Camberwell, or New Cross or Deptford, wherever. I mean, I came out of New Cross but you all sorta knew one another an' it was a definite sorta die-hard crowd an' the others stood by, y'know?

The distinctiveness of Millwall, then, is best regarded in an historical sense as a heightened form of working-class sociality with its content and shape determined by commonalties of experience in specific urban contexts.[4] Most obviously, it is an expression of a desire for collective and unifying experience for men drawn from a variety of contemporary social locations.

The ultimately respectable David, whose life trajectory has taken him a long way from his New Cross beginnings, nevertheless retains a desire for a sphere of experience that can only be accomplished by a return to his old stamping grounds, and a ritual steepening in the old class-based modes of participation and expression. Like Paul, he identifies a central element of the appeal of Millwall as residing in 'the fact of being one of a small band. Its not a glamour club, you're not one of 100 million Man U. supporters, or whatever.' Less preoccupied with questions of authenticity than many of his peers, David is more concerned with the coming together itself :

> You go down there and you know you're all on the same wavelength. They might be people from different walks of life and we might have nothing in common in the world except that shared passion for the club . . . but there's something there, and everybody feels the same thing.

The interpretive community at Millwall, and the atmosphere or feeling-space generated by it, is thus able to contain a range of perspectives and meet a variety of needs. Points of entry into this aggregative congregation may, within a restricted range of possibilities, be differently motivated and sustained in overlapping spheres of participation and meaning. Whatever the personal priorities of the participants, common themes emerge which revolve around a primary impulse toward a collective experience of *de-differentiation* (Girard 1977). Gathering in the company of those wanting the same things, and having the commonality of these desires ritually played out and confirmed is a very precise 'wavelength', with the desire and the capacity to tune into it a way of defining belonging. The experiential charge made possible by frequent immersions in the Millwall atmosphere, centred as it has been on generating those heightened and condensed actualizations of specific modes of consciousness and being, make the club a cultural resource of enormous power. This power lies in providing a context for collective experiences from which individuals may, as well as contributing themselves, draw strength, confirmation and sustenance of the deepest kinds.

Elective Association

The affective force and experiential richness of this context is sufficient to draw in and retain a minority of 'outsiders' from well beyond the cultural limits of the blood tradition. Here, as in the case of Martin, the role of Millwall as a concrete and highly specific marker of identity may be used more instrumentally, as something that is consciously adopted and nurtured:

> I just love the club. I love everything about it. It's like – I know this is a cliche – but it's the *passion* that you get at Millwall. That's what really made an impression on me, when I first went down there. To the old Den. It was a really boring game – against Coventry – freezing cold and wet, terrible weather, but in the second half the crowd just started to go *mental*. I couldn't really understand why, but the noise was unbelievable. It wasn't really like there was anything to shout about . . . I got the bug after that, started going all the time. The football left a bit to be desired but the atmosphere, y'know, the banter, the characters, the *humour*, that's what got me going.

Martin soon found that he was calling himself a Millwall fan. In time he graduated from simply attending the Den on a regular basis, to travelling away with a group of men he had met through work in the post office. These were deeply confirming experiences which he appears to have enjoyed even more than the home games: 'It was such a laugh. I'd never really done anything like that before. Its that whole day-out thing – turn up somewhere, have a good drink, go to the game, have another drink . . .' Sustained exposure at both work and play to Millwall fans and their activities led in a sense to him *becoming Millwall*, and placing increasing emphasis in his daily life on his support for the club:

> I moved around a lot when I was younger, and even though I sort of came to south London by accident, without really knowing anything about it, it's the first place in my adult life that I've really called home. I mean, it's a bit like Millwall itself, it doesn't really look very promising, but if you get to know the people, they're alright . . . they've got a great sense of humour. When I worked in the post office, I was scared of a lot of the blokes at first, 'cos they have this sort of *image*. It was like, if they weren't acting menacing, or whatever, they were always winding you up, cuntin' you off, fuckin' you about. It was like being in school, only worse. I took a lot of stick, a *lot* of stick. But once you get to know them . . . And its like that with Millwall: once you feel part of it, it gives you something to feel proud of, it gets right into you.

If Martin's new-found home and his Millwallism appear to be indivisibly linked in his own peculiar brand of purposefully downward social mobility, Keith's adoption of the club is much more tightly circumscribed by the boundaries of the institution itself. Though he displays little of Martin's generalized affection for south-east London and sees himself moving on when it becomes convenient, the origins of his fascination with Millwall are strikingly similar:

> I've always watched a lot of football, wherever I've been. But Millwall is something special. The passion that you get at Millwall is extraordinary, especially for a small club. I always associated that kind of passion with big clubs, you know, big crowds. But at Millwall there can be six-thousand people, and the atmosphere will still be incredible – even if the football isn't.

This indefinable extra-footballing *atmosphere* is what continues to draw Keith back to Millwall time and time again (he has been a season-ticket holder for four years) over and above any need to watch the game of football itself being played. This need borders on the obsessive, and he continues to attend various other London grounds when Millwall are not playing – but he has become addicted to the peculiarities of Millwallism:

> Its not the same at the other clubs. Millwall's got its own unique character, its got something *real* about it, which appeals to me. At a lot of the bigger clubs, like Arsenal, Man. U., Liverpool, the fans are like sheep, they'll put up with anything for their 'undying love of the club'. They're not like that at Millwall – they love the club, but they're critical, not passive. They've got this incredible passion, but it can become negative very quickly, and turn very sour. Sometimes its very uncomfortable – I find it hard sometimes to just sit there while some idiot shouts abuse at black players, or whatever. But I keep going back . . .

With no sense of regional or localist patriotism and a relatively distanced and reflexive relationship with Millwallism, Keith still feels compelled to return game after game, to immerse himself in a pervasive *atmosphere* of which, by his own account, he has an outsider's understanding. It is in those moments of collective effervescence and the constitution of Millwall's distinctive semantic-field and anti-charisma that supporting the club appears to have its affective centre, for Keith and the small number of those like him. It is clear that, for all his biographical distance from the social sources of the 'blood tradition', a factor which does not necessarily preclude attachment, Keith participates in match-day rituals at a deep and intensive level, but not on his own terms. Despite occasional misgivings, he buys into the cultural life of the club, warts and all. At the other end of the biographical spectrum of support from Keith are those for whom such participation engages and draws upon the deepest constituents of the self.

All the Old Cockney Things

Consider Bob, whose return to watching Millwall following an absence forced by convalescence from major surgery seemed integral to the recovery of his vigour and sense of self. After months cooped up at home, Bob found himself visiting the Den not just for the football, but 'for the atmosphere', especially the humour and its concomitant sense of the carnivalesque:

> I love bein' in wiv the crowd. The banter an' all that, the same old abuse the referees always useta get . . . oh, at Millwall you get all the funny ones. The comedians are unbelievable, they've always bin the same. They come out wiv the same cracks – I mean, I useta love goin' just to listen – it's the *verbal*, the jokes an' the cracks. It's all the old cockney things, unnit?

Banter and having a laugh is, for Bob, the primary medium in which the sense of a whole culture – 'all the old cockney things' – is held, sustained and conveyed. Ludic orality, a worldly philosophy implacably opposed to pretension and hubris, and a style of mind sharpened by metropolitan practice are coterminous in Bob's understanding.[5] His return to Millwall enabled him to locate, remember and replenish the social sources of himself. Getting back in touch with these things in so collectively heightened a context – his spell of recuperation coincided with some glorious successes against Crystal Palace and Arsenal – was of inestimable value to him. Bob's sense of himself, of who he is, and his feelings for Millwall and what *being* Millwall means, are indivisible. Indeed, he can barely achieve the distance required to separate and describe them. The symbolic relationship between Millwall and the self is one in which they are intimately connected. And faced with the long and difficult process of reclaiming his health and vigour, his instinct was to bring the two closer together. This was not a rhetorical gesture however, for it was fundamentally predicated on participation, upon an active steepening in a particular medium of expressive being.

For Bob this meant a return to being able to scream, to shout, to laugh, and once again to take possession of his body. To talk the talk and walk the walk. To be himself in the company of others like him. What Bob needed, it became clear, were large doses of grotesque realism and the carnivalesque, to consolidate his gradually returning vigour and sense of his own (declamatory, combative, difficult) self. Feeding off the clamour around him in the stadium, informing the match officials that they were less well equipped to control the game than his own wife, laughing at the waves of coruscating banter rolling across the seats, and singing 'Fuck 'em all!' for the first time in years, Bob reactivated his sense of what it meant to *be* Millwall.

For him, this was very close to a definition of being alive itself. Though this experience could carry its benefits back into everyday life, re-establishing his relationship with the club meant finding the centre of Millwallism in its ritual forms. To a large degree, his love of the atmosphere and 'the verbal' at Millwall is a love of the continuity it provides, and participation comes as naturally to him as it does to most fans.

That naturalness and spontaneity however lies in a familiarity with collective forms that have no precise equivalent in everyday experience. Rather they represent a heightening and a condensing of the performative and expressive aspects of working-class masculinity, and of which the participants themselves may be unaware. John remembers being shocked by his girlfriend's perception of him in action at the Den:

> I took me girl one day, an' we come 'ome an' she said 'you're totally different down there, you was talkin' different'. An' I said 'what d'ya mean like? I wasn't!' an' she said 'your voice changed, you was all standin' the same – there was about fifteen of us – an' you all spoke the same'. I think there's certain words, not rhymin' slang, but . . . I never say 'em except at Millwall, an' . . . she couldn't believe 'ow different I was. I thought 'you must've got it wrong', but she said 'nah'. I think I know what she meant. It's like, when you're drinkin' wi' ya mates, you pick up their sayin's an' their little mannerisms . . . an' when you get twenty blokes spendin' the 'ole day together – when you go away – an' you get drunk together, you take on each others personalities. I s'pose that's a lot of it.

The very language that John uses to tell his story demonstrates the extent to which his sense of identity is socially embedded (*pace* the work of Bernstein). Only deeply shared understandings and embodiments of identity are able to order inter-subjective experience of this kind. For the forms of consciousness that underpin this mode of performative inter-subjectivity, context is almost everything. Language and other forms of symbolic communication are barely required to explicate it. To *be* Millwall at this level is to draw in a heightened, actualizing and overwhelmingly implicit way, on the fundamental orientations of working-class, masculine sociality. This is a critical sphere of experiential continuity for both the individual and the collective. Bob, who is now past sixty, learned these patterns as a boy and he still lives in them in a fundamentally unchanged way. This is a difficult thing to talk and write about, but it is not a difficult thing to enact and symbolize. It should come as no surprise it has remained inaccessible to intellectualist–monological enquiry (Taylor 1995: 49). A central mechanism of the *habitus*, which structures and makes possible these personal interrelationships despite the grounded differentiation of individuals with increasingly varied life-trajectories, is the process of symbolization. Through its symbols such a form of life and experience becomes apprehendable. And to the men whose voices are presented here, Millwall is primary amongst such symbols. It is a distillation of a sense of self, of the group and of the world with which these things interact. It structures high moments of collective ritual experience, and, at a lower level, occupies a central place in the interactive dynamics of daily existence. In its ontological dimension, the symbol has an enormous potential and use, while the commitment to and investment in the club is of equal significance, for it has no existence outside those collectively generated processes that produce, define and sustain it. *Being Millwall* is a category of experience that does not only manifest itself on Saturdays and the occasional Wednesday nights. In the next section I will suggest some of the ways in which individuals experience and use Millwallism as a constituent part of themselves.

'We are, We are Millwall': Self, Class and Symbols of Solidarity

Roots

David's successful career in the diplomatic service and resultant upward mobility would appear to be a classic example of the 'opportunities' afforded by the post-war loosening of the boundaries around class identity and occupational progress. His process up the diplomatic career ladder has been swift and sure. But he has not renounced an identity, and a sense of the world, forged in New Cross as a youngster. Indeed he has made a virtue of it. Millwall is

> something there that's part of me and I don't actually think I should deny it. In the Foreign Office – which is a very un-'south London' occupation, in a sense – curiously enough, it's allowed me to carve out a niche, for straight talking, frankness, no bullshit an' what you see is what you get. That, in a sense, was the general sort of effect in the airy-fairy world of diplomacy – it means you're notably different from the others.

Thus does David articulate a critical distance between himself and his peers in the service. He is one of them, but not of them. The values and expressive repertoire of his youth have accompanied him in complex and adaptive forms throughout a life which, in employment and status terms, could scarcely have been less predictable. His animated talk about 'roots', connections and values is far from being mere rhetoric. What comes across most clearly in his account is that he is not *one* of them. His sense of distinction is further heightened by his experience of his neighbours: 'We live in Tonbridge, but we're not Tonbridge people, and never would be.'

David's disavowals of the culture of the workplace and area in which he finds himself underscore a critical but frequently neglected point. While his successful institutional career and six-bedroomed house in Kent suggest membership of the upper middle class, his values, mode of communication and personal aesthetic embody working-class south London. In a profound sense, David is both of these things, and neither. Happily prosperous and secure in his relative privilege, but still in touch with what he regards as the core of himself, he understands and uses Millwall as a metaphor for and a summation of his cultural personality. With its distinctive structure of feeling and sense of the world, it marks and symbolizes the continuing presence of the past in his radically transformed present.

David, it is clear, uses his relationship with Millwall to help define himself, order his sense of things. It is bound up with his most deeply held perspectives, which he is keen to try to pass on to his children, whom he feels will be unable to understand him without exposure to Millwall:

> I live a privileged existence . . . I say to her [oldest daughter] 'the world is not actually like that, the world is like the people you see down at Millwall, that's what the world is really like'. In a fourteen, fifteen year old – if they're gonna be streetwise, which is what Millwall've got – . . . I want 'er to understand that, I think its a link in that sense with the real world. The kids need to know where I'm comin' from. The younger one doesn't like Millwall, but at least she's got a sense of what it means.

David is secure in the knowledge that he is providing the best for his family, though he would not dream of returning to New Cross 'under any circumstances'. With his social and familial links to inner south-east London all but completely severed, his regular trips back begin to take on the appearance of ritual visits to a symbolically charged ancestral stamping ground resonant with the voices and atmosphere of the past. An enthusiastic performer of *No One Likes Us*, he uses the past, which is manifest as the core predispositions of his personal *habitus*, to help negotiate and enhance the present. This kind of adaptive or dialectical development of the personality is precisely enabled by David's irreplaceably formative experience of locality and community. It is the work of the *habitus* not only to constrain, but to allow for development in its framing of the modalities of social activity. However, this development must have a ground to push against, a set of formative experiences from which to launch its trajectory. The complexity of experience framed by such a trajectory produces a dialectical synthesis predicated not on the rejection of unwanted cultural baggage, but on the project of keeping it alive, relevant and useful in the present.[6] 'Successful' working-class people, contrary to popular conception, need not simply acculturate themselves in a journey away from the parochial, but frequently embark upon the imaginative transposition of formative experiences and dispositions to altered social and material circumstances.

David's identity, then, is clearly dual in some sense. But *being Millwall* helps him to understand and order the complex nature of his experience. He remains, despite the changes in his life, largely who he was. His identity seems not to have spiralled off into a postmodern stratosphere of flux, ontological anxiety and multiple personhood. Participation in Millwallism, the interjection of accumulated dispositions and orientations towards the world into his present, helps keeps him whole, vigorous and sane in a milieu seldom encountered by the majority of his class peers.

In a Class of Their Own

David's general experience and use of Millwall, though perhaps exceptional in some of its detail, is emblematic. The suburbs of Kent are full of men who have, by a variety of means, been successful enough to move out into big houses with nice gardens. Many of them would be as difficult to classify as David in their various blends of ostensibly bourgeois material culture and working-class aesthetic and performative dispositions. As the folk-truism would have it, you can take 'the boy out of the Walworth Road, but *you cannot take the Walworth Road out of the boy*'. Still less can you take the boy out of his body, for it is the first site of cultural knowledge, consciousness and reproduction. Terry M. and his Millwall loving friends are spread across south-east London and north Kent. Homeowners surrounded by fruits of the material culture of which they, like so many of their London forebears, are such advocates, their capacity for vital expression and the performative aesthetics of working-class masculinity appears undiminished:

> It's just what they're used to, they're used to quality, not so much wi' Millwall, but they wanna better themselves. Livin' in south London, they want better, better, better. They want everything, either for their family or themselves, an' if they support Millwall, they wannit for Millwall. An' they don't wanna come down 'ere an' see, y'know, shit! They wanna actually see . . . a bit a pride an' *be* shit, y'know, go out there an' *fight*, jus' go out there an' do it for the club. That's why they go potty.

They 'want the best' and 'go potty' when they they don't get it. Dunning *et al.* (1988) argued for a working-class incorporation into middle-class forms and material culture that was assumed to be behavioural–cultural as well as material.

However there is a clear discontinuity between the structures of feeling described here and this received wisdom, which should force us to ask 'how are these men to be classified?' It is clear that their experience cannot be contained within the increasingly creaky apparatus and categories of conventional class analysis (Butler and Savage 1995). They appear to be working class and yet not working class. They appear to be embourgoisified and yet not embourgeoisified. Who are they? They know, and this knowing somehow has Millwall bound up with it. Millwall swells their chests with pride and wracks their beings with rage. It is somewhere at the centre of themselves, and they use it to enhance their lives and to make them both richer and more solid. The experiential and symbolic possibilities that inhere in Millwallism hold for everybody, regardless of the point along the social continuum from which they engage in it. For David, being Millwall helps him negotiate, survive and prosper in new and challenging circumstances. He lives at a distance from the working-class traditions that shaped him, but is able and eager to reconnect with them.

On the other hand for John, who enjoys keeping as little distance as possible from those traditions, *being Millwall* sustains and enhances his everyday performative persona and is intimately bound up with the details of his social identity. It adds spice to many of his interactions, and is continuous with his sense of *south Londonness*:

> Deep down, I love the idea of comin' from somewhere where, you know, it's got a reputation, an' . . . I've gotta 'old me 'ands up, you know what I mean? . . . I do sort of *play on it* sometimes. It's like, sometimes I go over north London wi' me girlfriend, 'ave a drink wiv 'er mates over there. An' when I first met 'em it was sort've, 'where you from?' an' I said 'Old Kent Road', an' it's like, 'whoa!' . . . like I say to people, 'I go down Millwall', an' all of a sudden, it's like, people look at ya a bit strange, like there's gotta be *something more to ya.*

This indefinable something more, with its ontologically secure and self-believing resourcefulness, is more an experiential reality than it is an externally attributed myth. And it is this – he calls it 'pride' – which Martin, coming from a non-London, middle-class background, found so compelling in his first contacts with Millwall and south-east London:

> I'd never really come across that before. People round here (Bermondsey) seem a bit unforgiving, but they're proud. Proud to be who they are, even if they've got nothing. And its like that with Millwall – people are proud of the club, of supporting Millwall, even if they never win anything. That's where the passion comes from: pride.

If at times the psycho-social sources of the latter remain obscure to him, Martin clearly sees it as a desirable thing, and brings himself closer to the experience of it through his adoption of Millwall and immersion in its culture. All of these men, with the possible exception of Keith, use *being Millwall* in this kind of way. In their interactions at work and play, with colleagues, and with new acquaintances and old friends the idea, the experience, and the symbol of Millwall works by its mere invocation, referencing and activating a specifically understood identity, sense of the world and peculiarly atmospheric mystique (or anti-mystique). The significance of this mystique lies in a particular aesthetics of working-class performative embodiment. The incipiently and dramatically heightening nature of this performativity has its source in the uniquely dialectical complexities of the identity itself, in the lived interconnections between embodied local culture, metropolitan history, public-sphere-notoriety, and folk-taxonomic mythicization. These themes, each contained in the personal biographies and life-trajectories of individuals, are brought to bear on the negotiation of rapid social change and a cultural upheaval that is characteristic of contemporary life in the region. And at the centre of the embodied struggle to hold cultural attenuation and dissipation at bay is the impulse to keep ontological coherence, continuity, and a sense of history itself alive.

Will the Circle be Unbroken?: A Tradition of Support and the Spine of History

Then and Now

The values and preferences with which Millwallism is associated, for group identifications and affective bonds, the ontological relationship between self and place, and the desire to transmit a coherent and integral sense of the particularities of these things to succeeding generations, have proven remarkably resistant to the best attempts of liberal–progressive ideology and pedagogy to erase them. Millwall is one example of the ways in which working-class cultural activity continues to manifest a preoccupation with what I will to call the *spine of history*. The insistent reproduction of a collective repertoire of understanding and expression defines its status as a bulwark against the culturally attenuating effects of both progressivist ideology and the economic restructurings and global imperatives of late capitalism.

The accounts of Millwall and cultural continuity presented here give the lie to the frequently banal, radical claims about the 'essentialism' of such working-class men. As Stromberg observes, the process that we call history is nothing but a relentless and ongoing transformation of customs. Some traditions are indeed preserved through countless generations, but are not therefore impervious to change: 'It is not custom and tradition that order social life; rather, social life is ordered by an enormously complex interaction between custom and the exigencies of historical situations. That interaction occurs in the medium of human activity' (Stromberg 1986: 9).

It is patently obvious that Mick and John, for example, are fully aware of the nature and consequences of these contemporary exigencies. Their participation in Millwallism is not based on an adherence to primordial essences. On the contrary, it represents a dialectical tracking between past and present, with prior and current sets of experiences illuminating one another. Older Millwall fans may use their participation in what may be defined as a part of the unavoidable existential project of maintaining a grounded sense of self in a changing world. John, however, takes his son to Millwall not to immerse him in an immemorial identity, but as part of an attempt to equip him with transferable qualities and resources (mutual bonding and self reliance, mental and physical toughness, manly dignity, a sense of humour, practical acuity) which he believes will help him to negotiate an increasingly complex and uncertain present. A simplified attempt to seek refuge in an idealized past is not the inevitable consequence of a distaste for the direction in which history appears to be heading.

There is no doubt, however, that the spine is being subjected to increasing pressure. Those Millwall fans aged over thirty know this well, and contemporary participation in supporting the club can be read as an attempt to ground the self in a set of practices and experiences aimed at keeping history alive. However, if talk of the death of history at Millwall is premature, there are also apparent signs of serious injury. And whether or not the injury can be sustained over the longer term remains to be seen.

Though things are changing, Mick feels the club has a resistant core:

> People say to me 'why d'you support Millwall', an' it's because I come from the area, its the loyalty to the club, like the traditional clubs were I suppose. In an area like Millwall it's 'cos, still, yer roots are in the area and you support the local club, unnit? . . . I personally think the club reflects the environment an' the area, y'know, the supporters that is, reflects the area to a good balance in the sense that it's workin' class people – or unemployed people even, now – um, very local to the area, or 'ad been local and moved out but still kept strong roots, strong sort've ties with family an' connections with the area.

Mick feels, though, an acute sense that the most intense and interesting phase of Millwallism has passed. Now a law abiding family man – 'we're all respectable now, ain't we?' – he speaks with enormous pride about the days when Millwall was *really* special, *really* unique:

> I don't feel, with the young ones, that its perhaps as strong as it was, an' I don't think the new ground's 'elped that either. You know, the new ground certainly . . . y'know, its more invitin' to away supporters to come, its more open an' everything. When I'm cabbin'

> . . . you get talkin' to people, y'know, northeners or wherever they come from, about football, an' nigh on every customer I've ever spoken to, they go 'oh I went there once, it was like goin' to a party uninvited, you'd gatecrashed, you shouldn't a been there', y'know, an' its unique, that. Whether they're Newcastle fans or Man City fans or wherever they come from, they've all come out with the same expression about the old Den . . . I certainly think there was a deep fear and a deep respect for the old stadium, an' I think that's gone. The myths carry on, but its certainly not the same. Nothin' like the same, the atmosphere's not the same.

This is much more than a paean to the days when Millwall ruled hooligan culture. It is an acknowledgement that the former intensity of commitment, the seriousness and power of the bond that spontaneously grew up between the club and boys in the area in his day, has weakened. The sheer variety of leisure alternatives militates against the forming of a deep bond to one specific cultural institution:

> I think its not as fashionable now with the younger kids. The whole concept of what we used to do in the 70s is not so strong now because the culture's changed, there's a lot more for kids to do, doin' other sort've sports or entertainments, whatever. Whereas in the 70s, that was yer Saturday out, yer day out, y'know, from early mornin' to whatever time you got 'ome at night, y'know, that was a big culture thing, an' I don't thinks its so strong now.

This local culture, premised on a relatively narrow range of leisure options, seems to have made up in its depth and tightness of focus and identification what it lacked in breadth. Until the 1980s many local boys at a decisive time in the development of the personality and its symbolized identifications *became* Millwall, a becoming sustained and strengthened by its non-footballing social sources in urban experience. Mick talks about this passing of a cohesive fit between local culture and Millwall with a palpable sense of regret. And it is a regret generated by a fundamental but imprecise suspicion that young people have changed.

Assimilating the Junior Lions

Anxiety about the possible consequences of this change – in a more common variant of David's need to demonstrate his roots to his children – is the often explicit motivation of many fans to induct their children into the cultural life of the club. Loyalty to Millwall is, in this view, indivisible with broader loyalties and values. John takes his son to Millwall because

> I wan' 'im to 'ave that sort've thing that we 'ad, that goes along wiv growin' up round 'ere. I don't wan' 'im to grow up without knowin' about that. Y'know 'e lives out there

> now (in the suburbs), wiv 'is mum, an' when I see 'im, it's like, 'es not gettin it. She (John's ex-wife) don't like it, she don't want me takin' 'im down there when 'es wiv me. But I wan' 'im to know about all that.

John's anxieties about his son's cultural identity are stimulated by his perception of the differences between himself and his younger brother, who moved out of London with his parents in the early 1980s while John and his older brother stayed: 'My younger brother's different, he comes to Millwall sometimes, but 'es not so streetwise, 'e don't talk like me an' me older brother.' He is concerned that his son, like his younger brother, will miss out on the uniqueness of his own experience, and fail to absorb his understanding of the unwritten code of the street and of the manly honour central to it. His concern is intensified by his observation that the spine of history is under more general pressure, and that his (and the interviewer's) generation represent the last one to fully absorb this coherent and identifiably local culture:

> I mean, me old man always talks about the Teddy Boys an' all that, you know, the violence an' all that, but I think what's changed is that, um, like we're the last generation who've got, I could say *morals*, but there's certain things, certain rules that . . . you could go into a pub, wherever it was, an' if you was drinkin' on yer own you'd never get a clump – 'cos you was on yer own. There 'ad to be certain rules, y'know, an' even, like, the people I go Millwall wiv, a lot of 'em was *at it* sort've thing, y'know, an' they'd break the law every week for the last thirty years when they went to football, like, but anythin' else is . . . that's a *liberty*, robbin' people, breakin' into peoples 'ouses, that's wrong.

For John, supporting Millwall betokens adherence to a particular moral code and set of values. That these values are under such pressure on a range of fronts makes their survival at Millwall all the more vital.[7] This is the point at which all the talk of pride, passion and commitment comes into sharpest focus: Millwall is a repository of these absolutely core values and expressions, but its health depends upon them being appropriately sustained and confirmed. The sense of cultural crisis examined in the last chapter is concentrated on this point. For if these things cannot be thrown into high relief and experienced in symbolically condensed ways at Millwall, then where are they to be?

100 Per Cent Millwall?

The crisis of morale at Millwall is therefore a microcosmic and metaphorical instance of the broader pressures to which traditionalist working-class masculine values are being subjected. Millwall presents a version of reality in which toughness is primary but measured and competed for by equal forces, where manly honour and dignity are to be struggled over and earned, and where impassioned loyalty is the cardinal virtue. The social reality it expresses may be tough, sometimes brutal, and usually uncompromising, but is a reality firmly bounded by moral sensibilities. All of this is symbolically at stake whenever Millwall play, and the gradual disappearance of these qualities and perspectives from contemporary football mirrors their perceived attenuation in social life more generally. It is for this reason that Millwall fans react with such scorn when their players fail to represent them adequately. For if *Millwall* is a crucial metaphor for these structures of feeling and a symbol with which individuals have intimate personal relationships, then its failure to live up to the standards set for it registers deeply, at the level of practical identity itself. Millwall's recent failures on the field and its footballing marginalization thus become a metaphor for what is perhaps the final decline of those particular ways of life and senses of the world that have slowly but continuously been dissipating since the advent of modernity.

Investment in the symbolic life of the club is, therefore, no small matter. The primary bearers of the symbolic burden generated by the intensity of these relationships are the players themselves. Thus, when fans make observations upon the performances of particular players they are engaged in making micro-statements about their cultural universe as a whole. This is why the constant complaints about players' lack of conviction and commitment are of such significance because, like 'young people' in general, *players* have changed. And players have changed because the world is changing, and the world is changing in ways that appear inimical to previously obtaining forms of life and value: old ladies are being attacked in the street, everyone's house is being burgled, and *Millwall players can't be bothered*. Where is the pride, the manly dignity, in these things?

Terry, like so many others, organizes his articulation of these concerns around a contrast between the traditional stalwart and the newer, mercenary breed of footballer:

> Chris Malkin wants to win. 'Es workin' very 'ard, 'es been my player of the season. When 'e started an' 'e were'nt gettin' goals, 'is work rate was brilliant. 'E never let 'is 'ead go down. But you know, wiv *Uwe* (Fuchs), players like that, they're out there to get their money. An' Millwall supporters 'ate that. Wiv Millwall, they'll let you know, if you're shit they'll let you know, they're not like the Liverpools, they won't get behind ya – they won't try an' lift yer 'eads, they're on ya straight away.

Paul believes that it is pride, 'pride in the area' and its symbolic representatives, that makes the mercenary attitude so hard to swallow:

> A Millwall team's expected to give 100%, an' if they do lose, it ain't through lack of tryin'. They wanna win, the desire is there to win, but if they do lose, the majority of

> the time, then they've given 100%, an' you can't say fairer than that . . . I mean, that is part of bein' Millwall, we want the team to be as passionate as we are . . . that's what it is for Millwall, mate, its pride, proud of the people.

But this pride needs appropriate emblems and representatives. Bob's conviction that there are no 'proper' Millwall players anymore is underpinned by a belief that contemporary players have no *character*:

> There ain't no characters now. I mean, goin' back years ago when I was a kid there was. Neary. Played centre forward, great big, powerful, got one shot on target in twenty. 'E was absolutely useless, but 'e was a crowd puller . . . Well, 'e was playin' for the Lions 'till 'e dropped. 'E would charge around the pitch like a ragin' bull for twenty minutes an' wouldn't get *near* the ball. But 'e never stopped tryin', an' when 'e did score, through 'is own efforts, 'e was the 'ero, weren't 'e? 'E was the 'ero anyway. 'E used to knock 'em over (this was when they could attack goalkeepers, jump wiv goalkeepers, know what I mean?). 'E knocked more goalkeepers into the net than you know. Not the ball very often, but the goalkeeper went. That was when it was good, good team then.

Bob thinks of this kind of sporting picaresque as firmly rooted in the past. It was what drew him to games, this chance to see a bit of refereed rough-and-tumble and bodily contest. Pat Neary compensated for his lack of technique with clamorously received exhibitions of embodiment. He did this because he had character, forged in the vicissitudes and demands of the golden age of working-class life. That so many Millwall fans are concerned about the lack of contemporary equivalents of Neary demonstrates the way in which the club functions as a site of cultural continuity.

Millwall fans need these kinds of players to represent them, to assist them in their attempt to keep the spine of history from breaking down and to keep a particular sense of the world alive. Without a Harry Cripps, a Barry Kitchener, a Terry Hurlock or a Keith Stevens, Millwall culture flounders without a touchstone, without an imaginative thread with which to bind the present to the past. The burden of keeping historical continuity alive without inspirational symbolic representatives on the field of play falls entirely onto the shoulders of the fans themselves, and is becoming increasingly onerous. They need something to get their teeth into. Without it, Millwall, as a material institution and a symbolizing and constituent aspect of the self for many individuals, may become drained of its vigour and charge. Millwall fans know well what is at stake in all of this, and it is this awareness that motivates and gives added force to their well-known vituperativeness and capacity for righteous anger as the guardians of a cultural tradition under threat of dissipation. The protection, maintenance and celebration of local culture and character in the guise of Millwallism is, then, the central mechanism of cultural practice at the club, and it is driven by a deep and long-term engagement in an embodied, attritional cultural war against the forces of disintegrating social change and universalizing progressivism. The continuing power of these older dispositions and orientations is exemplified by the seriousness and passion with which fans approach their participation in Millwallism – as one of the primary activities and resources in their lives. The intensity of experience that the club makes possible derives not only from its function as a repository of specific traditions and values, but also, out of its extraordinary capacity to metaphorically represent, both experientially and conceptually, broader strains of experience and cultural conflict.

This metaphoricity works on two interconnected levels, beginning with the specific and working outward toward the more general. First, as I have demonstrated in some detail, *Millwall* condenses and exemplifies particular modes of south-east-London masculinity; second, this has become particularly acute since the club's relegation to the second division, with all of *its* provincial and anachronistic atmospheres and overtones. *Millwall* means football of the more old-fashioned, unglamorous, excessively local-partisan and unenlightened sort, the sort that must be either marginalized, swept away or re-branded by the newer, hyper-commercial and universalizing ethos of the game in the 1990s. Millwall's market-unfriendly mythological baggage has combined, in a genuinely spectacular example of bad timing, with a downward footballing spiral which has seen the club plummet to mediocre obscurity in a second division becoming increasingly, and perhaps definitively, remote from the resources and glamour of the new era. Millwallism is, in all probability, irreconcilable with the climate of freshness, change and novelty now pervading the professional game. In the public imagination, this makes Millwall *yesterday's* football, *yesterday's* culture, *yesterday's men.* Millwall's Collective Imaginary is to a large extent organized around a shared awareness of this cultural baggage. And the long-suffering and dedicated fans who protect and maintain the Imaginary's core meanings draw on these themes in those critical ritual moments when *Millwall* is brought most fully alive.

Notes

1. My use of the concept of *commitment* draws on Peter Stromberg's (1986) account of faith in the Immanuel Church in Sweden. Stromberg defines commitment systems, voluntarily entered into by individuals in complex societies, as revolving around uniquely meaningful and emotionally charged

relations between actors and the symbols that express the deepest spiritual propositions to which they adhere.

2. If there is an element of *construction* in the constitution of these accounts, it lies in the use of Millwall to exemplify and amplify salient themes in local, everyday experience. Individuals seldom *invent* or *construct* themselves as Millwall fans in the fictive sense: rather, they tend to use their participation in Millwallism as a means of metaphorically/symbolically expressing, encapsulating and dramatizing characteristic varieties of social identity and consciousness. They do not, therefore, have the status of unmediated versions of any unified reality, but they *do* allow for widely held senses of embodied identity to be placed within common frameworks of reference and interpretation. Their construction, which draws from everyday, intimate, familiar and widely shared details, helps individuals to talk about their experiences but entails neither 'self-creative' novelty nor distance from their social sources.
3. Carl Prosser, editor of *The Lion Roars* fanzine, supports this observation. Though 'we've got a lot of subscribers, we haven't got that many that actually live near the ground, they're all out in areas like Welling, Sidcup . . . a lot of our fan's families have grown up and probably the mum and grandparents are still up in Bermondsey – not so much Peckham, I'd say Bermondsey – Walworth, Elephant, Rotherhithe, Surrey Quays, Deptford, but as the family has grown up it's spread out into south, not so much southwest London, but Sidcup, Feltham (Kent), and going by our magazine sales we sell really well, we sell more in say Feltham or Sidcup . . . than we would in say Brockley or New Cross . . . it has spread out, even going down to Gillingham, Rochester.' I am indebted to Les Back for the use of this personal communication (1997).
4. Mick's account clearly emphasizes the extent to which Millwall's affective power has historically been grounded in the high levels of both *material* and *moral density* (Durkheim 1984) – each of which are necessary to the underpinning of any attachment to a *conscience collective* – formerly characteristic of these corners of the capital. As Collins (1988: 112) notes, 'The sum of the daily experiences of . . . small isolated communities is an overall situation of very high moral density, hence resulting in highly reified symbols of group membership.' Though the specific urban situation which contained these densities has become much more diffuse, the power of the exemplifying symbols generated therein has not. The strength and constancy of these symbols – *Millwall, south-London, the Lion, etc.* – structures the adherence to Millwallism of both the displaced south-London populations *and* those like Martin and Keith who are looking for something more substantial than the 'abstract, universalistic' symbols (Collins 1988: 112) of the modern nation-state.
5. Bob likes to talk about his comedy favourites almost as much as he likes to talk about the Lions. He regards Del Boy Trotter (see Chapter Two) as an

altogether appropriate fictional exemplar of his own cultural milieu: 'E is a typical south Londoner. Without any shadow of a doubt. 'Es a ducker 'n diver, a jack the lad tryin' to better 'imself all the time, get in front. 'Es a modern spiv, a modern one a them – "it fell off the back of a lorry" job, anything. In actual fact a *money getter*, an uneducated moneygetter, an' there's a lot of 'em about, who've got a lotta money. They're, like, workin'-class businessmen, that's the only way I can put it. They'll bend the rules any way they can, an' do their best to keep out the nick. Do their utmost !'

6. Lasch (1996: 131) writes, in connection with New York, of the 'many autobiographers who have evoked both the rich background of New York's insular communities and the break with the old neighbourhood, at once painful and exhilarating, that enabled ambitious young people to make themselves at home in the international republic of letters. To reduce this complex narrative to the conventional saga of upward mobility . . . is to simplify it almost beyond recognition. The break is not irrevocable unless the object is conceived as success in the crudest sense of the term. Finding the world implies, above all, finding oneself through an imaginative return to one's roots, not losing oneself in the struggle to succeed or to acquire the cultural distinctions that go with material success. It is a common mistake to think that exposure to the world's culture necessarily leads to the loss or renunciation of one's particular subculture. Except for those whose only aim is complete assimilation – the ostentatious display of all the trappings of one's power and status – moving beyond ones parochial identity leads to a more complex, even to a painfully divided identity.'
7. John is very anxious about Millwall's future. Though he has never had a penchant for violence himself, the broader culture of which it was a part was what made Millwall uniquely meaningful for him. His general ambiguity in these matters does not prevent him from expressing unease about the possible consequences of the pressures on this tradition: 'I know a lotta the old blokes don't go no more, a lot of 'em ended up gettin' nicked for other reasons – credit cards an' all that – an' you don't really see 'em no more. They've sort of been lost, an' I don't know if there's anyone else . . . I mean, I'm not sayin' its a good thing or a bad thing but it bothers me that, like, not so much the *reputation*, but the *atmosphere* side of it will be just dead, we'll be like Charlton, or any a them.' John therefore notes, with some relief, a smaller-scale continuation of customary practices at the younger end of the support in recent seasons: 'I look at them kids behind the goal, an' they're nickin' the ball an' abusin' the goalkeeper, the little kids, y'know . . . I s'pose it'll always go on in different forms, y'know, there's bound to be a little 'ooligan mob, always will be.'

– 6 –

The Collective Imaginary and Ritualization: Bringing *Millwall* Alive

The deeply personal phenomenon of symbolization considered in the preceding chapter is the basis of individual participation in the Collective Imaginary. The accumulated experiences and meanings of what it is to *be* Millwall, sedimented as they are in the embodied agency of the majority of fans, are the primary resources out of which the transformations of match-day ritual are achieved. In this final chapter I will use descriptive fieldnotes from two additional games to explore how Millwallism is put into motion in the fullest sense.

Remembering the Tradition: A Death in the Family. Millwall *v.* Leicester City, 1.1.96

A little over two-and-a-half years after the last day at the Den, the death of Harry Cripps in December 1995 has precipitated a period of profound mourning among Millwall fans, in particular those in their mid-thirties and beyond who have personal memories of watching him play. Younger fans, aware by way of the inter-generational reproduction of the tradition of the significance of Harry's iconic status as the personification of Millwallism, understand the outpouring of grief in their own ways. At the first home fixture against Leicester following his death, Harry is honoured with a one-minute commemorative silence before the game.

It is a bitterly cold and grey afternoon. The bleakness of the sky presents a perfect backdrop for the sombre crowds moving slowly toward the all-seated, rationally planned and fully convenienced New London Stadium, half a mile or so from the old Den. Immediately outside the main entrance to the stadium is a kind of folk-shrine which has become popular with football fans since the 1989 Hillsborough disaster, with flowers, scarves, a portrait of Harry, and written messages covering the whole. All who pass it stop to observe, stamping their feet against the cold as a freezing wind rustles the cellophane and flowers. The funereal atmosphere of the stadium's environs is carried over into the breeze-block thoroughfares, grey four-square stands and blue plastic seats of the interior.

The ground is half full with mute figures huddled inside coats and collars. Shortly before kick-off the one minute silence is announced, and the crowd of

9,953 rises as one to its feet. Absolute silence is maintained for the minutes duration by 9,952 of those present. In the upper tier of the East Stand one individual, clearly the worse for drink, punctures the silence with a series of indecipherably slurred exhortations. Baseball cap askew and red face glazed over, he appears at every moment to be on the verge of collapse. He is assiduously ignored by those around him who are intent on honouring Harry, perhaps remembering who he was, what he meant and even meditating on the unlikelihood of a man of his type ever representing the club again. His death is a serious blow, for he was the primary living symbol of Millwallism, a figure occupying a nodal point on that spine of remembered history that connects the present with the past. His untimely death has come in a moment when that spine and the expressive culture that structures its perception and brings it to life are under increasing threat of dissipation. There is much to remember and consider, and the silence – with this one exception – is profound in its weight, and pregnant with undischarged emotions of the deepest kind.

As the silence ends, the drunk is immediately surrounded by an angry crowd infuriated with his spectacularly disrespectful behaviour. Beginning in the shouts and gestures of heated argument, the scene soon shifts to pushing and shoving. The culprit, who appears to be angry about something himself, offers no display of contrition, and is buffeted from side to side as others join the confrontation. An awareness of the confrontation spreads out across the stand in ever larger waves, as a local incident gradually attracts the attention of everyone in the section. Not everybody is sure of its cause. Is it a Leicester fan in the wrong place? A confrontation with a policeman or steward? Increasing numbers of individuals, as they become appraised of the facts, are rising from their seats, turning, and being drawn directly into the fray. Two entire blocks of seating begin to demand his removal from the stadium. There are calls to 'Smack the cunt!' '*Do* the cunt!' 'Show some fuckin' respect! 'Sort 'im out, for fuck's sake!' 'DO THE FUCKIN' CUNT!'

Still he refuses to budge. Someone approaches from behind and punches him in the back of the head, which snaps forward violently almost throwing him to the ground. He corrects himself and stands upright. Immediately another man comes from the side and lands a full and open-handed slap across the front of his face. He is struck more blows as the huddle around him intensifies. He gives the appearance of being in the eye of a hurricane, but is being kept upright by the pinioning effects of the narrow seating aisles. He is buffeted this way and that in a maelstrom of punches, screams and shouts from faces thrust forward, generating a blanket of breath-mist and spittle. The game kicks off with the situation unresolved, for the culprit, beaten and buffeted as he is, will not voluntarily stand down.

For the moment, the game has become an irrelevance. A consensus emerges that events cannot proceed until the culprit has been completely removed from sight: 'Get the cunt out of it so we can watch the game!' Stewards are called for and move in, but are their usual incompetent selves in the face of what is by now a bitterly enraged crowd. At this stage something virtually unprecedented happens, in that many in the crowd are calling for the police to resolve things by making an arrest. Six policemen move up the crowded steps, settle a seething mob still throwing abuse and occasional punches at the recalcitrant, and remove him from his seat. He is marched down the steps and out of the ground to massed chants of 'Scum! Scum! Scum! Scum!' The police, rewarded with cries of 'Well done old Bill!' receive what may for them be a first at Millwall, when they are given a round of good-natured and appreciative applause.

The game is now five minutes old, and as the last of the arresting officers disappears out of sight, attention turns to the field of play. The already heightened atmosphere is now crackling with raw emotion, spine-tingling in its intensity. There are shouts of 'Let's do it for 'arry boy!' and chants of the long dormant favourite 'Oh 'arry, 'arry, 'arry, 'arry, 'arry, 'arry, 'arry Cripps . . .'. From the same era, 'Ra ra, zigga zagga Kitchener' echoes from some of the older fans. Nothing which takes place on the pitch in the first half – Millwall are in indifferent form – resonates with the incendiary atmosphere of the beginning of the game, and things eventually quieten down. However, halfway through the second half, the entire tempo of the game and atmosphere are raised by one incident. Ben Thatcher, a young defender enormously popular at Millwall for his guile, tenacity and emergent aura of personal inviolability, robs a Leicester forward of the ball on the Millwall eighteen-yard line. He sets off on a long, surging run with all of the vigour, passion and aggression of Cripps himself. Now the collective has something to bite on, and within moments the ground is alive with noise, movement, clamour. *No one likes us*, *Fuck 'em all* and *The Lion's Roar* swell up, clash and surge around the stadium, punctuated by cries of 'Oh, 'arry 'arry . . .' as the mimetic repertoire of cathartic corporeal remembrance and celebration is played out with raised arms, clenched fists, wild eyes and frenetically shaking bodies. The ghost of Harry Cripps looms ever larger over the proceedings now as *Millwall*, with the full weight of its fierce and passionate, volatile and inviolate, unforgiving and hilarious past, comes alive, rises up and hangs in the air like an experiential fog. It is no longer a 'metaphor' or a 'symbol' but a state of heightened consciousness and being connected to the past, alive to the moment and projected into the future. The space of the stadium and almost all those within it are crackling with raw pride, convulsed by an electrifying cascade of sound, movement and emotional release. It almost seems to be 1970 again, back in the old and true Lion's Den, inviolate, sacred, irreplaceable: Harry is on the rampage, the opposition forwards are running scared, and *the lions are roaring*.

The death of Millwall's defining, exemplary player-symbol throws into the highest possible relief the uncertainties maturing beneath the surface of Millwallism since the move from the Den. Harry's memorial game is therefore perhaps the best place to look for insight into the ways in which the Collective Imaginary manages to maintain its shape and integrity in these straitened times, and is an exemplary – if extraordinary – example of the workings of ritualization. The depth of ritualization's affective sources is indicated first of all by the ferocity – and unanimity – of the response to the ritual-defaulter. An event that was always going to be emotionally highly charged was ignited and made devastatingly raw by this transgressive puncturing of the semantic field structuring the commemorative ritual. This violation of the implicit rules of appropriate practice was, perhaps, all the more shocking for being isolated. The disturbance of the solemnity of the occasion and its necessarily distinctive psychic atmosphere tore at raw emotional nerves in the very moment that was designed to contain and express them. A silence created for an essential experience of collective commemoration and meditation was destabilized by a lack of ritual mastery, which cut to the heart of and undermined the seriousness of the occasion. The lack of respect for Harry's memory and for the deepest perspectives of Millwallism itself, simply had to be punished, and the transgressor removed from the very space of ritual itself. The unanimity of the crowd was immediate, implicit and absolute, demonstrating a shared feel for a correct practice that was clearly prior to any discursive explication or argumentation. The collective knew, as one, that it was *just wrong*. Given this, the intensity of atmosphere manifest later in the proceedings can be regarded not only as an extraordinary response to already extraordinary circumstances, but as a concerted effort to defend the integrity of ritualization and the impulses of practical mastery themselves.

Consider then the range of techniques whereby the collective brings *Millwall* alive and actualizes it in the present. The pervasively ritualized nature of linguistic expression at Millwall, which is characterized by a particular form of individual comment, song and chant, marks the beginning-point of the transformation. Situated between collectively formalized and free-individual expression is a stratum of fixed linguistic formulae which, while uttered spontaneously, nevertheless constitutes a stable repertoire of ritual invocation. In a situation in which Millwall players are failing to sufficiently press the ball in midfield the cry is 'Put 'em under!' (i.e. pressure). Lack of team cohesion is met with 'Sort it out Millwall!'. Millwall players faced with a particularly aggressive or difficult opponent will be urged to 'Do 'im!' The ubiquitous 'Come on Millwall!' speaks for itself. The significance of these utterances is that they mark the borderline, in terms of individual participation in the flow of the game and ritual, between individual expression and collective ritualization. For they are already restricted, codified in usage, and are appropriate in generally understood and specific contexts. That inchoate roar of the aroused crowd (short of expressive unison) which attends particular moments of drama is largely composed of these utterances, and others like them. They are best understood, therefore, as representing the first point of engagement on the upward curve to a unified ritual expression, a nodal point in the activation of the ritual consciousness brought into being at the point where creative individual comment and free expression trail off. This use of linguistic formulae, while obviously rooted in everyday vernacular, represents a decisive break with everyday speech. Disassociated from the dialogical flows of routine social discourse, they allow for an intermediate stage of expression which, despite this disassociation, connects participants to those social contexts beyond the stadium from which they are drawn. Thus are they the first point of departure from discursive language, and are in their restriction the foundation blocks of genuinely ritualistic activity.

Here this actualization has both specific and general components. Following the individual cries of 'Come on Millwall!', 'Come on you Lions!' and the more specific 'Let's do it for 'arry!', the chants of *oh, 'arry 'arry!* and *ra ra, zigga zagga, Kitchener!* are the first to occupy the semantic void left by the end of the minute's silence and the expulsion of the ritual defaulter, and may never have been heard before by a sizeable minority of the crowd who are below twenty-five years of age. These chants are summoned up by the guardians of Millwall's older lore, the men in their mid-thirties and beyond who have vivid memories of Harry in action and a sense of Millwallism as deeply connected to its past. The mnemonic effect of reviving these chants is instantaneous, recollecting and harnessing an embodied sphere of affective memory and experience accumulated over years spent in ritual space and time, and igniting the atmosphere for *everybody* in the stadium.

Once ignited, the more contemporary and universally known elements of the repertoire come into play in a spontaneous fashion. These solidify and stabilize the nascent moment of collective consciousness and affective unity and set up the expressive semantic field in all of its customary dimensions. Thousands of voices, immediately and spontaneously pick up and move through the invariant incantations, so that distanced or neutral observation quickly become all but impossible. *No One Likes Us*, *Fuck 'em All* and *The Lion's Roar* swirl around in and completely fill the psychic space of the stadium until one's perception of events is drastically altered. The quickening of the blood and a humming, incandescent emotionality are overwhelming, but there is no transcendental loss of self. Rather, the socially specific self expands into an extraordinarily heightened but demotically *situated* magnification of its everyday modalities. An anthropologically distinct and all-encompassing sense of archetypal being (*Millwall, south London*) is summoned up and, as I have noted, hangs in the air as a field of experiential possibility in which the individual members of the collective engage in their own ways on the basis of personal commitment and ritual expertise.

The core of this expertise lies in a feel for matching appropriate modes of physical and vocal expression to the playing-out of events in the stadium as a whole. The speed with which these are picked up and circulated around the crowd is critical, allowing the collective to activate its full dimensions as if possessed of a group mind. This gives ritual its unorchestrated but reliable, essential *form* (Connerton 1989: 52), and constitutes match-day activity not as the expression of certain things but as the *only way* of expressing a shared sense of the world. The very absence of formal leadership and orchestration in itself indicates the fact that this sense of things is embodied and tacitly understood by the majority of participants.

The collective is drawn together and unified by an absorption in a body of expression characterized by the qualities of *invariance*, *formalization* and *restriction*. The embodied participant is, among other things, a repository of specific knowledge and experience and it requires only immersion in these customary forms for the deeply sedimented memory and consciousness of what it means to *be* Millwall to be mnemonically and mimetically triggered. The commitment to singing the same songs, performing the same motions and being in the same place time and again generates a block of ritualized experience in which the body, once replaced in the context in which these experiences were accumulated, can become literally and affectively saturated with the sense of *being* Millwall. These biographical and pre-conscious dispositions require only the congregational summoning up of the Millwall atmosphere to rise to the surface and, for the duration of the ritual, to take over the person. This is what *The Lion's Roar*, *No One Likes Us* and their attendant modes of physical expression – always the same, always there, always effective – are for. As absolutely central ritual utterances, they could not be of more import.

'You Can't Argue with a Song: Liturgy and Memory

Defining the role and nature of 'liturgical' or congregational language is central to an understanding of how collective orientation/memory is organized in the ritual context. Connerton makes two main points about how liturgical language – critically endowed with *invariance* – works. First, '. . . it does not employ forms of communication which have propositional force'. Second, and as a corollary of this, liturgical language is 'a certain form of action and puts something into practice. It is not a verbal commentary on an action external to itself; in and of itself liturgical language *is* action' (Connerton 1989: 57). It is in its powerfully mnemonic aspect that ritual language is most significant. This mnemonic force is derived from two central characteristics of such a language: it is both performative and formalized. The thinking of Maurice Bloch in a related area can help us to understand the significance of these points.

Proceeding from the assertion that it is unsatisfactory to both isolate symbols from ritual processes and subsequently interpret them simply as meaning-containing units, Bloch argues that

> Symbols in ritual cannot be understood without a prior study of the nature of the communication medium of ritual in which they are embedded, in particular singing and dancing, and that once this has been done we find that symbols cannot any more be understood as units of meaning on the Saussurian signifier/signified model. (Bloch 1989: 19)

It is the formalized aspects of ritual language which Bloch regards as most characteristic. Adapting Bernstein's general schema, he argues that in ritual ordinary forms of verbal communication are changed in favour of a 'restricted' mode which is centred upon highly stylized speech and singing. We cannot, therefore, assume in this kind of language the semantic processes of a more ordinary communication. This occurs because, as a form of language is being operationalized in which syntax does not articulate freely, the capacity of language to convey argument is reduced, and the propositional force of language is transformed. It is in this context that Bloch laments a generalized anthropological disinterest in linguistic analysis, arguing that ritualized speech, singing and dancing are of a communicative piece and may be approached theoretically as constituent parts of a communicatively formalized whole.

In this view, song and dance appear not as secondary or alternative manifestations of communicative practice, but as integral components of the mnemonics and mimetics of ritual. Citing an example from his own work, Bloch suggests that

> the bodies of the participants are not used in the same way as they would be in a non-ritual context, that is to say the participants dance. The voices of the participants are not used in an everyday way, that is, the participants use their language in a particular way: formalized speech and singing. A purely formal analysis of the symbols of the ceremony would simply miss out this central fact. (1989: 22)

It is the central purpose of ritual language and communication, then, not to somehow discursively represent particular social or moral forms and the identities located in them, but to operationalize, enact and experience them. For – to give Bloch's examples – speech-making, intoning spells and singing all occur as part of a process of transformation *from* 'secular discursive language' (1989: 22).

Bloch does not suggest that formalized ritual language is meaningless, but rather contends two types of meaning. If logic depends upon the flexibility of features of linguistic articulation, then the effect of 'removing the possibility of alternatives from the mode of communication, as is done by formalization, makes what is being said beyond logic' (Bloch 1989: 32). Following J.L. Austin, Bloch locates meaning in formalized language not in discursive articulation but in illocutionary or performative force. If illocutionary force prevails at the expense of its propositional counterpart in the language of ritual, a critical question emerges as to how it communicates without explanation. It is this point which calls into question the hermeneutic enterprise. If rituals manage to generate and sustain semantic fields of communicative expression without explaining anything, then to what extent is it valid to ask of ritual expression 'what does it explain/say/mean?'

Bloch's account of ritual intonation leads him into an analysis of song, and illustrates the significance of the concept of illocutionary force in the analysis of ritual. Religious rituals, to take the most obvious example, have a number of central characteristics. To begin with, intonation involves restricting the range of choice of vocabulary, the choice of syntactic forms, the range of acceptable illustrations, and the body of knowledge from which suitable illustrations can be drawn. Next, the characteristically sing-song nature of these intonations places them midway between singing and speaking, with the effect of further reducing the possibility of variation in vocabulary, syntax, style and so on. Intonation thus consists in nothing but repeating what has already been said previously. Indeed the difference between intoning and singing is slight:

> It consists first of the ever more complete denial of choice of intonation and rhythm, and secondly in moving towards rhythms and intonations more remote from the norms of formal speech . . . Song is, therefore, nothing but the end of the process of transformation from ordinary language which began with formalization. From the point of view of ritual this transformation is, however, a most important stage since singing is so often and so prominently an integral part of religious action. (Bloch, 1989: 37)

Millwall's Collective Imaginary, then, can be thought of as articulated through a semantic field characterized by a primarily *illocutionary* communicative repertoire. Ritual singing tends to have as a central feature a fixity of articulation that leaves little or no space for individual variation, as

> the propositional force of all song is less than that of spoken words in an ordinary context. The songs sung by groups of people in unison which characterize so much of ritual are particularly extreme examples of lack of individual creativity. (Bloch 1989: 36)

This lack of individual creativity is seen by Bloch as the prelude to the possibility of authoritarian domination, in which participants may be led inexorably towards a state of affective subjugation and conformity by the internal momentum and structure of the ritual process. But if this model is persuasive in the context of a pedagogy of 'traditional authority', other readings of ritual using these ideas are possible. At Millwall these spontaneously generated restrictions on expression derive from a fundamental understanding of the need for conformity of participation. This is the prerequisite and the great strength of the ritualization process. Forms of expression – verbal, corporeal or sartorial – are restricted within a relatively narrow range, and in general are structured by those commonly understood frames of cultural reference that enable participation to proceed through inference and implication, metaphor and mimesis. In their very structure and application, songs and chants express all of these tendencies.

Brought into play in response to highly specific but ritually predictable circumstances, the Millwall songs, which in terms of expression are always the same and admit no individual variation, cohere the collective on the basis of unified performance and shared understandings of appropriate use. Once a song or chant is established in the repertoire it tends to find its place in the run of ritual events in these kinds of terms. All songs and chants are simple and repetitive, and the more popular tend to be intensely, cyclically performed.

This preoccupation with discursively restricted but affectively and psychologically unifying songs is exemplified by the way in which the one word – Millwall – comprises the entire lyric content of no less than five pieces. These I will deal with shortly, but it is worth noting here that this represents restricted language-use of a profound order, and is generated from within the collective itself. It bears repeating that no 'leadership', authoritarian or otherwise, is involved. Events are neither formally led nor absolutely statically objectified. This kind of ritual activity is based upon a participant use of what Bourdieu calls *ritual mastery.* This is an aspect of the more general conception of *practical mastery,* a sphere of experience grounded in those systems of classifying schemes – or *habitus* – and which, as we have seen, act as instruments for ordering the world possessed by similarly socialized agents. These schemes of practical mastery 'come to be embedded in the very perceptions and dispositions of the body and hence are known only in practice as the way things are done' (Bourdieu 1977: 94). In this context, ritual mastery is closely related to everyday social practice and relates to that implicit sense of knowing how particular things are done, and the inculcation of which in individuals is a primary characteristic of the *habitus.* Ritual stems from a 'practical mastery of the schemes of ritualization as an embodied knowing, as the sense of ritual seen in its exercise . . . *a cultural sense of ritual cannot be isolated from the other senses of the ritualized person*' (Bell 1992: 107, my emphasis).

This, in essence, is Bourdieu's idea of ritualization, with ritual practice characterized not by 'ritual' as a static or reified entity, but as a central and pervasive component of practical existence. At Millwall such ritualization proceeds on the basis of a collective participation, demonstrating an apparently spontaneous application of invariant expressive forms, which is underpinned by an implicit awareness in individuals of what is appropriate in any given context. Ritual practice is therefore organized around the constitution of a communicative, experientially inhabited semantic field in which these overwhelmingly invariant forms find expressive application according to both the rhythm of a game as it unfolds, and a concomitant sense of the rhythm of ritual embodied by participants. In this context Bloch's anxieties about the lack of individual creativity are misplaced. Collective participation of this kind is premised most obviously in the singing of songs, and on a powerfully desired experience of univocality which is far less concerned with 'discursively' explaining something than with summoning up an intensely experiential, 'commemoratively' felt identity and manner of being.

If the central and most apparent characteristic of ritualized expression at Millwall is to be found in singing, and most clearly in the effectively wordless unisonance in the seemingly primordial drone-like *Lion's Roar*, then it is in the very extremity of its formalization that its strength as a ritual resource is located. As Bloch says, 'You cannot argue with a song' (1989: 37). Such songs are not for arguing with because ritual thus enacted is neither explanatory nor discursive. Its core purpose and power lie in its capacity to activate an experiential sphere located, as Bourdieu has it, on the other side of discourse.[1] This is the real significance of embodiment and 'practical consciousness' in processes of ritualization, and Millwall is, in its resolutely non-bourgeois cast of culture, an exemplary case.

Returning to Connerton, we can appreciate more fully the vital role that formalized language plays in the ritual process. The significance of the concept of illocutionary force, as applied to ritual, is that is an essentially performative, communicative practice. Ritual language forms presuppose

> certain attitudes . . . which come into effect at the moment when, by virtue of the annunciation of the sentence, the corresponding act takes place. Or better : that act takes place in and through the enunciation. Such verbs do not describe or indicate the existence of attitudes: they effectively bring those virtues into existence by virtue of the illocutionary act. (Connerton 1989: 58)

Thus a rendition of *No One Likes Us*, or *The Lion's Roar* does not – and here the limitations and distortions of hermeneutic textualization are clear – primarily constitute a discursive formulation of a collective identity. Rather, the effect of such invocations at moments of high collective emotion is to mnemonically trigger, both as an expression and an effect of ritual mastery, an experientially intense and embodied activation of that identity for those individuals who invest in achieving it. It is in this sense that the process of ritualization at Millwall is more commemorative and experientially embodied than representational or discursive. The level of embodied, tacit cultural know-how required to generate such experiences and forms is itself an important expression of practical mastery – these things do not happen by mistake. And it is implicit that these experiences may not be reproduced at the individual level.

Consider the process whereby ritualization is accomplished. The crowd arrives for a game and socializes informally on a small group and individual basis. Gradually something that begins to look like a collective accumulates within the space of the stadium. This is followed by series of conventionalized and invariant songs and chants in particular sections of the crowd in the lead up to kick-off. By the time the game kicks off the crowd is ready (at least momentarily, often in more sustained ways on big occasions) to come alive, generate its semantic–affective field, and constitute and experience itself as *Millwall.*[2]

Critically, Connerton notes that the performatives that structure this kind of congregational activity are also encoded in postures, gestures and movements, that the formalization of bodily expression mirrors the same process in the sphere of language, and that the

> limited resources of ritual posture, gesture and movement strip communication clean of many hermeneutic puzzles . . . such performative 'doings' are particularly effective, because unequivocal and materially substantial, 'ways of saying'; and the elementariness of the repertoire from which such 'sayings' are drawn makes possible at once their performative power and their effectiveness as mnemonic systems. (1989: 58)

The apparent informality of physical culture at Millwall should not obscure the essentially ritualistic invariability that it communicates. This invariability is, again, the product of particular forms of ritual mastery and embodiment. The bodily hexis of given groups expresses the ways in which individuals incorporate the dispositionary and perceptual schemes of the *habitus*. Socialization, as Margaret Mead (1964: 61) noted, can involve orientations acquired at a deep level by means not of imitation, which presupposes a conscious effort, but mimesis. This mimetic instinct is at the core of the ritualization process. The rehearsal of *habitus*-grounded, implicitly formalized bodily practice and expression involves a 'practical reactivation which is opposed to both memory and knowledge . . . below the level of consciousness, expression and the reflexive distance which these presuppose' (Bourdieu 1986: 69). This is emphatically not a matter of deliberate, calculated 'performance', as 'the body believes in what it plays at: it weeps if it mimes grief. It does not memorise the past, it enacts the past, bringing it back to life' (Bourdieu 1986: 69).

It is this mimetic capacity which makes possible that activated bodily experience so characteristic of the ritual context at Millwall, when collective, unified singing and particular physical postures are fused in a rendition of the core *doing songs*. In this way participation is focused less upon saying/describing anything than activating a state of being and Millwall fans demonstrate a mastery of subtle and powerful ritual processes:

> every social order systematically takes advantage of the disposition of the body and language to function as depositories of deferred thoughts that can be triggered off at a distance in space and time by the simple effect of re-placing the body in an overall posture which recalls the associated thoughts and feelings, in one of the inductive states of the body which, as we know, give rise to states of mind. (Bourdieu 1986: 69)

The repetitive and ongoing experience of attending Millwall games, of being in the stadium week after week, year after year, makes the club an exemplary site of mnemonically triggered collective experience. In the collective mnemonics of ritual practice, the personal history of participation and the general history – the tradition – of the club become fused. In the context of the new stadium, this has placed a premium on the capacity to inhabit the new space in the old ways. Enforced spatial disruption has highlighted the foundational fact of Millwallism: *Millwall* is not its owners, its administrators, its players or even its ancestral ground. Its essence is embodied in the fans themselves, in a specific sphere of reproducible and ongoing collective experience and memorialization. It is this commemoration and experiential perpetuation of the tradition, in what at times appears to be an inimical physical environment to these purposes, that lies at the heart of the Collective Imaginary's expressive practices. If the intensity of these practices has been somewhat reduced in recent seasons, there are still infrequent occasions, exemplified by those such as I have described, when the full weight of the tradition and its extraordinarily powerful affective force are summoned up by the collective memory.

Thus the implicit and unelaborated ritual mechanisms that create the *Millwall We* are brought into being in the space of the stadium. They are the most fundamental aspect of Collective Imaginary activity and constitute the core attraction in allegiance to Millwall. However, their foundational status makes other things possible. By bringing the experientially tangible Collective Imaginary alive and making it real, ritualized contests with other, contradistinctive regional and footballing identities become possible. Ritualization processes, therefore, should be thought of as having the capacity to bring *Millwall* alive as an end in itself, *and* to organize specific rivalries into a hierarchical taxonomy of regional, masculinist cultural formations.

Who the Fucking Hell Are *You*?: Doing, Saying and Ritual Contest

I noted earlier that a central feature of English football culture lies in the ritualized juxtaposition of contradistinctive senses of collective identity. In constituting these subcultural rivalries in this vital sphere of practice, the fans again exhibit an expertise concerned with the contrastive manipulation of binary oppositions. Many anthropological studies have shown these to be practically universal, and such deeply rooted tendencies towards rituals of polarization may thus be thought of as expressions of the kinds of analogical categorization and interpretation that are characteristic of the 'savage mind' (Levi-Strauss: 1966). The workings of ritual contestation at Millwall represent a concrete case of the continued persistence of forms of reflection and expression generated by immersion in an essentially pre-modern 'science of the concrete':[3] the social world is categorized, thought through and made sense of via procedures that owe less to an abstracting, logical rationality than to a form of *habitus*-grounded intuitive sense.[4] Most obviously at Millwall, the we/you, what-we-are/what-you-are (or are-not) polarization organizes the constitution of an expressive–semantic field upon which the ritual contest of identities is played out. This proceeds, as Connerton makes plain, via the invariant congregational constituting of the 'we' as, for example in '*We* are, *we* are Millwall,' or 'No one likes *us*' or '*We* are the Millwall and *we* are the best, *we* are the Millwall so fuck all the rest!' However, these assertions are not designed to always stand alone, for though they represent the foundational core of ritual activity, they may be complemented, for example, with 'Who the fucking hell are *you*?' '*You're* just a bunch of wankers' or '*You* dirty Northern bastards'. The inclusion of such pieces in the repertoire indicates a clear and central purpose of the ritual drama, in their unambiguous and schematizing contrast between sets of fans and the forms of collective identity which they are taken to represent. Such simple oppositions are merely a beginning however, for as Bell observes in relation to the thinking of Robert Hertz, Victor Turner, Terence Turner and Bourdieu,

> one set of relations comes to be related to another set: right–left is analogised to inside–outside or good–evil, while male–female is linked to right–left, front–back and so on. These relationships both generate and presuppose complex chains of associations and taxonomic relations. (1992: 102)

At Millwall the juxtaposing of identities and those qualities held to inhere in them allows the semantic field to constitute and sustain some detailed, if largely implicit, understandings of these contrasts. The symbolic binaries and sets of positive and negative taxonomic associations around which the Collective Imaginary at Millwall revolves include, as central,

Male/Female, Virile/Effete, White/Black, Natural/Cultivated, Hard/Soft,
Strong/Weak, Passionate/Dispassionate, Volatile/Pacified, Metropolitan/Provincial,
Southern/Northern, Authentic/ 'Gloryhunting'.

Though some of the categories are not without a degree of ambiguity, Millwallism is understood, embodied and articulated for the most part via the positive qualities in these oppositions. For big or important games, these meanings may be activated in contrastive ways to constitute the *We* as characterized by all of the former positives and the *You* as (at least some of) the latter negatives. The semantic field that contains the Millwall *We* can be constructed, in the choice of songs, chants, expressive movements and the nature of their renderings, with differing dimensions and mnemonically triggered taxonomic sets to suit particular cases.

The ritual forms in which these associations are expressed, then, may be bitterly cruel and entirely devoid of empathetic fellow-feeling. Ultimately it is the psycho-social efficacy of two broad and simultaneous processes which are at stake in this contest. The first is concerned with the ritual constitution of internal cohesion in and through the use of division (Bourdieu 1977: 163); the second with the establishment of hierarchic relationships based on the ritually achieved and demonstrated superiority of *Millwall*. The latter functions here as a metaphor for specific forms of embodied social agency ranked, according to the internal logic of Millwallism's system of heuristic categories, at the top of the folk-taxonomic league table of England's masculine cultural formations. Millwall, when used in this experientially metaphorical sense, connects the club with its historical backdrop of south-east-London cultural traditions and forms in an implicit articulation of a peculiarly combative and metropolitan–masculinist understanding of the cultural universe: *We are the Millwall/south-east London, and we are the best.*

Beneath an ostensible similarity of expression the Collective Imaginary can generate, depending on the game and its context, very different atmospheres. Patterns and histories of rivalry and conflict, as well as the level of siginificance of the fixture itself, therefore help to determine the ways in which the semantic expressive field at a game will be inflected. Although the core qualities of Millwallism are symbolically invariant, certain of them may be prioritized for expression depending on context. It is clear that the central organizing principle of this flexibility lies in the use of song, two broad types of which are analytically distinguishable. These frame and determine the ways in which *Millwall* can be both *said* and *done*.

Saying Songs and Doing Songs

Saying Songs

These contain explicit discursive messages designed for communication with a juxtaposed imaginary. They are intended to insult, hurt, abuse and annoy that other on the one hand, and to confirm and exalt Millwallism on the other. They are made available to textual interpretation, once placed in the semantic field of a given occasion of rivalry. These kinds of song play a central, vituperative role in traducing the opposed imaginary, and the *saying* songs are therefore invariably coupled with those performing the opposite function, so that, in the game against Crystal Palace:

Palace, Palace, who the fuck are Palace?
Who the fucking hell are you?
Ooh aah Eric Cantona
You're just a bunch of wankers
You're shit and you know you are

are alternated with Millwall *doing* songs in order to set up and maintain a semantic–expressive field around the game and maintain the illocutionary force of performative Millwallism. The juxtaposition, as we saw in Chapter Three, is between *Millwall* as Inner-Urban, Working-class, Tough, Virile, Passionate, Volatile and Dangerous set against *Palace* as Suburban, Middle-class, Weak, Effete, Dispassionate, Pacified and Harmless.

In the case of the match against Everton, where the virility and toughness of the ideal-type 'scouse' other is accepted rather than challenged, the performance of the saying songs is intended to revile the identity of Liverpudlians in a more general sense. Thus

In your Liverpool slums
I would rather be a Paki than a Scouse
Does the social know you're here?
Sign on, sign on
Sing when you're stealin'
Oh Merseyside is full of shit

express a contrast between *Millwall* as Metropolitan ('Cockney'), Witty, Sharp, Hostile, Ready and Passionate and *Everton* as Provincial northern ('Scouser'), Stupid, Dull, Docile, Styleless and Dispassionate.

In games against West Ham United (the 'Hammers') – probably the club with a Collective Imaginary that looks most like Millwall's – the contest is played out entirely in terms of toughness, virility and cultural authenticity within *Londonness*:

Millwall as	**West Ham** as
Very Tough	Tough
Very Dangerous	Dangerous
Extremely Volatile	Volatile
'Authentic' London	'Plastic' Cockney

The hateful and frequently violent nature of this particular rivalry is signalled by a specifically tailored repertoire. This includes songs that say

He's only a poor little 'ammer,
His face is all tattered and torn,
He made me feel sick
So I hit him with a brick,
And now 'e don't sing anymore!
He's only a poor little 'ammer. . .

and

Chim-chimenee,
Chim-chimenee,
Chim-chim cheroo,
We hate those bastards in claret and blue!

One further example from games against Arsenal will serve to illustrate the way in which taxonomic components are adaptively recombined to suit particular circumstances. The semantic field for these games is organized around some of the themes already presented, but with different points of focus and emphasis. The most important thing to bear in mind here is the cultural tension between the north and south of the river. *Arsenal* stands in for north London itself, with all of the regionalist associations that *that* triggers for those from south of the river. The Millwall saying songs rendered at these games tend, therefore, to be of the generic *Who the fucking hell are you?*, *You're just a bunch of wankers* variety, intended to demonstrate that north Londoners, and Arsenal fans in particular, are not to be taken too seriously. It is the passion of rendition itself as an aspect of the Millwall *pageant* that is significant here, as the Millwall Collective Imaginary performs a ritualized drama of contrast between the two broad sets of class-based moral forms around which much of the overall argument of this work is organized:

Millwall as	**Arsenal** as
Working-Class virile	Middle-Class effete
Strong	Weak
Volatile	Pacified
Authentic Committed	Consumerist Gloryhunting
Characterful	Anodyne
Exuberant	Constrained

In addition to the saying songs outlined, there are a number of core, invariant ritual pieces which are brought into play in all games (with the obvious exception of 'Maybe it's Because I'm a Londoner' in local derbies), and which should be thought of as comprising both *saying* and *doing* elements. Here explicitly communicative and illocutionary elements are combined in order to simultaneously express and confirm the *Millwall We*, *and* discursively make a point:

'Fuck 'em all' (Melody: 'Bless 'em all')
Fuck 'em all,
Fuck 'em all
United, West Ham, Liverpool,
'Cos we are the Millwall and we are the best,
We are the Millwall so FUCK ALL THE REST

'Maybe it's Because I'm a Londoner'
Maybe it's because I'm a Londoner,
That I love London Town,
Maybe it's because I'm a Londoner,
That I think of her, wherever I go (whoah!),
I get a funny feelin' insida me (spunk!),
Jus' walkin' up an' down,
Maybe it's because I'm a Londoner,
That I love London Town (get off me sister!)

Doing Songs

These songs on the other hand, bereft as they are of instrumental semantic elements, carry the burden of actualizing and maintaining the Collective Imaginary. They are, given their critical role in generating the psycho-affective conditions in which this actualization can occur, the primary means through which everyday, discursive language is transformed into ritual utterance. The non- or para-linguistic nature of these is an example of the renunciation of propositional discourse in favour of illocutionary force.

The most heightened and intense example of this is *The Lion's Roar*, discussed below in connection with the game against Ipswich Town. The extraordinary drone-like utterance of this formula is entirely illocutionary, consisting of an excursion into pure vocalese on the basis of just the one word: Millwall.

'The Lion's Roar'
Miiiiieeeewuuuuuuuull

But it is not alone in this respect, as *Millwall* comprises the entire lyric content of four other central elements of the repertoire:

'Millwall' (Melody: 'Che sera sera')
Millwall, Millwall,
Millwall, Millwall, Millwall,
Millwall, Millwall, Millwall,
Millwall, Millwall.

'Millwall' (Melody:'Marching through Georgia')
Millwall, Millwall, Millwall,
Millwall, Millwall, Millwall,
Millwall, Millwall, Millwall,
Millwall, MILLWALL

'Millwall' (Melody: 'You'll Never Walk Alone')
Millwall, Millwall,
Millwall, Millwall,
Millwall, Millwall, Millwall,
MILLWALL, Millwall, Millwall . . .

'Millwall' (Melody: 'Amazing Grace')
Millwall, Millwall,
Millwall, Millwall,
Millwall, Millwall, MILLWALL,
Millwall, Millwall,
Millwall, Millwall,
Millwall, Millwall, Millwall . . .

These songs employ ritually restricted language of a high order, and in the utter absence of any discursive content are the exemplary *doing* songs: the *form* of them is the thing. As such they will confound forms of conventional sociological analysis derived from monological–intellectualist perspectives. Though these songs will be deployed in every game Millwall play, no juxtaposed identity is required for them to take off and achieve ritual efficacy; they are the foundational and constitutive elements of the expressive practices that bring *Millwall* into being. This is also the case, despite its rather more explicit and discursive tenor, with the anthem *No One Likes Us.*

In both its jubilant and defiant modes, this song is used to convey a much greater illocutionary force than its limited propositional content would appear to indicate. The most frequently rendered of all the Millwall songs, it is as likely to be the cornerstone of the achieved collective atmosphere at games where there is little or no interest in opposition fans as it is to structure the kinds of intensive contest examined above. Thus, while its at times limited discursive content makes it a notional *saying* song, its ritual centrality is derived, like the almost and wordless and counter-propositional pieces, from its *doing* function.

These *doing* songs, centrepieces of the repertoire and ritual forms in their own right, are the most enduring and significant pre-requisites of collective experience at Millwall. This is where the Collective Imaginary's constitution of *Millwall* – as a specifically altered state of ritual being – takes place, for Millwall fans alone. And some of the most spectacular manifestations of Millwallism in recent years have revolved less around high-profile juxtapositional conflicts, than what appear to be internal themes and preoccupations. The last game at the old Den and Harry Cripps's memorial fixture are two such extraordinary examples. The vital relegation game at Ipswich detailed involving no intensive juxtapositionary contest of rival identities was another illustration of the variability and flexibility of intention and purpose made possible by practical ritual mastery.

Millwallism's Pageant

Conceptions of the carnivalesque and grotesque realism can, as we have seen, be adapted to the analysis of Collective Imaginary ritualization. The carnival instinct remains strong among significant sections of Millwall's support, and the practice of symbolic inversion – most obviously of the moral order now obtaining in British football – has been a central characteristic of ritual activity in recent seasons. This is especially true in highly charged and important games. However, these practices neither end with symbolic inversions nor suggest moments of quasi-utopian possibility: they represent, through the ritual actualization of the Millwall identity, an experience that is not merely symbolic but *symbolized.* The setting up of a semantic and experiential field enables people to *be* Millwall in ways that are neither discursive nor merely gesturally oppositional to the prevailing (bourgeois–hegemonic) moral order within and without football. This is a point seriously neglected in the contemporary literature on carnival and transgression. Even the most insightful and important of these (Stallybrass and White 1986) overlooks the centrality of embodiment in the maintenance of the carnivalesque sensibility, and searches in the wrong places for contemporary manifestations of its survival. An obsession with texts and textuality obscures the fact that the persistence of the carnivalesque as an ontologically grounded cultural imperative does not, and cannot, find full expression in literary production, but exists in action. At the furthest reaches of their expression, grotesque–realist practices can achieve an extraordinarily affective, almost primordial power which no text could contain. Getting a grip on how these things work in what is often volatile, messy and unpleasant practice requires the search be undertaken in some hitherto unfashionable places.

Millwallism is one of these places. Opposition (or 'otherness') here is not rhetoricized, declaimed or discursively elaborated, rather it is instanced and lived. It resides not merely in words, but in deeds, not in explicate formulation but in specific and immemorial practices of the body. Any meaningful empirical manifestation of carnivalesque consciousness will, by definition, involve practices and sensibilities to some extent pre-dating the personality structures and perspectives of bourgeois modernity. It is vital to consider that their contemporary maintenance is likely to characterize cultural formations in which practical consciousness and embodied cultural reproduction has, to some extent, secured their survival. Carnivalesque activity in Millwallism does not express a simple transgression of norms and values in favour of discursively notional alternatives. Rather it activates a sphere of being and of experience that asserts its claim to (counter) legitimacy on the basis of historical continuity and practical reproduction. It contains no novelty, offers no fresh perspectives, generates no radical reappraisals. It operationalizes a world of experience and a mode of consciousness that say, simply, *here we are, we haven't gone away. This is what we're like, and we'll be staying around.*

All of this is accomplished through the ritualization process which, in the following example, is focused not so much on 'us versus them', as on 'this is us'. It is a peculiar sort of carnival, for it holds no promise of a better world. It celebrates the persistence of the relatively stable and embodied sense of the world of ritual activists which perhaps looks less like a carnival than a *pageant*: an invariable and dramatic enactment of expressively stable historical tableaux.

Ipswich v. *Millwall, 5.5.96*

This game at Ipswich is vitally important for Millwall. The Lions need to win in order to avoid what the fans consider to be a catastrophic relegation to the Nationwide second division, and there are 4,000–5,000 Millwall fans in attendance for this last league fixture of the season. All of the classical elements necessary for a serious carnival excursion are therefore in place. This is a vital game with a large away following, and that spirit of abandon – of a ritual ending in cyclical (seasonal) time – peculiar to the last day of the English football season.[5]

The area surrounding the Portman Road stadium in Ipswich is, as is usual on such occasions, swarming with many hundreds of Millwall fans who are giving mostly good humoured offence to the locals. The walk to the ground from the station, car parks and pubs in which many have been ensconced for the last couple of hours sets the general tone for what follows. The full panoply of Millwall-embodiment is brought to bear on the build up to the game: the easy, swaggering, confident bowling, raucous good humour and a sense of implicitly menacing collective inviolability which the overwhelmingly male Millwall following carries with it sets up the distinctive and unmistakeable atmosphere of a mobile cultural collectivity, of south Londoners in a provincial town. It is a case of *Millwall on tour.*

An hour before the game the Millwall section of the ground is raucous and chaotic, and appears, despite the all-ticket status and numbered seating allocation, to be overcrowded. Amidst this chaotic inhabitation of the stadium – standing on seats and in aisles, remonstrating with stewards and police – the congregation is finding its voice. *The Roar*, *Fuck 'em all* and repeated renderings of *No One Likes Us* establish the atmosphere.

The first moment of high drama comes just as the game starts. A number of cameramen, one with a video recorder, focus their lenses on the Millwall section of the crowd as it emerges into volatile life in the final moments before the kick off. This is a never popular activity with Millwall fans, many of whom are never slow to express their contempt for the various institutions of state authority and the mass media (see Chapter Two). The ferocity of collective objection to their presence, screaming, jeering, whistling, gesticulating and chants of *fuck off you cunts*, is sufficient to drive all but one (club? television? police?) video cameraman away.[6] His persistent scanning of the crowd becomes the focus of vituperative collective attention:

Who's the wanker,
Who's the wanker,
Who's the wanker with the camera?
Who's the wanker with the camera?
(Melody: 'Bread of Heaven')

The cameraman's personal battle of wills with the Millwall section concentrates the crowd's energies and heightens the already volatile atmosphere to a level which alarms the police, who (after perhaps three minutes) escort him from the touchline. He leaves to cheers and an almost deafening chorus of *No One Likes Us*.[7] This heightens an already fervent atmosphere and assures that much of the game will be played out against, in the Millwall section at least, an explosive and febrile backdrop.

With the game underway, the crowd becomes a hive of kinetic expression. People are standing in groups on chairs, in aisles and walkways. Chorus after chorus of *No One Likes Us* cascades across the stand. Shouts, screams, whoops and whistles, growls and roars fill the intermittent gaps between collective incantation. There is jumping, dancing, turning. Heads are angled back to open the throat and chest, the space above them filled with punching and gesticulating arms and hands. At the back of the stand a group of fifty or so voices sings (to the tune of 'She'll Be Coming round the Mountain') *There'll Be Nothin' Left of Ipswich if We Lose*. The general tenor of proceedings is a kind of churning affective wildness in which everything else in existence falls away to reveal an atemporal existential essence, composed of two aspects: We are Millwall, and we have to win.

However, Millwall do not win, and show few signs of being able to do so throughout a dreary and uneventful game. Little of the drama played out on the field is able to compete with or significantly contribute to the affective intensity of what is happening in the crowd as the first half grinds on. It is towards the end of the half that the Bakhtinian character of Millwallism's pageant comes into clearest focus, and centres on an instance of the well-established Millwall crowd favourite of keeping the ball.

The atmosphere moves up a gear in intensity when the ball flies high into the Millwall crowd, precipitating a spontaneous rugby-style scrum for possession of it. Once brought to ground, it is concealed for a few moments before being used for a game of crowd-volleyball, accompanied by shouts, from a majority, to 'keep it, keep it!' This is countered by a minority of more gentlemanly voices, calling for the ball to be returned. The general response is of spontaneous ludic hilarity, as the bulk of the crowd revel in the opportunity to savour the change in atmosphere that the ball keeping initiates.

The first effect is to entirely disrupt the momentum of the occasion and refocus attention onto the collective itself. With the drama of the game held in suspension, events shift to a new perceptual plane on which time and the linear motion of activity appear to be in stasis. This plane or plateau is the perfect experiential context for Millwall's carnivalesque pageant, for at this point in time, in the space of the stadium, the world is distilled down into one thing, which is admitting of no distractions. Millwallism is being spontaneously brought to life, condensed and paraded.

A specific form of ritual mastery and embodied participation orders what follows, as thousands unite in *being* Millwall under a heightened public gaze. Once activated and asserted in this way, a collectively playful and anarchic spirit pushes hard against the social and physical structures containing the event. A zestful and intuitive undermining of the regulative norms that frame the event – panopticized and pacified social space, restrained individualist conduct, sporting good manners and generally appropriate consumerist conduct – sweeps aside the previously obtaining atmosphere of competitive seriousness and replaces it with mischievous joy and wild hilarity.

The semantic hierarchy of the event is ritually reordered; from order to chaos; from seriousness to the loud laugh of grotesque realism; from a universalized 'respectable' and hegemonic social order to the particularized and irreverent instantiation of an embodied alternative to it.[8] It is not a momentary, discursive challenge to a prevailing moral order, but a collectively activated demonstration of the perspectives, orientations and varieties of embodied social consciousness that that order is elsewhere believed to have succeeded. For *We are Millwall*, this display seems to urge: read *We are vital, embodied, non-bourgeois, playful, volatile – and difficult . . .*

Thus the Collective Imaginary sets up and enacts a sphere of perceptorily heightened activity in which, through the mnemonic and mimetic capacities of the process of ritualization, individual symbolizations of Millwallism feed into moments of aggregative transcendence. The ball-keeping incident lasts less than two minutes, but completely alters the atmosphere. With the game once more underway the collective, in its effervescent and transfigured sense of itself and its openness to the moment, has only one place left to go: *into the Roar*.

Being effectively wordless, and lacking any decisive harmonic resolution, this merging of the resonating individual voice with sustained collective performance produces an atmosphere of extraordinary intensity, a kind of sonic field in which time stands still and being itself hangs, static and unelaborated in the air. As the roar of one singers dies another begins, crashing into and rolling over one another against the sustained aural backdrop of thousands of open throats and resonating chests. The collective is unified at a psychological level of profound depth. This is collective mnemonic immersion of the most extraordinary kind, and represents – despite being seen from without as savage, inchoate and moronic – an exemplary ritualizing practice which draws upon a deeply rooted and anthropologically widespread musical technique: the sonic constitution and activation of a group's implicit sense of the world. Such singing not only welds participants into a communal whole, it unites that whole to a larger whole which, as Turnbull suggests in a rather different context, includes 'the central fire, the camp itself, the clearing in which the camp is built, the forest in which the clearing stands, and whatever . . . contains the forest' (in Tuan 1993: 86).

Thus is a ritualizing community able to summon up and connect with a sense of the world lying beyond the ritual context, in this case a *habitus*-grounded sense of *south-east London* and the characteristic myths, social and moral forms and structures of feeling and experience this generates. The roar brings the collective and its world alive, and can overwhelm both participants and observers.[9] It lies at the affective epicentre of Millwallism, and once activated as the deepest possible experience of being Millwall, is not easily dissipated. It bears repeating that the 'discursive' dimension of all of this is negligible.

A prolonged invocation of the roar tends to make Millwall fans exhilarated, sure of themselves and *serious*. Its use on this occasion in Ipswich is followed by an extended period of relative calm, which obtains well into the second half of the game. Only as the game enters its final fifteen minutes does the collective intensively activate itself again when, conscious of the urgent need to score in a game in which Millwall have subjected the Ipswich goal to little pressure, the choruses of *No One Likes Us* and chants of *Millwall, Millwall, Millwall . . .* become more frequent and intense. With five minutes remaining the collective has worked itself, in its urgent promptings and roars of support, into a condition of manic emotional and physical effervescence.[10] The tension is all but unbearable, and the sense emerges of a build up of anxiety and emotion which may become difficult to contain.

Still the clock ticks on. The game is virtually over now, with Millwall repeatedly heaving the ball high into the Ipswich half in successive and desperate attempts to snatch last-minute salvation. The atmosphere reaches its fevered crescendo just as the whistle blows, arresting the Millwall section in its flight: Ipswich 0 – Millwall 0. Relegation. There is a momentary hiatus in which time again appears to stand still. And then all hell breaks loose.

A number of Ipswich fans at one end of the stadium turn spontaneously towards the Millwall section to administer the ritual *coup de grâce*: *Going down, going down, going down* is rendered with tangible satisfaction and some venom. Millwall fans are divided between a stunned, head-shaking silence and bitter anger. Within seconds first one, then two, and finally a shower of blue and white plastic seats are torn from their frames and hurled towards the Ipswich fans responsible for the slight, who retreat under the spinning shards and make their exit from the ground. The onslaught is soon redirected towards the police and stewards attempting to cope with the situation, culminating in a face-off between the sizeable minority of Millwall fans hurling seats and abuse, and the line of gradually retreating keepers of order. For many this explosion of destructive outrage appears to be the only viable form of catharsis on this day of heightened and negative emotion and wounded pride. The rest of the Millwall crowd, perhaps a half, confine themselves to a resigned silence and the familiar trance-like experience of absorbing profound disappointment.

Whether expressed in quiet desolation, vituperative articulation or destructive action, the sources of despair are common: the days are long gone when Millwall fans would revel in the anti-charisma of failure, and this relegation hurts. It is the responses which differ in these first moments of engagement of what will become, for many, a period of genuine depression.[11] The symbol and the self are as fused in defeat and despair as they are in victory and triumph, and a disconsolate hush gradually descends over the bulk of the collective for the gloomy shuffle towards the exits. Everyone is literally drained. The massive, extraordinary and frustrating emotional investment in ritual which the afternoon represents has not, despite its inherent satisfactions, been resolved by the hoped-for catharsis of triumphal glory.

The example of the Ipswich game, like those in the game against Bristol Rovers given in the last chapter and Leicester City earlier, throw into high relief the central expressive and ritual practices of the Collective Imaginary, characterized most of all by a kind of spontaneous invariance. Not all games generate such spectacular examples of the bringing alive of *Millwall*. Many less important games are played out against less intensive backdrops. And yet there tend to be at least one or two moments, however momentary and fleeting, of heightened rituality in every game that Millwall play. The sources of ignition of these moments are not always predictable, and according to the rhythms and sensibilities of practical mastery, often arise out of apparently slight moments in the drama of the game or crowd dynamics. Beneath the surface of events, this alertness, readiness and instinctive feel for appropriate participation is always present. Whether fully operational or not, the air at Millwall is at all times pregnant with the possibility for it, and the irreplaceable moments of experience that the Collective Imaginary is able to open up. The peculiarities of such moments – such pageantry – cannot be replicated elsewhere.

Over and above the pleasures of the game itself, this is what draws fans back, match after match, season after season. And this instinctive sacralizing love of the club provides a unique connection between the confirmed, exhilarating and expanded experience of a distinctive regional identity, and the mundane social contexts in which the sources of that identity are grounded.

The central importance of the expressive forms developed by groups such as Millwall's Collective Imaginary does not lie, as is widely and mistakenly believed, in discursive representation. A distinctive sphere of collective orality functions, rather, as an illocutionary aspect of an experiential ritual whole. This whole anchors and activates a powerfully affective sense of collective identity the more acute for its juxtaposition with contradistinctive others and/or its internally generated positioning within a hierarchy of regional masculine subcultures. It is as an expression of collective ritual and consequent practical mastery, and as an intensely lived experience whose significance extends far beyond the stadium, that football-based practice of this sort has its primary interest and force. Charged up, confirmed and strengthened, the participants can thus return to mundane reality, carrying the experience with them until next time.

At the level of practical ritualization, individuals with particular kinds of disposition and orientation have moulded an ostensible leisure institution to meet their identificatory and expressive needs. The maintenance of senses of collective and individual identity and social memory in changing historical circumstances within this medium has involved the purposeful development of a particular symbolic corpus (the primary symbol being something we can only call *Millwall* itself) derived from commonalities of social context and experience. People in complex societies only become committed to specific institutions and practices because they find them particularly, and probably uniquely, meaningful. Though the experience of being Millwall is made possible by a deeply personal fusion of symbol and self, it is brought most fully alive through participation in processes of ritualization. It is the experiential, affective and transformative capacity of ritual which enables an aggregative community of disparate individuals to fully cohere and make manifest modes of experience becoming increasingly rare in an age of pacific football consumption (with its burgeoning culture of ersatz 'carnival') in particular, and the civil privatism of liberal–indvidualist culture in general.

Notes

1. Like Bloch, Bourdieu's thinking is fully opposed to the 'textual' rendering of ritual forms based upon practical mastery: '. . . simply by bringing to the level of discourse – as onc must, if one wants to study it scientifically – a practice which owes a number of its properties to the fact that it falls short of discourse

(which does not mean it is short on logic) one subjects it to nothing less than a change in its ontological status the more serious in its theoretical consequences because it has every chance of passing unnoticed' (Bourdieu 1977: 120). As Bell notes, Bourdieu 'avoids all semblance of verbal or literary analysis . . . he eschews terms like metaphor, metonymy, analogy . . . ritual practice is always much fuzzier, avoiding the distinctive change in state that occurs when things are brought to the level of explicit discourse' (Bell 1992: 113).

2. Connerton provides a general model of congregational-liturgical formation, and the parallels are startling. After noting, as we have seen, that actions and attitudes are activated by illocutionary acts, he writes (1989: 59) that 'Liturgical language makes special use of "us" and "those"; the plural form, in "we" and "us", indicates that there are a number of speakers but that they are acting collectively, as if they were only one speaker, a kind of corporate personality. Prior to such pronomial utterance there exists an undifferentiated preparedness, expressed by the presence of all the participants in the place where the liturgy is to be celebrated. Through the utterance of the "we" a basic disposition is given definitive form, is constituted, among the members of the liturgical community. The community is initiated when pronouns of solidarity are repeatedly pronounced. In pronouncing the "we" the participants meet not only in an externally definable space but in a kind of ideal space determined by their speech acts . . . Performative utterances are as it were the place in which the community is constituted and recalls to itself the fact of its constitution.' A number of things follow from this. First, it alerts us to the importance of recognizing the fact that such collectives are far less interested in telling the world stories about themselves than in activating for themselves experiences of who and what they are. Second, it makes clear that the informal ritual processes developed by English football fans relate closely to the kinds of well established practice associated with the various cultic, religious and political rituals in which Connerton is interested . Third, it confirms the correctness and importance of Bourdieu's use of the concepts of practical and ritual mastery in accounting for the ways in which social groups use ritual processes to confirm, sustain and perpetuate the central identificatory principles of their *habitus*.
3. This 'science', in Levi-Strauss, orders the building of models of reality, of the self and the social world, in the 'savage' consciousness. But, as Geertz observes (1975: 352), 'they ['savages'] do so not as modern scientists do by integrating abstract propositions into a framework of formal theory, sacrificing the vividness of perceived particulars for the explanatory power of generalized conceptual systems, but by ordering perceived particulars into immediately intelligible wholes. The science of the concrete arranges directly sensed realities into immediately intelligible wholes . . . These become structural models representing the underlying order of reality as it were analogically.' Many people in

even late-modern societies continue to cognitize and interpret the world, I would suggest, in this kind of way; most especially populations still characterized by high levels of connectedness-to-background and 'concrete' social experience.

4. 'Intuitive sense', that is, as distinct from Levi-Strauss's universal structures of the human mind, alleged to govern all empirical configurations regardless of social conditions. Incorporating the role of the latter in ritual practices means, as Bourdieu observes, 'reconstructing the socially constituted system of inseparably cognitive and evaluative structures that organizes perception of the world and action in the world in accordance with the objective structures of a given state of the world. If ritual practices and representations are practically coherent, this is because they arise from the combinatorial functioning of a small number of generative schemes which are linked by relations of practical substitutability, that is, capable of producing results that are equivalent in terms of the "logical" requirements of practice. This systematicity remains loose and approximate because the schemes can receive the quasi-universal application they are given only in so far as they function in the practical state, below the level of explicit statement and therefore outside the control of logic, and in relation to practical purposes which require of them and give them a necessity which is not that of logic' (Bourdieu 1992: 94).
5. The maintenance of an alternative temporal sense in which life can continue to be imagined as a structure of exemplary recurrences outside of rational, linear time is of course vital in the lives of football fans, and in itself represents an orientation towards experience deeply antithetical to the cognitive structures of modernity. Under the conditions of the latter, Connerton notes (1989: 64), the celebration of recurrence can never be anything more than a compensatory strategy 'because the very principle of modernity itself denies the idea of life as a structure of celebrated recurrence. It denies credence to the thought that the life of an individual or community either can or should derive its value from acts of consciously performed recall, from the reliving of the prototypical. Although the process of modernisation does indeed generate invented rituals as compensatory devices, the logic of modernisation erodes those conditions which make acts of ritual re-enactment, of recapitulative imitation, imaginatively possible and persuasive.' The deep investment made in calendrical repetition by many football fans has clearly run counter to this erosion, and the continuing tendency towards the sacralization of specific times and places should be regarded as a durable expression of the mytho-poetic imagination. See also, in this connection, Eliade (1954, 1963).
6. It is again interesting to note, contra Foucault (1977), the effect that filmed surveillance has on many in the crowd. Passive capitulation to the so-called 'gaze' of authority is not the norm. For many it acts as an incitement to move up a gear and *intensify* their unacceptable behaviour. In this case the attention

of the cameras precipitated *more* wanker signs, screamed obscenities, standing in the aisles and jumping on seats than would otherwise have occurred.

7. This one incident, turned into ritual by the fans, is a concrete encapsulation of the Millwall experience of the last thirty years, exemplifying all the central themes: folk–popular notoriety ('let's watch the animals, see what they do'); a bitter relationship with the media ('get the cunt off the pitch, all they ever fuckin' do is stitch us up!'); and the assertion of a collective pride and being which contests any attempt to traduce them. *No One Likes Us* summons up, actualizes and expresses these things and their affective underpinnings.
8. This kind of manifestation of popular culture, as Stuart Hall (in Morley and Chen 1996: 468) observes, has origins in 'the pleasures, the memories, the traditions of the people. It has connections with local hopes and aspirations, local tragedies and scenarios that are the everyday practices and everyday experiences of ordinary folks. Hence, it has links with what Mikhail Bakhtin calls "the vulgar" – the popular, the informal, the underside, the grotesque. That is why it has always been counterposed to elite or high culture, and is thus a site of alternative traditions. And that is why the dominant tradition has always been suspicious of it.'
9. Bill, a West Ham supporter, remembers his first visit to the old Den for this most intensively contested of derbies: 'We all got there early, an' we was singin' an' shoutin' an' that, 'avin' a great time. Millwall was really quiet. We was well takin' the piss. Then all of a sudden this noise started, like moanin', they was all sorta *moanin'*. I thought, "what the fuck's goin' on 'ere?" It was so fuckin' *loud*, an' they was all doin' it, an' it went *on* an' *on* an' *on* . . . West 'am just shut up.'
10. In such a moment as this, the experience of *being* Millwall could hardly be deeper, more profound, or engage and draw upon a more complete range of human experience and resource. I use the notion of *effervescence* here in its definitive Durkheimian sense, as a collective phenomenon 'linked not only to powerful passions which are experienced as a physical force (a "somatic" component), but to people's material and moral density . . . (a "behavioural" component), and to the stock of knowledge contained within the *conscience collective* which imparts meaning to emotional experiences (something which can loosely be approximated to a "feeling" component)'. (Shilling 1997: 204).
11. The gloom precipitated for fans by this demoralizing return to the lower divisions, following the most successful era in the clubs history – two seasons in the old first division, and more or less convincing challenges for promotion to the Premiership throughout the nineties – proved difficult to bear for many fans, and their loved ones. Maureen's account was typical of the moment: 'I left 'im to it. I went to me mums'. 'E would'nt talk – 'e was so *miserabl*e, y'know, just sittin' about. I don't understand it' (from fieldnotes).

Bibliography

Abu-Lughod, L. (1986) *Veiled Sentiments: Honor and Poetry in a Bedouin Society.* Berkeley: University of California Press.

Alexander, J. (1988) *Durkheimian Sociology: Cultural Studies.* Cambridge: Cambridge University Press.

Allan, J. (1989) *Bloody Casuals: Diary of a Football Hooligan.* Aberdeen: Famedram.

Anderson, B. (1983) *Imagined Communities.* London: Verso.

Apte, M. (1985) *Humor and Laughter: An Anthropological Approach.* Ithaca: Cornell University Press.

Archer, J. (1994) *Male Violence.* London: Hutchinson.

Archetti, E. (1992) 'Argentinean Football: A Ritual of Violence?', *International Journal of the History of Sport* 9,2, pp.209–35.

Armstrong, G. (1998) *Football Hooligans: Knowing the Score.* Oxford: Berg.

Armstrong, G. and Giulianotti, R. (eds) (1997) *Entering the Field: New Perspectives on World Football.* Oxford and New York: Berg.

Armstrong, G. and Harris, R. (1991) 'Football Hooligans: Theory and Evidence', *Sociological Review* 39,3, pp.427–58.

Armstrong, G. and Young, M. (1997) 'Legislators and Interpreters: The Law and "Football Hooligans"', in G. Armstrong and R.Giulianotti (eds), *Entering the Field: New Perspectives on World Football.* Oxford and New York: Berg.

Ash, M. (1971) *A Guide to the Structure of London.* Bath: Adams and Dart.

Back, L. (1996) *New Ethnicities and Urban Culture.* London: UCL Press.

Back, L., Crabbe, T. and Solomos, J. (1996) *Alive and Still Kicking: An Overview Evaluation of Anti-Racist Campaigns in Football.* London: Commission for Racial Equality.

Bakhtin, M (1965) *Rabelais and his World.* Bloomington: Indiana University Press.

Bale, J. (1993) *Sport, Space and the City.* London: Routledge.

Ball, P. (1986) 'Postscript', in E. Dunphy, *Only a Game?: The Diary of a Professional Footballer.* Harmondsworth: Penguin.

Ball, S., Bowe, R. and Gewirtz, S. (1995) 'Circuits of Schooling: A Sociological Exploration of Parental Choice of School in Social Class Contexts', *Sociological Review* 43, 1, pp.57–78.

Bateson, G. (1978) 'A Theory of Play and Fantasy', in G. Bateson (ed), *Steps to an Ecology of Mind.* London: Paladin.

Bell, C. (1992) *Ritual Theory, Ritual Practice.* New York and Oxford: Oxford University Press.

Berger, J. (1972) *Ways of Seeing.* Harmondsworth: Penguin.

Berger, P. (1984) 'On the Obsolescence of the Concept of Honour', in M.J. Sandel (ed.) *Liberalism and its Critics.* Oxford: Basil Blackwell.

Bernstein, B. (1971) *Class, Codes and Control*, Vol. 1. St Albans: Paladin.

Bernstein, B. (1975) *Class, Codes and Control*, Vol. 3. London: Routledge and Kegan Paul.

Bernstein, B. (1979) 'Social Class, Language and Socialisation', in J. Karabel and A.H. Halsey (eds) *Power and Ideology in Education.* New York: Oxford University Press.

Bernstein, B. (1990) *The Structuring of Pedagogic Discourse.* London: Routledge.

Bloch, M. (1989) 'Symbols, Song, Dance and Features of Articulation: Is Religion an Extreme Form of Traditional Authority?', in M. Bloch, *Ritual, History and Power.* London: The Athlone Press.

Bloch, M. (1991) 'Language, Anthropology and Cognitive Science', *Man* 26, pp.183–98.

Bourdieu, P. (1977) *Outline of a Theory of Practice.* Cambridge: Cambridge University Press.

Bourdieu, P. (1978) 'Sport and Social Class', *Social Science Information* 17, pp.819–40.

Bourdieu, P (1979) *Algeria 1960.* Cambridge: Cambridge University Press.

Bourdieu, P. (1986) *Distinction: A Social Critique of the Judgement of Taste.* London: Routledge.

Bourdieu, B. (1990) *In Other Words: Essays Towards a Reflexive Sociology.* Cambridge: Polity Press.

Bourdieu, B. (1991) *Language and Symbolic Power.* Cambridge, Mass.: Harvard University Press.

Bourdieu, P. (1992) *The Logic of Practice.* Cambridge: Polity Press.

Bourke, J. (1994) *Working Class Cultures in Britain 1890–1960.* London: Routledge.

Brimson, D. and Brimson, E. (1996) *Everywhere We Go: Behind the Matchday Madness.* London: Headline.

Bromberger, C. (1993) '"Allez l'O.M., Forza Juve": The Passion for Football in Marseille and Turin', in S. Redhead (ed.), *The Passion and the Fashion: Football Fandom in the New Europe.* Aldershot: Avebury.

Burke, P. (1977) 'Popular Culture in Seventeenth Century London', *London Journal* 3, 2, pp.142–62.

Butler, T. and Savage, M. (eds) (1995) *Social Change and the Middle Classes.* London: UCL Press.

Byrne, R. (1989) *Prisons and Punishments of London.* London: Grafton.

Caine, M. (1992) *What's it all About?* London: Arrow.

Calhoun, C., Lipuma, E. and Postone, M. (eds) (1995) *Bourdieu: Critical Perspectives*. Cambridge: Polity Press.

Campbell, D. (1994) *The Underworld.* London: BBC Books.

Campbell, D. and Shields, A. (1993) *Soccer City: The Future of Football in London.* London: Mandarin.

Canetti, E. (1962) *Crowds and Power*. London: Victor Gollancz.

Carby, H. (1982) 'Schooling in Babylon', in Centre for Contemporary Urban Studies *The Empire Strikes Back: Race and Racism in 70s Britain.* London: Hutchinson.

Clarke, A. (1991) 'Figuring a Better Future', in E. Dunning and C. Rojek (eds), *Sport and Leisure in the Civilising Process.* London: Macmillan.

Clarke, J. (ed.) (1976) *Working Class Culture: Studies in History and Theory.* London: Hutchinson.

Clifford, J. (1994) *The Predicament of Culture: Twentieth Century Ethnography, Literature and Art.* Cambridge, Mass., and London: Harvard University Press.

Cohen, A. (1955) *Delinquent Boys.* New York: The Free Press.

Cohen, A.P. (1989) *The Symbolic Construction of Community.* London: Routledge.

Cohen, P. (1971) 'Policing the Working Class City' in B. Fine, R. Kinsey, J. Lea, S. Pociotto and J. Young (eds), *Capitalism and the Rule of Law.* London: Hutchinson.

Cohen, P. (1996) 'All White on the Night?: Narratives of Nativism on the Isle of Dogs', in T. Butler and M. Rustin (eds), *Rising in the East.* London: Lawrence and Wishart.

Cohen, P. and Robins, D. (1978) *Knuckle Sandwich: Growing* Up *in the Working-Class City.* Harmondsworth: Penguin.

Cohen, S. (1971) *Folk Devils and Moral Panics.* London: Paladin.

Cohen, S. and Young, J. (1973) *The Manufacture of News*. London: Constable.

Collins, R. (1988) 'The Durkheimian Tradition in Conflict Sociology', in J.C. Alexander (ed.), *Durkheimian Sociology: Cultural Studies.* Cambridge: Cambridge University Press.

Connell, R.W. (1983) *Which Way is Up?: Essays on Sex, Class and Culture.* London: Allen and Unwin.

Connerton, P. (1989) *How Societies Remember.* Cambridge: Cambridge University Press.

Crawford, R. (1987) 'Cultural Influences on Prevention and the Emergence of a New Health Consciousness', in N. Weinstein (ed), *Taking Care: Understanding and Encouraging Self-Protective Behaviour*. Cambridge: Cambridge University Press.

Critcher, C. (1979) 'Football since the war', in J. Clarke (ed.), *Working Class Culture: Studies in History and Theory.* London: Hutchinson.

Csordas, T. (ed.) (1994) *Embodiment and Experience: The Existential Ground of Culture and Self.* Cambridge: Cambridge University Press.

Cunningham, H. (1980) *Leisure in the Industrial Revolution c. 1780–1880.* London: Croom Helm.

Curran, J., Ecclestone, J., Oakley, G. and Richardson, A. (eds) (1986) *Bending Reality: The State of the Media.* London: Pluto Press.

Daly, M. and Wilson, M. (1988) *Homicide.* New York: Aldine de Gruyter.

Dentith, S. (1995) *Bakhtinian Thought: An Introduction.* London: Routledge.

Dickens, C. (1985 [1837]) *Oliver Twist.* Harmondsworth: Penguin.

Douglas, M. (1973) *Natural Symbols.* London: Barrie and Jenkins.

Dunning, E. (ed.) (1971) *The Sociology of Sport: A Collection of Readings.* London: Frank Cass.

Dunning, E., Murphy, P. and Williams, J. (1988) *The Roots of Football Hooliganism: An Historical and Sociological Study.* London: Routledge and Kegan Paul.

Dunning, E. and Rojek, C. (eds) (1991) *Sport and Leisure in the Civilising Process.* London: Macmillan.

Dunphy, E. (1986) *Only a Game?: The Diary of a Professional Footballer.* Harmondsworth: Penguin.

Durkheim, E. (1961) *The Elementary Forms of the Religious Life.* New York: Collier Books.

Durkheim, E. (1984) *The Division of Labour in Society.* London: Macmillan.

Dyos, H.J. and M. Wolff (eds) (1973) *The Victorian City: Images and Realities,* Vol. 2. London: Routledge and Kegan Paul.

Eliade, M. (1954) *The Myth of Eternal Return.* New York: Harper and Row.

Eliade, M. (1963) *Myth and Reality.* New York: Harper and Row.

Elias, N. (1982) *The Civilizing Process: State Formation and Civilization.* London: Basil Blackwell.

Elias, N. and Dunning, E. (1986) *Quest for Excitement: Sport and Leisure in the Civilizing Process.* Oxford: Basil Blackwell.

Foucault, M. (1977) *Discipline and Punish.* London: Allen Lane.

Foucault, M. (1980a) *Power/Knowledge,* (ed.) C. Gordon. Brighton: Harvester.

Foucault, M (1980b) 'Body/Power', in Michel Foucault, *Power/Knowledge*, ed. C.Gordon. Brighton: Harvester.

Francis, M. and Walsh, P. (1997) *Guvnors*. Bury: Milo Books.

Fraser, F. (1994) *Mad Frank: Memoirs of a Life of Crime.* London: Warner.

Fryer, P. (1984) *Staying Power: The History of Black People in Britain.* London: Pluto Press.

Gavron, H. (1966) *The Captive Wife.* Harmondsworth: Penguin.

Geertz, C. (1975) *The Interpretation of Cultures*. London: Hutchinson.

Giddens, A. (1979) *Central Problems in Social Theory: Action, Structure and Contradiction in Social Analysis.* London: Macmillan.

Giddens, A (1991) *Modernity and Self-Identity: Self and Society in the Late Modern Age.* Cambridge: Polity Press.

Gilmore, D. (1990) *Manhood in the Making: Cultural Concepts of Masculinity.* New Haven, Conn.: Yale University Press.

Gilroy, P. (1987) *There Ain't No Black in the Union Jack.* London: Hutchinson.

Gilroy, P. (1988) 'Cruciality and the Frog's Perspective: An Agenda of Difficulties for the Black Arts Movement in Britain', *Third Text* 5, pp.33–44.

Gilroy, P. (1993) *The Black Atlantic: Modernity and Double Consciousness.* London: Verso.

Girard, R. (1977) *Violence and the Sacred.* Baltimore: John Hopkins University Press.

Giulianotti, R. (1993) 'Soccer Casuals as Cultural Intermediaries', in S. Redhead (ed.), *The Passion and the Fashion: Football Fandom in the New Europe.* Aldershot: Avebury.

Giulianotti, R. (1996) 'A Sociology of Scottish Fan Culture', University of Aberdeen, Department of Sociology, unpublished PhD thesis.

Goldberg, A. and Wagg, S. (1991) 'It's Not a Knockout: English Football and Globalisation', in J. Williams and S. Wagg (eds), *British Football and Social Change: Getting into Europe.* Leicester: Leicester University Press.

Gorer, G. (1955) *Exploring English Character.* London: Cresset Press.

Green, H. (1988) *Informal Carers: A Study.* London: OPCS HMSO.

Halbwachs, M. (1980) *The Collective Memory*. London: Harper and Row.

Hall, S. (1986) 'Media Power and Class Power', in J. Curran, J. Ecclestone, G. Oakley and A. Richardson (eds), *Bending Reality: The State of the Media.* London: Pluto Press.

Hall, S. (1990) 'Cultural Identity and Diaspora', in J. Rutherford (ed.) *Identity: Community, Culture, Difference.* London: Lawrence and Wishart.

Hall, S. (1993) 'For Allon White: Metaphors of Transformation', introduction in A. White (ed.), *Carnival, Hysteria, Writing*. Cambridge: Cambridge University Press.

Hall, S., Critcher, C., Jefferson, T., Clarke, J. and Roberts, B. (1978) *Policing the Crisis: 'Mugging', the State, and Law and Order.* London: Macmillan.

Hargreaves, J. (1993) *Sport, Power and Culture.* Cambridge: Polity Press.

Hargreaves, J.A. (ed.) (1982) *Sport, Culture and Ideology.* London: Routledge.

Hartsock, N. (1983) 'The Feminist Standpoint: Developing the Ground for a Specifically Feminist Historical materialism', in S. Harding and M.B. Hintikka (eds), *Discovering Reality*. Dordrecht and London: Reidel

Hastrup, K. (1995) *A Passage to Anthropology: Between Experience and Theory.* London: Routledge.

Hebdige, D. (1974a) *The Style of the Mods*. Sub and Popular Culture series, stencilled paper no. 20. Birmingham: CCCS.

Hebdige, D. (1974b) *The Kray Twins: A Study of a System of Closure*. Sub and Popular Culture Series, stencilled paper no. 21. Birmingham: CCCS.

Hebdige, D. (1979) *Subculture: The Meaning of Style*. London: Routledge.

Herbert, D.T. and Raine, J.W. (1976) 'Defining Communities within Urban Areas', *Town Planning Review* 47, pp.41–60.

Hewitt, R. (1986) *White talk, Black Talk: Inter-racial Friendship and Communication among Adolescents*. Cambridge: Cambridge University Press.

Hewitt, R. (1996) *Routes of Racism: The Social Basis of Racist Action*. Stoke-on-Trent: Trentham Books.

Hill, C. (1969) *Reformation to Industrial Revolution*. London: Pelican.

Himmelfarb, G. (1973) 'The Culture of Poverty', in H.J. Dyos and M. Wolff (eds), *The Victorian City: Images and Realities*. London: Routledge and Kegan Paul.

Hobbs, D. (1988) *Doing the Business: Entrepreneurship, the Working Class and Detectives in the East End of London*. Oxford: Clarendon Press.

Hobbs, D. and Robins, D. (1991) '"The Boy Done Good": Football Violence, Change and Continuities'. *Socoilogical Review* 39, 3, pp.489502.

Hoberman, J. (1984) *Sport and Political Ideology*. London: Heinemann.

Hobsbawm, E. and Ranger, T. (eds) (1993) *The Invention of Tradition*. London: Verso.

Hogg, A., McDougall, J. and Morgan, R. (1988) *Bullion: Brink's Mat. The Story of Britain's Biggest Gold Robbery*. London: Penguin.

Holt, R. (1989) *Sport and the British*. Oxford: Oxford University Press.

Horne, J., Jary, D. and Tomlinson, A. (1987) *Sport, Leisure and Social Relations*. London: Routledge.

Humphries, S. (1984) *Hooligans or Rebels?: An Oral History of Working Class Childhood and Youth 1889–1939*. Oxford: Blackwell.

Hutton, R. (1996) *The Rise and Fall of Merry England*. Oxford: Oxford University Press.

Jary, D., Horne, J. and Bucke, T. (1991) 'Football "Fanzines" and Football Culture: A Successful Case of "Cultural Contestation"', *Sociological Review* 39, 3, pp.581–98.

Jenkins, R. (1996) *Social Identity*. London: Routledge.

Jenks, C. (1996) *Childhood*. London: Routledge.

Jenks, C. and Lorentzen, J. (1997) 'The Kray Fascination', *Theory, Culture and Society* 14, 3, pp.87–107.

Johnson, D. (1968) *Southwark and the City*. London: Oxford University Press.

Johnson, M. (1987) *The Body in the Mind: The Bodily Basis of Meaning, Imagination and Reasoning*. Chicago: University of Chicago Press.

Johnson, P. (1996) 'Economic Development and Industrial Dynamism in Victorian London', *London Journal* , 21,1, pp.29–37.

Jones, G.S. (1971) *Outcast London: A Study in the Relationship Between Classes in Victorian Society.* Oxford: Oxford University Press.

Jones, G.S. (1983) 'Working-Class Culture and Working-Class Politics in London 1870–1900: Notes on the Remaking of a Working-Class', in Jones, *Languages of Class; Studies in Working-Class History 1832–1982.* Cambridge: Cambridge University Press.

Karabel, J. and Halsey, A.H. (eds) (1979) *Power and Ideology in Education.* New York: Oxford University Press.

Kelland, G. (1993) *Crime in London.* London: HarperCollins.

Kimmel, M. (ed.) (1987) *Changing Men: New Directions in Research on Men and Masculinity.* Newbury Park, Calif.: Sage.

King, J. (1996) *The Football Factory.* London: Jonathan Cape.

King, M. and Knight, M. (1999) *Hoolifan: 30 Years of Hurt.* Edinburgh: Mainstream.

Krieken, van, R. (1997) 'Sociology and the Reproductive Self: Demographic Transitions and Modernity', *Sociology* 31, 3, pp.445–471.

Kuzmics, H. (1987) 'Civilization, State and Bourgeois Society: The Theoretical Contribution of Norbert Elias', *Theory, Culture and Society* 4, pp.515–37.

Lakoff, G. (1990) *Women, Fire and Dangerous Things: What Categories Reveal about the Mind.* Chicago: University of Chicago Press.

Lasch, C. (1979) *The Culture of Narcissism: American Life in an Age of Diminishing Expectations.* New York and London: W.W. Norton.

Lasch, C. (1996) *The Revolt of the Elites and the Betrayal of Democracy.* New York and London: W.W. Norton.

Lave, J. (1988) *Cognition in Practice.* Cambridge: Cambridge University Press.

Levi-Strauss, C. (1966) *The Savage Mind.* Chicago: University of Chicago Press.

Linebaugh, P. (1993) *The London Hanged.* London: Penguin.

Malcolmson, R. (1973) *Popular Recreations in English Society 1700–1850.* Cambridge: Cambridge University Press.

Marsh, P., Rosser, R. and Harre, R. (1978) *The Rules of Disorder.* London: Routledge and Kegan Paul.

Mason, M. (1994) *The Making of Victorian Sexuality.* Oxford: Oxford University Press

Massey, D. (1994) *Space, Place and Gender.* Cambridge: Polity Press.

Mayhew, H. (1969 [1862]) *London's Underworld.* London: Spring Books.

Mays, J.B. (1954) *Growing up in the City: A Study of Juvenile Delinquency in an Urban Neighbourhood.* Liverpool: Liverpool University Press.

McCarthy, B. (1994) 'Warrior Values', in J. Archer (ed.), *Male Violence.* London: Routledge.

McDowell, L. (1983) 'Towards an Understanding of the Gender Division in Public Space', *Environment and Planning* D,1.

McMullan, J.L. (1984) *The Canting Crew: London's Criminal Underworld 1550–1700.* New Brunswick: Rutgers University Press.

McRobbie, A. (1994) *Postmodernism and Popular Culture.* London: Routledge.

Mead, M. (1964) *Continuities in Cultural Evolution.* New Haven, Conn.: Yale University Press.

Mercer, C. (1976) *Living in Cities: Psychology and the Urban Environment.* Harmondsworth: Penguin.

Moerman, M. (1974) 'Accomplishing Ethnicity', in R.Turner (ed.), *Ethnomethodology.* Harmondsworth: Penguin.

Morgan, G. (1993) 'Frustrated Respectability: Local Culture and Politics in London's Docklands', *Society and Space* 11, pp.523–541.

Morley, D. and Chen, K.H. (eds) (1996) *Stuart Hall: Critical Dialogues in Cultural Studies.* London: Routledge.

Morton, J. (1994) *Gangland: London's Underworld.* London: Warner.

Murphy, P., Williams, J. and Dunning, E. (1990) *Football on Trial: Spectator Violence and Development in the Football World.* London: Routledge.

Murray, J. (1988) *Millwall: Lions of the South.* London: Indispensable Books.

Newson, J. and Newson, E. (1970) *Infant Care in the Urban Community.* Harmondsworth: Penguin.

Newson, J. and Newson, E. (1971) *Four Years Old in an Urban Community.* Harmondsworth: Penguin.

Newson, J. and Newson, E. (1976) *Seven Years Old in the Home Environment.* London: Unwin and Allen.

Oakley, A. (1974) *The Sociology of Housework.* Oxford: Martin Robertson.

Oakley, A. and Rajan, L. (1991) 'Social Class and Social Support: The Same or Different?', *Sociology* 25,1, pp.231–240.

O'Day, R. and Englander, D. (1993) *Mr Charles Booth's Enquiry: Life and Labour of the People in London Reconsidered.* London: Hambledon Press.

Opie, I. and Opie, P. (1969) *Children's Games in Street and Playground.* Oxford: Clarendon Press.

Pahl, J. (1980) 'Patterns of Money Management', *Journal of Social Policy* 9, 3, pp.313–335.

Parker, G. (1990) *With Due Care and Attention: A Review of Research on Informal Care.* London: Family Policy Studies Centre.

Pearson, G. (1983) *Hooligan: A History of Respectable Fears*. London: Macmillan.

Pelling, H. (1979) *Popular Politics and Society in Late Victorian Britain.* London: Macmillan.

Polk, K. (1994) 'Masculinity, Honour and Confrontational Homicide', in T. Newburn and E.A. Stanko (eds), *Just Boys Doing Business?: Men, Masculinities and Crime.* London: Routledge.

Porter, R. (1994) *London: A Social History.* London: Penguin.

Pritchett, V.S. (1986) *London Perceived.* London: Hogarth Press.

Redhead, S. (1991) *Football with Attitude.* Manchester: Wordsmith.

Redhead, S. (1993) *The Passion and the Fashion: Football Fandom in the New Europe.* Aldershot: Avebury.

Richardson, C. (1992) *My Manor.* London: Pan.

Rock, P. (1973) 'News as eternal recurrence', in S. Cohen and J. Young (eds), *The Manufacture of News*. London: Constable.

Rooks, C. (1899) *The Hooligan Nights*. London: Grant Richards.

Rose, G. (1993a) *Feminism and Geography: The Limits of Geographical Knowledge.* Cambridge: Polity Press.

Rose, G. (1993b) *Limited Livelihoods: Gender and Class in Nineteenth Century England.* Berkeley: University of California Press.

Roy, D.F. (1960) '"Banana time" job satisfaction and informal interaction', *Human Organisation*, 18, pp.156–68.

Rutherford, J. (ed.) (1990) *Identity: Community, Culture, Difference.* London: Lawrence and Wishart.

Seabrook, J. (1984) *What Local Politics Should Be About: The Idea of Neighbourhood.* London: Pluto Press.

Seidler, V. (1994) *Unreasonable Men: Masculinity and Social Theory.* London: Routledge.

Sennett, R. (1994) *Flesh and Stone: The Body and the City in Western Civilisation.* London: W.W. Norton.

Shilling, C. (1991) 'Educating the Body: Physical Capital and the Production of Social Inequalities', *Sociology* 25, 4, pp.652–673.

Shilling, C. (1993) *The Body in Social Theory*. London: Sage.

Shilling, C. (1997) 'Emotions, Embodiment and the Sensation of Society', *Sociological Review*, 45, 2, pp.195–219.

Shipley, S. (1983) 'Tom Causer of Bermondsey: A Boxer Hero of the 1890s', *History Workshop Journal,* 15, pp.28–59.

Sinclair, I. (1997) *Lights Out for the Territory.* London: Granta.

Spiegel, J. and Machotka, P. (1974) *Messages of the Body.* New York: The Free Press.

Stallybrass, P. and White, A. (1986) *The Politics and Poetics of Transgression.* London: Methuen.

Stromberg, P. (1986) *Symbols of Community.* Tucson: University of Arizona Press.

Suttles, G.D. (1971) *The Social Order of the Slum: Ethnicity and Territory in the Inner City.* Chicago: University of Chicago Press.

Suttles, G.D. (1972) *The Social Construction of Community*. Chicago: University of Chicago Press.

Taylor, C. (1993) 'To Follow a Rule . . .', in C. Calhoun, E. Lipuma and M. Postone (eds), *Bourdieu: Critical Perspectives.* Cambridge: Polity Press.

Taylor, I. (1971) 'Football Mad: A Speculative Sociology of Football Hooliganism', in E. Dunning (ed.), *The Sociology of Sport: A Collection of Readings*. London: Frank Cass.

Taylor, I. (1982) 'On the Sports Violence Question: Football Hooliganism Revisited', in J.A. Hargreaves (ed.), *Sport, Culture and Ideology*. London: Routledge.

Taylor, I. (1991) 'English Football in the 1990s: Taking Hillsborough Seriously?', in J. Williams and S. Wagg (eds), *British Football and Social Change: Getting into Europe*. Leicester: Leicester University Press.

Thomas, K. (1971) *Religion and the Decline of Magic*. Harmondsworth: Penguin.

Thompson, E. H. and Pleck, J.H. (1987) 'The Structure of Male Role Norms', in M.S. Kimmel (ed), *Changing Men: New Directions in Research on Men and Masculinity*. Newbury Park, Calif.: Sage.

Thompson, E.P. (1963) *The Making of the English Working Class*. Harmondsworth: Penguin.

Thompson, E.P (1967) 'Time, Work-Discipline and Industrial Capitalism', *Past and Present,* 38, pp.56–97.

Thompson, F.M.L. (1988) *The Rise of Respectable Society: A Social History of Britain, 1830–1900.* London: Fontana Press.

Tolson, A. (1977) *The Limits of Masculinity*. London: Tavistock.

Tuan, Y.F. (1993) *Passing Strange and Wonderful: Aesthetics, Nature and Culture.* Washington D.C.: Island Press.

Turnbull, C. (1961) *The Forest People.* London: Jonathan Cape.

Turner, R. (ed.) (1974) *Ethnomethodology.* Harmondsworth: Penguin.

Turner, B. (1984) *The Body and Society.* Oxford: Basil Blackwell.

Turner, T. (1994) 'Bodies and Anti-bodies: Flesh and Fetish in Contemporary Social Theory', in T. Csordas (ed.), *Embodiment and Experience: The Existential Ground of Culture and Self.* Cambridge: Cambridge University Press.

Turner, V. (1967) 'Symbols in Ndembu Ritual', in Turner, *The Forest of Symbols.* Ithaca: Cornell University Press.

Vaught, C. and Smith, D.L. (1980) 'Incorporation and Mechanical Solidarity in an Underground Coal Mine', *Sociology of Work and Occupations* 7, 2, pp.159–187.

Walkowitz, J. (1992) *City of Dreadful Delight: Narratives of Sexual Danger in Late Victorian London.* Chicago: University of Chicago Press.

Ward, C. (1977) *The Child in the City*. London: The Architectural Press.

Ward, C (1989) *Steaming In: Journal of a Football Fan*. London: Sportspages.

Weber, M. (1985) *The Protestant Ethic and the Spirit of Capitalism*. London: Counterpoint.

Weinstein, N. (ed.) (1987) *Taking Care: Understanding and Encouraging Self-Protective Behaviour*. Cambridge: Cambridge University Press.

Werlen, B. (1993) *Society, Action and Space: An Alternative Human Geography.* London: Routledge.

White, A. (1993) *Carnival, Hysteria, Writing*. Cambridge: Cambridge University Press.

Williams, J. (1991) 'Having an Away Day: English Football Spectators and the Hooligan Debate', in J. Williams and S. Wagg (eds), *British Football and Social Change: Getting into Europe.* Leicester: Leicester University Press.

Williams, J. (1994) 'The Local and the Global in English Soccer and the Rise of Sattelite Television', *Sociology of Sport Journal* 11.

Williams, J. and Wagg, S. (eds) (1991) *British Football and Social Change: Getting into Europe.* Leicester: Leicester University Press.

Williams, R. (1973) *The Country and the City.* London: The Hogarth Press.

Willis, P. (1988) *Learning to Labour: How Working Class Kids Get Working Class Jobs.* Aldershot: Gower.

Willmott, P. (1986) *Social Networks, Informal Care and Public Policy*. London: Policy Studies Institute.

Willmott, P. (1987) *Friendship Networks and Social Support.* London: Policy Studies Institute.

Wright, I. (1996) *Mr Wright: The Explosive Autobiography of Ian Wright.* London: HarperCollins.

Wright, P. (1993) *A Journey through the Ruins: A Keyhole Portrait of Post-War British Life and Culture.* London: Flamingo.

Wolfgang, M.E. (1958) *Patterns in Criminal Homicide*. New York: Wiley.

Wrightson, K. (1982) *English Society 1580–1680*. London: Hutchinson.

Television Programmes

BBC Television (1977) *Panorama* Millwall Special.

Channel 4 Television (1993) *Champions.*

Channel 4 Television (1989) *'No one likes us'.*

Index